Defoe Abbott Marx Hardy Melville Machiavelli Chesterton Cooper Emerson Joyce Austen Hugo Eliot Grimm

Stoker Carroll Christie Montaigne Haggard Molière Byron Schiller Wilde Maupassant Engels Smith Kafka Hall

Garnett Goethe Einstein Fitzgerald Hawthorne Dostoyevsky Kipling Doyle Willis

Baum Henry Nietzsche Balzac Leslie Dumas Flaubert Turgenev Crane Stockton Vatsyayana Verne Burroughs Vinci

Curtis Tocqueville Gogol Busch Homer Widger Tolstoy Whitman Darwin Thoreau Twain Scott Plato Harte

Potter Freud Zola Lawrence Dickens Burton Hesse Kant Jowett Stevenson

Andersen London Descartes Cervantes Voltaire Cooke Poe Aristotle Wells Irving Hale James Hastings Shakespeare Bunner Richter Chekhov Chambers da Shaw Wodehouse Benedict Alcott Doré Dante Swift Pushkin Newton

 tredition®

tredition was established in 2006 by Sandra Latusseck and Soenke Schulz. Based in Hamburg, Germany, tredition offers publishing solutions to authors and publishing houses, combined with world-wide distribution of printed and digital book content. tredition is uniquely positioned to enable authors and publishing houses to create books on their own terms and without conventional manu-facturing risks.

For more information please visit: www.tredition.com

TREDITION CLASSICS

This book is part of the TREDITION CLASSICS series. The creators of this series are united by passion for literature and driven by the intention of making all public domain books available in printed format again - worldwide. Most TREDITION CLASSICS titles have been out of print and off the bookstore shelves for decades. At tredition we believe that a great book never goes out of style and that its value is eternal. Several mostly non-profit literature projects provide content to tredition. To support their good work, tredition donates a portion of the proceeds from each sold copy. As a reader of a TREDITION CLASSICS book, you support our mission to save many of the amazing works of world literature from oblivion. See all available books at www.tredition.com.

Project Gutenberg

The content for this book has been graciously provided by Project Gutenberg. Project Gutenberg is a non-profit organization founded by Michael Hart in 1971 at the University of Illinois. The mission of Project Gutenberg is simple: To encourage the creation and distribution of eBooks. Project Gutenberg is the first and largest collection of public domain eBooks.

The Old Masters and Their Pictures For the Use of Schools and Learners in Art

Sarah Tytler

Imprint

This book is part of TREDITION CLASSICS

Author: Sarah Tytler
Cover design: Buchgut, Berlin – Germany

Publisher: tredition GmbH, Hamburg - Germany
ISBN: 978-3-8472-3371-8

www.tredition.com
www.tredition.de

PREFACE TO FIRST EDITION.

I wish to say, in a very few words, that this book is intended to be a simple account of the great Old Masters in painting of every age and country, with descriptions of their most famous works, for the use of learners and outsiders in art. The book is not, and could not well be, exhaustive in its nature. I have avoided definitions of schools, considering that these should form a later and more elaborate portion of art education, and preferring to group my 'painters' according to what I hold to be the primitive arrangements of time, country, and rank in art.

PREFACE TO NEW EDITION.

The restrictions with regard to space under which the little volume called "The Old Masters" was originally written, caused me to omit, to my regret, many names great, though not first, in art. The circulation which the book has attained induces me to do what I can to remedy the defect, and render the volume more useful by adding two chapters—the one on Italian and the other on German, Dutch, and Flemish masters. These chapters consist almost entirely of condensed notes taken from two trustworthy sources, to which I have been already much indebted—Sir C, and Lady Eastlake's version of Kugler's "Handbook of Italian Art," and Dr. Waagen's "Handbook,"—remodelled from Kugler—of German, Dutch, and Flemish art, revised by J.A. Crowe. I have purposely given numerous records of those Dutch painters whose art has been specially popular in England and who are in some cases better represented in our country than in their own.

CONTENTS.

THE OLD MASTERS AND THEIR PICTURES.

CHAPTER I.

EARLY ITALIAN ART—GIOTTO, 1276-1337—ANDREA PISA-NO. 1280-1345—ORCAGNA, 1315-1376 GHIBERTI, 1381-1455—MASACCIO, 1402-1428 OR 1429—FRA ANGELICO, 1387-1455.

A pencil and paper, a box of colours, and a scrap-book, form so often a child's favourite toys that one might expect that a very large portion of men and women would prove painters. But, as we grow in years and knowledge, the discrepancy between nature and our attempts to copy nature, strike us more and more, until we turn in dissatisfaction and disgust from the vain effort.

There was only one old woman in an Esquimaux tribe who could be called forward to draw with a stick on the sand a sufficiently graphic likeness of the Erebus and the Terror. It is only a few groups of men belonging to different countries, throughout the centuries, who have been able to give us paintings to which we turn in wonder and admiration, and say that these are in their degree fair exponents of nature. The old painter's half-haughty, half-humble protest was true—it is 'God Almighty,' who in raising here and there men above their fellows, 'makes painters.'

But let us be thankful that the old propensity to delight in a fac-simile, or in an idealized version of nature, survives in the very common satisfaction and joy—whether cultivated or uncultivated—- derived from looking at pictures, thinking over their details, striving to understand the meaning of the painters, and proceeding farther to consider the lives and times which throw light on works of genius. Music itself is not more universally and gladly listened and responded to, than pictures are looked at and remembered.

Thus I have no fear of failing to interest you, my readers, in my subject if I can only treat it sympathetically,—enter at a humble distance into the spirit of the painters and of their paintings, and place before you some of the paintings by reverent and loving word-painting such as others have achieved, and such as I may strive to attain to, that you may be in a sort early familiar with these paintings, before you see them in engravings and photographs, and on canvas and in fresco, as I trust you may be privileged to see many of them, when you may hail them not only for what they are, the glories of art, but for what they have been to you in thoughts of beauty and high desires.

Of the old Greek paintings, of which there are left isolated specimens dug up in Herculaneum and Pompeii, I cannot afford to say anything, and of the more modern Greek art which was spread over Europe after the fall of Constantinople I need only write a few words. While Greece was to Europe the birthplace of painting as of other arts, that Greek painting which illustrated early Christianity, was painting in its decline and decay, borrowing not only superstitious conventionalities, but barbaric attributes of gilding and blazoning to hide its infirmity and poverty. Virgins of the same weak and meaningless type, between attenuated saints or angels, and doll-like child-Christs in the one invariable attitude holding up two fingers of a baby hand to bless the spectator and worshippers, were for ever repeated. In a similar manner the instances of rude or meagre contemporary paintings with which the early Christians adorned their places of worship and the sepulchres of their dead in the basilicas and catacombs of Rome, are very curious and interesting for their antiquity and their associations, and as illustrations of faith; but they present no intrinsic beauty or worth. They are not only clumsy and childish designs ill executed, but they are rendered unintelligible to all save the initiated in such hieroglyphics, by offering an elaborate ground-work of type, antitype, and symbol, on which the artist probably spent a large part of his strength. Lambs and lilies, serpents, vines, fishes, dolphins, phœnixes, cocks, anchors, and javelins played nearly as conspicuous a part in this art as did the dead believer, or his or her patron saint, who might have been supposed to form the principal figure in the picture.

Italian art existed in these small beginnings, in the gorgeous but quaintly formal or fantastic devices of illuminated missals, and in the stiff spasmodic efforts of here and there an artist spirit such as the old Florentine Cimabue's, when a great man heralded a great epoch. But first I should like to mention the means by which art then worked. Painting on board and on plastered walls, the second styled painting in fresco, preceded painting on canvas. Colours were mixed with water or with size, egg, or fig-juice—the latter practices termed *tempera* (in English in distemper) before oil was used to mix colours. But painters did not confine themselves then to painting with pencil or brush, else they might have attained technical excellence sooner. It has been well said that the poems of the middle ages were written in stone; so the earlier painters painted in stone, in that mosaic work which one of them called — referring to its durability — 'painting for eternity;' and in metals. Many of them were the sons of jewellers or jewellers themselves; they worked in iron as well as in gold and silver, and they were sculptors and architects as well as painters; engineers also, so far as engineering in the construction of roads, bridges, and canals, was known in those days. The Greek knowledge of anatomy was well-nigh lost, so that drawing was incorrect and form bad. The idea of showing degrees of distance, and the management of light and shade, were feebly developed. Even the fore-shortening of figures was so difficult to the old Italian painters that they could not carry it into the extremities, and men and women seem as though standing on the points of their toes. Landscape-painting did not exist farther than that a rock or a bush, or a few blue lines, with fishes out of proportion prominently interposed, indicated, as on the old stage, that a desert, a forest, or a sea, was to play its part in the story of the picture. So also portrait-painting was not thought of, unless it occurred in the likeness of a great man belonging to the time and place of the painter, who was the donor of some picture to chapel or monastery, or of the painter himself, alike introduced into sacred groups and scenes; for pictures were uniformly of a religious character, until a little later, when they merged into allegorical representations, just as one remembers that miracle plays passed into moral plays before ordinary human life was reproduced. Until this period, what we call dramatic expression in making a striking situation, or even in bringing the look of joy or sorrow, pleasure or pain, into a face, had hardly been attained.

Perhaps you will ask, what merit had the old paintings of the middle ages to compensate for so many great disadvantages and incongruities? Certainly before the time I have reached, they have, with rare exceptions, little merit, save that fascination of pathos, half-comic, half-tragic, which belongs to the struggling dawn of all great endeavours, and especially of all endeavours in art. But just at this epoch, art, in one man, took a great stride, began, as I shall try to show, to exert an influence so true, deep, and high that it extends, in the noblest forms, to the present day, and much more than compensates to the thoughtful and poetic for a protracted train of technical blunders and deficiencies.

Giotto, known also as Magister Joctus, was born in 1276 near Florence. I dare say many have heard one legend of him, and I mean to tell the legends of the painters, because even when they are most doubtful they give the most striking indications of the times and the light in which painters and their paintings were regarded by the world of artists, and by the world at large; but so far as I have heard this legend of Giotto has not been disproven. The only objection which can be urged against it, is that it is found preserved in various countries, of very different individuals—a crowning objection also to the legend of William Tell. Giotto was a shepherd boy keeping his father's sheep and amusing himself by drawing with chalk on a stone the favourites of the flock, when his drawings attracted the attention of a traveller passing from the heights into the valley. This traveller was the well-born and highly-esteemed painter Cimabue, who was so delighted with the little lad's rough outlines, that getting the consent of Giotto's father, Cimabue adopted the boy, carried him off to the city of Florence, introduced him to his studio, and so far as man could supplement the work of God, made a painter of the youthful genius. I may add here a later legend of Giotto. Pope Boniface VIII, requested specimens of skill from various artists with the view to the appointment of a painter to decorate St Peter's. Giotto, either in impatient disdain, or to show a careless triumph of skill, with one flourish of his hand, without the aid of compass, executed a perfect circle in red chalk, and sent the circle as his contribution to the specimens required by the Pope. The audacious specimen was accepted as the most conclusive, Giotto was chosen as the Pope's painter for the occasion, and from the incident arose the Italian proverb 'round as the o of Giotto.' Giotto was the friend of Dante, Petrarch, and Boccaccio, especially of Dante, to whom the grandeur of some of the painter's designs has been vaguely enough attributed. The poet of the 'Inferno' wrote of his friend:

> '— — Cimabue thought
> To lord it over painting's field; and now

The cry is Giotto's, and his name eclipsed.'

Petrarch bequeathed in his will a Madonna by Giotto and mentioned it as a rare treasure of art. Boccaccio wrote a merry anecdote of his comrade the painter's wit, in the course of which he referred with notable plain-speaking to Giotto's 'flat currish' plainness of face.

The impression handed down of Giotto's character is that of an independent, high-spirited man, full of invention, full of imagination, and also, by a precious combination, full of shrewdness and common sense; a man genial, given to repartee, and at the same time not deficient in the tact which deprives repartee of its sting. While he was working to King Robert of Naples, the king, who was watching the painter on a very hot day, said, with a shrug, 'If I were you, Giotto, I would leave off work and rest myself this fine day, 'And so would I, sire, if I were *you*,' replied the wag.

I need scarcely add that Giotto was a man highly esteemed and very prosperous in his day; one account reports him as the head of a family and the father of four sons and four daughters. I have purposely written first of the fame, the reputed character, and the circumstances of Giotto before I proceed to his work. This great work was, in brief, to breathe into painting the living soul which had till then—in mediæval times—been largely absent. Giotto went to Nature for his inspiration, and not content with the immense innovation of superseding by the actual representation of men and women in outline, tint, and attitude, the rigid traditions of his predecessors, he put men's passions in their faces—the melancholy looked sad, the gay glad. This result, to us so simple, filled Giotto's lively countrymen, who had seldom seen it, with astonishment and delight. They cried out as at a marvel when he made the commonest deed even coarsely life-like, as in the case of a sailor in a boat, who turned round with his hand before his face and spat into the sea; and when he illustrated the deed with the corresponding expression, as in the thrill of eagerness that perceptibly pervaded the whole figure of a thirsty man who stooped down to drink. But Giotto was no mere realist though he was a great realist; he was also in the highest light an idealist. His sense of harmony and beauty was true and noble; he rose above the real into 'the things unseen and eternal,' of which the real is but a rough manifestation. He was the first to paint a crucifixion robbed of the horrible triumph of physical power, and of the agony which is at its bidding, and invested with the divinity of awe and love.

Giotto's work did not end with himself; he was the founder of the earliest worthy school of Italian art, so worthy in this very glorious idealism, that, as I have already said, the men whose praise is most to be coveted, have learned to turn back to Giotto and his immediate successors, and, forgetting and forgiving all their ignorance, crudeness, quaintness, to dwell never wearied, and extol without measure these oldest masters' dignity of spirit, the earnestness of their originality, the solemnity and heedfulness of their labour. It would seem as if skill and polish, with the amount of attention which they appropriate, with their elevation of manner over matter, and thence their lowered standard, are apt to rob from or blur in men these highest qualifications of genius, for it is true that judges miss even in the Lionardo, Michael Angelo, and Raphael of a later and much more accomplished generation, and, to a far greater extent, in the Rubens of another and still later day, the perfect simplicity, the unalloyed fervour, the purity of tenderness in Giotto, Orcagna, Fra Angelico, and in their Flemish brethren, the Van Eycks and Mabuse.

The difference between the two classes of painters in not so wide as that between the smooth and brilliant epigrammatic poets of Anne's and the ruggedly rich dramatists of Elizabeth's reign, neither was there the unmistakable preponderance of such a mighty genius as that of Shakespeare granted to the first decade, still the distinction was the same in kind. [1]

I wish you, my readers, to note it in the very commencement, and to learn, like the thoughtful students of painting, to put aside any half-childish over-estimate of the absurdity of a blue stroke transfixing a huge flounder-like fish as a likeness of a sea, (which you have been accustomed to see translucid, in breakers and foam, in modern marine pictures,) or your quick sense of the ugliness of straight figures with long hands, wooden feet, and clinging draperies, while your eyes have been familiar with well-modelled frames and limbs and flowing lines. But we must look deeper if we would not be slaves to superficial prettiness, or even superficial correctness; we must try to go into the spirit of a painting and value it more in proportion as it teaches art's noblest lesson—the divinity of the divine, the serenity of utmost strength, the single-heartedness of passion.

I have only space to tell you of three or four of the famous works of Giotto. First, his allegories in the great church, in honour of St Francis, at Assisi, in relation to which, writing of its German architect, an author says: 'He built boldly against the mountain, piling one church upon another; the upper vast, lofty, and admitting through its broad windows the bright rays of the sun: the lower as if in the bowels of the earth—low, solemn, and almost shutting out the light of day. Around the lofty edifice grew the convent, a vast building, resting upon a long line of arches clinging to the hill-sides. As the evening draws nigh, casting its deep shadows across the valley, the traveller beneath gazes upwards with feelings of wonder and delight at this graceful arcade supporting the massy convent; the ancient towers and walls of the silent town gathering around, and the purple rocks rising high above—all still glowing in the lingering sunbeams—a scene scarcely to be surpassed in any clime for its sublime beauty.' The upper church contains frescoes wonderfully fresh, by Cimabue, of Scriptural subjects, and frescoes of scenes from the life vowed to poverty of St Francis. In the lower church, over the tomb of St Francis, are the four master-pieces with which we have to do. These are the three vows of the order figuratively represented. Mark the fitness and grandeur of two of the figures, the suggestion of which has been attributed to Dante, the woman Chastity seated beyond assault in her rocky fortress, and Obedience bowing the neck to curb and yoke. The fourth fresco pictures the saint who died, 'covered by another's cloak cast over his wasted body eaten with sores,' enthroned and glorified amidst the host of Heaven.

I have chosen the second example of the art of Giotto because you may with comparative ease see it for yourselves. It is in the National Gallery, London, having belonged to the collection of the late Samuel Rogers. It is a fragment of an old fresco which had been part of a series illustrating the life of John the Baptist in the church of the

Carmine, Florence, a church which was destroyed by fire in 1771. The fragment in the National Gallery has two fine heads of apostles bending sorrowfully over the body of St John. Though it is not necessary to do it, in strict justice, because good work rises superior to all accidents of comparison as well as accidents of circumstance, one must remember in regarding this, the stilted and frozen figures and faces, which, before Giotto broke their bonds and inspired them, had professed to tell the Bible's stories.

The third instance I have chosen to quote is Giotto's portrait of Dante which was so strangely lost for many years. The portrait occurs in a painting, the first recorded performance of Giotto's, in which he was said to have introduced the likeness of many of his contemporaries, on the wall of the Palazzo dell' Podestà or Council Chamber of Florence. During the banishment of Dante the wall was plastered or white-washed over, through the influence of his enemies, and though believed to exist, the picture was hidden down to 1840, when, after various futile efforts to recover it, the figures were again brought to light.

This portrait of Dante is altogether removed from the later portraits of the indignant and weary man, of whom the Italian market-women said that he had been in Hell as well as in exile. Giotto's Dante on the walls of the Council Chamber is a noble young man of thirty, full of ambitious hope and early distinction. The face is slightly pointed, with broad forehead, hazel eyes, straight brows and nose, mouth and chin a little projecting. The close cloak or vest with sleeves, and cap in folds hanging down on the shoulder, the hand holding the triple fruit, in prognostication of the harvest of virtue and renown which was to be so bitter as well as so glorious, are all in keeping and have a majesty of their own. The picture is probably known by engravings to many of my readers.

The last example of Giotto's, is the one which of all his works is most potent and patent in its beauty, and has struck, and, in so far as we can tell, will for ages strike, with its greatness multitudes of widely different degrees of cultivation whose intellectual capacity is as far apart as their critical faculty. I mean the matchless Campanile or bell-tower 'towering over the Dome of Brunelleschi' at Florence, formed of coloured marbles—for which Giotto framed the designs, and even executed with his own hands the models for the sculpture. With this lovely sight Dean Alford's description is more in keeping than the prosaic saying of Charles V., that 'the Campanile ought to be kept under glass.' Dean Alford's enthusiasm thus expresses itself:

'A mass of varied light written on the cloudless sky of unfathomed blue; varied but blended, as never in any other building that we had seen; the warm yellow of the lighter marbles separated but not disunited by the ever-recurring bands of dark; or glowing into red where the kisses of the sun had been hottest; or fading again into white where the shadows mostly haunted, or where the renovating hand had been waging conflict with decay.'

It is known that Giotto, together with his friend Dante, died before this—Giotto's last great work—was finally constructed by Giotto's pupil, Taddeo Gaddi, and that therefore neither of the friends could have really looked on 'Giotto's Tower,' though Italian Ciceroni point out, and strangers love to contemplate, the very stone on which 'Grim Dante' sat and gazed with admiration in the calm light of evening on the enduring memorial of the painter.

Giotto died in the year 1336 or 1337, his biographer adds, 'no less a good Christian than an excellent painter,' and in token of his faith he painted one crucifixion in which he introduced his own figure 'kneeling in an attitude of deep devotion and contrition at the foot of the Cross.' The good taste of such an act has been questioned, so has been the practice which painted the Virgin Mother now as a brown Italian, now as a red and white Fleming, and again as a flaxen-haired German or as a swarthy Spaniard, and draped her and all the minor figures in the grandest drama the world ever saw—as well as the characters in older Scripture histories, in the Florentine, Venetian, and Antwerp fashions of the day. The defence of the practice is, that the Bible is for universal time, that its Virgin Mother, its apostles and saints, were types of other mothers and of other heroes running down the stream of history; that even the one central and holy figure, if He may be represented at all, as the Divine brother of all humanity, may be clad not inaptly in the garments of all. It appears to me that there is reason in this answer, and that viewed in its light the criticism which constantly demands historic fidelity is both carping and narrow. I do not mean, however, to underrate historic accuracy in itself, or to depreciate that longing for completeness in every particular, which drives our modern painters to the East to study patiently for months the aspects of nature under its Oriental climate, with its peculiar people and animals, its ancient costumes and architecture.

Giotto was buried with suitable honours by a city which, like the rest of the nation, has magnified its painters amongst its great men, in the church of Santa Maria del Fiore, where his master Cimabue had been buried. Lorenzo de' Medici afterwards placed over Giotto's tomb his effigy in marble.

In chronicling ancient art I must here diverge a little. I have already mentioned how closely painting was in the beginning allied with working in metals as well as with sculpture and architecture. It is thus necessary to write of a magnificent work in metal, the study and admiration of generations of painters, begun in the life of Giotto, and completed in two divisions, extending over a period of nearly a hundred years. We shall proceed to deal with the first division, and recur to the second a little later.

Let me first say a word to explain the extent of the treasures of art in the old Italian cities. They were then the great merchant cities of the world, more or less republican in their constitution. They stood to the citizens, who rarely left their walls, at once as peculiar possessions and as native countries rather than as cities alone, while they excited all the patriotism, pride, and love that were elsewhere expended on a whole country—which after all was held as belonging largely to its king and nobles. The old Italian merchant guilds, and wealthy merchants as individuals, vied with each other in signalizing their good citizenship by presenting—as gifts identified with their names—to their cities, those palace buildings, chapels, paintings, gates, which are the delight of the world to this day. It was a merchant guild which thought happily of giving to Florence the bronze gates to the baptistery of San Giovanni or St John the Baptist, attached to the Cathedral. After some competition the gates were intrusted to **Andrea Pisano,** one of a great group of painters, sculptors, and architects linked together and named, as so often happened in Italy, for their place of birth, Pisa. Andrea executed a series of beautiful reliefs from the life of John the Baptist, which were cast in 1330, gilt, and placed in the centre door-way. I shall leave the rest of the gates, still more exquisitely wrought, till their proper time, only observing that the Pisani group of carvers and founders are supposed to have attained their extraordinary superiority in skill and grace, even over such a painter as Giotto, in consequence of one of them, Nicola Pisano, having given his attention to the study of some ancient Greek sarcophagi preserved at Pisa.

Passing for a while from the gates of St John of Florence, we come back to painting and a painter, and with them to another monument — in itself very noble and curious in its mouldering age, of the old Italians' love to their cities. **Andrea Orcagna,** otherwise known as **Andrea di Cione,** one of a brotherhood of painters, was born in Florence about 1315. His greatest works are in the Campo Santa of Pisa.

This wonderful 'holy field' is a grand legacy, so far as dilapidation, alas, will let it be, of the old painters. Originally a place of burial, though no longer used as such, it is enclosed by high walls and an arcade, something like the cloisters of a cathedral or college running round, and having on the north and east sides chapels where masses for the dead were celebrated. The space in the centre was filled with earth brought from the Holy Land by the merchant ships of Pisa. It is covered with turf, having tall cypress-trees at the corners, and a little cross in the centre. The arcade is pierced with sixty-two windows, and contains on its marble pavement hundreds of monuments — among them the Greek sarcophagi studied by Nicola Pisano. But the great distinction of the Campo Santa (of which there are many photographs) are the walls opposite the windows of the arcade painted with Scriptural subjects by artists of the fourteenth and fifteenth centuries, for the decoration of the walls was continued at intervals, during two hundred years. The havoc wrought by time and damp has been terrible; not only are the pictures faded and discoloured, but of the earliest only mutilated fragments, 'here an arm and there a head,' remain. Giotto's illustrations of the book of Job have thus perished. Still Orcagna's work has partially escaped, and left us indications of what it was in his and its youth, when Michael Angelo and Raphael did not disdain to borrow from it in design and arrangement. Dean Alford has thus described Orcagna's mournful, thoughtful 'Triumph of Death:'

'The picture is one of crowded action, and contains very many personages. The action may be supposed to begin in the lower corner on the right hand. There we see what appears to be a wedding-party seated in festivity under a grove of orange-trees laden with fruit. Over two of them a pair of winged loves flutter in the air, and musicians are entertaining them with merry strains. But close to them on the left comes swooping down on bats' wings, and armed with the inevitable scythe, the genius of Death. Her wild hair streams in the wind, her bosom is invulnerable, being closed in a trellised armour of steel. Beneath her, on the ground, are a heap of corpses, shown by their attire to be the great and wealthy of the world. Three winged figures, two fiends and one angel, are drawing souls, in the form of children, out of the mouths of three of these corpses. Above, the air is full of flying spirits, angels and demons: the former beautiful and saintly, the latter hideous and bestial. Some are dragging, or bearing upwards, human souls: others are on their way to fetch them from the heaps of dead: others, again, are flying about apparently without aim. Further yet to the left, a company of wretched ones, lame and in rags, are invoking Death with outstretched arms to come to their relief; but she sweeps by and heeds them not.

'Dividing one half of the picture from the other, is a high range of rocks, terminating in a fiery mountain, into which the demons are casting the unhappy souls which they have carried off. Beyond that seems to be a repetition of the same lesson respecting Death in another form. A party of knights and dames are issuing on horseback from a mountain pass. In the left hand of the picture there lie in their path three corpses in coffins, with coronets on their heads. One is newly dead; on the second, decay has begun its work; the third is reduced to a grinning skeleton. The impression produced on the gay party by the sight is very various. Some look on carelessly; one holds his nose in disgust; one, a lady jewelled and crowned, leans her head on her hand in solemn thought. Above, on a rising ground, an aged monk (it is said, Saint Macarius) is holding a scroll, and pointing out to passengers the moral of the sight which meets them. The path winds up a hill crowned with a church, and by its side at various points are hermits sitting in calm security, or following peaceful occupations. One of them is milking a doe; another is reading; a third is calmly contemplating from a distance the valley of Death. About them are various animals and birds. The idea evidently intended to be conveyed is that deliverance from the fear of death is to be found not in gaiety and dissipation, but in contemplation and communion with God.

'Such is the wonderful fresco, and the execution is as wonderful as the conception. Belonging as the painter did to a rude and early period of art, he yet had the power of endowing his figures with both majesty and tenderness of expression.'

The Last Judgment is no less solemn and sad, with hope tempering its sadness. Mrs Jameson's note of it is: 'Above, in the centre, Christ and the Virgin are throned in separate glories. He turns to the left, towards the condemned, while he uncovers the wound in his side, and raises his right arm with a menacing gesture, his countenance full of majestic wrath. The Virgin, on the right of her Son, is the picture of heavenly mercy, and, as if terrified at the words of eternal condemnation, she turns away. On either side are ranged the Prophets of the Old Testament, the Apostles and other saints, severe, solemn, dignified figures. Angels, holding the instruments of the Passion, hover over Christ and the Virgin; under them is a group of archangels. The archangel Michael stands in the midst holding a scroll in each hand; immediately before him another archangel, supposed to represent Raphael, the guardian angel of humanity, cowers down, shuddering, while two others sound the awful trumpets of doom. Lower down is the earth where men are seen rising from their graves; armed angels direct them to the right and left. Here is seen King Solomon, who, whilst he rises, seems doubtful to which side he should turn; here a hypocritical monk, whom an angel draws back by the hair from the host of the blessed; and there a youth in a gay and rich costume, whom another angel leads away to Paradise. There is wonderful and even terrible power of expression in some of the heads; and it is said that among them are many portraits of contemporaries, but unfortunately no circumstantial traditions as to particular figures have reached us.'

One of Orcagna's altar-pieces, that of 'the coronation of the Virgin,' containing upwards of a hundred figures, and with the colouring still rich, is in our National Gallery. As an architect, Orcagna designed the famous Loggia de' Lanzi of the grand ducal palace at Florence.

Now I must take you back to the bronze gates of the Baptistery in their triumphant completion nearly a hundred years after the first gate was executed by Andrea Pisano. I should have liked, but for our limits, to tell in full the legend of the election of Lorenzo Ghiberti, the step-son of a goldsmith, and skilled in chasing and enamelling, to design the second gate; when yet a lad of twenty-three, how he and two other young men, one of them still younger than Ghiberti, were declared the most promising competitors in the trial for the work; how the last two voluntarily withdrew from the contest, magnanimously proclaiming Lorenzo Ghiberti their superior; how all the three lived to be famous, the one as a founder in metal, the others as an architect and a sculptor, and remained sworn brothers in art till death.

Lorenzo Ghiberti has left us an expression of the feeling with which he set about his task, an expression so suggestive that, even had we no other indication, it is enough to stamp the true and tender nature of the man. He prepared for his achievement 'with infinite diligence and love'—the words deserve to be pondered over. He took at least twenty-two years to his work, receiving for it eleven hundred florins. He chose his subjects from the life and death of the Lord, working them out in twenty panels, ten on each side of the folding doors, and below these were eight panels containing full-length figures of the four evangelists and four doctors of the Latin Church, with a complete border of fruit and foliage, having heads of prophets and sibyls interspersed. So entire was the satisfaction the superb gate gave, that Lorenzo was not merely loaded with praise, he received a commission to design and cast a third and central gate which should surpass the others, that were thenceforth to be the side entrances.

For his second gate Lorenzo Ghiberti repaired to the Old Testament for subjects, beginning with the creation and ending with the meeting of Solomon and the Queen of Sheba, and represented them in ten compartments enclosed in a rich border of fruit and foliage, with twenty-four full-length figures of the Hebrew heroes and prophets, clearly and delicately designed and finished, occupying corresponding niches. This crowning gate engaged the founder upwards of eighteen years — forty-nine years are given as the term of the work of both the gates.

The single defect which is found in those marvellous gates — left to us as a testimony of what the life-long devotion of genius could produce — is that they abound floridly both in ornament and action, in place of being severely simple and restrained according to the classical standard.

Michael Angelo called these gates 'worthy to be the gates of Paradise,' and they are still one of the glories of Florence. Casts of the gates are to be found in the School for Art at Kensington, and at the Crystal Palace.

A young village boy learned to draw and model from Ghiberti's gates. He in his turn was to create in the Brancacci Chapel of the Church of the Carmine at Florence a school of painters scarcely less renowned and powerful in its effects than that produced by the works in the Campo Santa. You will find the Italian painters not unfrequently known by nicknames, quite as often by their father's trades as by their father's surnames, and still oftener by the town which was their place of birth or nurture. This **Tommaso Guido**, or Maso de San Giovanni (from his village birth-place), was commonly called Masaccio, short for Tomasaccio, 'hulking Tom,' as I have heard it translated, on account of his indifferent, slovenly habits. I think there is a tradition that he entered a studio in Florence as a colour boy, and electrified the painter and his scholars, by *brownie* like freaks of painting at their unfinished work, in their absence, better than any of his masters, and by the dexterity with which he perpetrated the frolic of putting the facsimile of a fly on one of the faces on the easels. His end was a tragic conclusion to such light comedy. At the age of twenty-six, he quitted Florence for Rome so suddenly that he left his finest frescoes unfinished. It was said that he was summoned thither by the Pope. At Rome, where little or nothing of Masaccio's life is known, he died shortly afterwards, not without a suspicion of his having been poisoned.

A curious anecdote exists of the identification of the time when he forsook Florence to meet his death in Rome. Just as we have read, that the period of the death of Massinger the dramatist has been settled by an entry in an old parish register, 'died, Philip Massinger a stranger,' so there has been found some quaint equivalent to a modern tax-paper which had been delivered at the dwelling of Masaccio when the word 'gone' was written down.

There is a further tradition—not very probable under the circumstances—that Masaccio is buried, without name or stone, under the Brancacci Chapel. Be that as it may, he very early rose to eminence, surpassing all his predecessors in drawing and colouring, and he combined with those acquirements such animation and variety of expression in his characters, that it was said of him 'he painted souls as well as bodies,' while his invention was not less bold and fresh.

It is difficult to indicate Masaccio's pictures because some of them have been repainted and destroyed. As to those in the Brancacci Chapel from the life of St Peter, (with the exception of two,) considerable confusion has arisen as to which are Masaccio's, and which belong to his scholar Filippino Lippi. The fresco which Masaccio left unfinished, that of the Apostles Peter and Paul raising a dead youth (from traditional history), was finished by Lippi. In the fresco of Peter baptizing the converts, generally attributed to Masaccio, there is a lad who has thrown off his garments, and stands shivering with cold, whose figure, according to authority, formed an epoch in art. Lionardo da Vinci, Michael Angelo, Andrea del Sarto, Fra Bartolommeo, all studied their art in this chapel. Raphael borrowed the grand figure of St Paul preaching at Athens in one of the cartoons, from one of Masaccio's or Filippo Lippi's frescoes. Masaccio's excellence as an artist, reached at an immature age, is very remarkable.

I have come to the last and probably the best appreciated among modems of the early Italian painters. Fra **Angelico da Fiesole**, the gentle devout monk whom Italians called '*Il Beato*,' the Blessed, and who probably did receive the distinction of beatification, a distinction only second in the Roman Catholic Church to that of canonization. He was born at the lovely little mountain-town of Fiesole near Florence, 1387, and his worldly name, which he bore only till his twenty-first year, was Guido Petri de Mugello. In his youth, with his gift already recognized, so that he might well have won ease and honour in the world, he entered the Dominican Convent of St Mark, Florence, for what he deemed the good and peace of his soul. He seldom afterwards left it, and that only as directed by his convent superior, or summoned by the Pope. He was a man devoid of personal ambition, pure, humble, and meek. When offered the Archbishopric of Florence as a tribute to his sanctity, he declined it on account of his unworthiness for the office. He would not work for money, and only painted at the command of his prior. He began his painting with fasting and prayer. Believing himself inspired in his work, he steadfastly refused to make any alteration in the originals. It is said that he was found dead at his easel with a completed picture before him. It is not wonderful, that from such a man should come one side of the perfection of that idealism which Giotto had begun. Fra Angelico's angels, saints, Saviour, and Virgin are more divinely calm, pure, sweet, endowed with a more exulting saintliness, a more immortal youth and joy, and a more utter self-abnegation and sympathetic tenderness than are to be found in the saints and the angels, the Saviour and the Virgin of other painters. Neither is it surprising that Fra Angelico's defects, besides that of the bad drawing which shows more in his large than in his small pictures, are those of a want of human knowledge, power, and freedom. His wicked—even his more earthly-souled characters, are weak and faulty in action. What should the reverent and guileless dreamer know, unless indeed by inspiration of the rude conflicts, the fire and fury of human passions intensified in the malice and anguish of devils? But Fra Angelico's singular successes far transcend his failures. In addition to the sublime serenity and positive radiance of expression which he could impart to his heads, his notions of grouping and draping were full of grace, sometimes of splendour and magnificence. In harmony with his happy temperament and fortunes, he was fond of gay yet delicate colours 'like spring flowers,' and used a profusion of gold ornaments which do not seem out of keeping in his pictures. The most of Fra Angelico's pictures are in Florence—the best in his own old convent of St Mark, where he lovingly adorned not only chapter-hall and court, but the cells of his brother friars. A crucifix with adoring saints worshipping their crucified Saviour is regarded as his master-piece in St Mark's. A famous coronation of the Virgin, which Fra Angelico painted for a church in his native town, and which is now in the Louvre, Paris, is thus described by Mrs Jameson: 'It represents a throne under a rich Gothic canopy, to which there is an ascent of nine steps; on the highest kneels the Virgin, veiled, her hands crossed on her bosom. She is clothed in a red tunic, a blue robe over it, and a royal mantle with a rich border flowing down behind. The features are most delicately lovely, and the expression of the face full of humility and adoration. Christ, seated on the throne, bends forward, and is in the act of placing the crown on her head; on each side are twelve angels, who are playing a heavenly concert with guitars, tambourines, trumpets, viols, and other musical instruments; lower than these, on each side, are forty holy personages of the Old and New Testament; and at the foot of the throne kneel several saints, male and female, among them St Catherine with her wheel, St Agnes with her lamb, and St Cecilia crowned with flowers. Beneath the principal picture there is a row of seven small ones, forming a border, and representing various incidents in the life of St Dominic.'

CHAPTER II.

EARLY FLEMISH ART—THE VAN EYCKS, 1366-1442—MABUSE, MATSYS, 1460-1530 OR 31.

In the Low Countries painting had very much the same history that it had in Italy, but the dates are later, and there may be a longer interval given to each stage of development. Religious painting, profuse in symbolism, with masses of details elaborately worked in, meets us in the first place. This style of painting reached its culmination, in which it included (as it did not include in its representation in the Italian pictures) many and varied excellencies, among them the establishment of painting in oil in the pictures of the Flemish family of painters—the Van Eycks.

Before going into the little that is known of the family history of the **Van Eycks,** I should like to call attention to the numerous painter families in the middle ages. What a union, and repose, and happy sympathy of art-life it indicates, which we appear to have lost in the restlessness and separate interests of modern life. The Van Eycks consisted of no less than four members of a family, three brothers, Hubert, John, and Lambert, and one sister, Margaret, devoted, like her brothers, to her art. There is a suggestion that they belonged to a small village of Limburg called Eyck, and repaired to Bruges in order to pursue their art. Hubert was thirty years older than John, and it is said that he was a serious-minded man as well as an ardent painter, and belonged to the religious fraternity of our Lady of Ghent. He died in 1426. John, though of so much consideration in his profession as to be believed to be 'the Flemish Painter' sent by Duke Philip the Good of Flanders and Burgundy with a mission to Portugal to solicit the hand of a princess in marriage, is reported to have died very poor in 1449, and has the suspicion attached to him of having been a lover of pleasure and a spendthrift. Of Lambert, the third brother, almost nothing is known; indeed, the fact of his existence has only lately come to light. Margaret lived and died unmarried, and belonged, like her brother Hubert, to the religious society of our Lady of Ghent. She died about 1432.

The invention of painting in oil, for which the Van Eycks are commonly known, was not literally that of mixing colours with oil, which was occasionally done before their day. It was the combining oil with resin, so as to produce at once a good varnish, and avoid the necessity of drying pictures in the sun, a bright thought, which may stand in the same rank with the construction, by James Watt, of that valve which rendered practicable the application of steam to machinery. The thought, occasioned by the cracking of a picture in tempera exposed to the sun, is due to Hubert Van Eyck.

The great picture of the Van Eycks, which was worked at for a number of years by both Hubert and John, and, as some reckon, touched by the whole family, is the 'Adoration of the Lamb,' at St Bavon's, Ghent. I should like to give a faint idea of this extraordinary picture, which was painted for a burgomaster of Ghent and his wife in order to adorn their mortuary chapel in the cathedral. It was an altar piece on separate panels, now broken up and dispersed, only a portion of it being retained in Ghent.

It may strike some as strange that a picture should be on panels, but those of the old pictures which were not on plastered walls were commonly on panels, many of them on the lids and sides of chests and presses which were used to hold sacred vessels and priestly raiment.

When the wings of the Van Eycks' altar-piece of the 'Adoration of the Lamb' were opened on festivals, the subjects of the upper central picture were seen, consisting of the Triune God, a majestic figure, and at his side in stately calm the Virgin and the Baptist. On the inside of the wings were angels, at the two extremities Adam and Eve. The lower central picture shows the Lamb of the Revelation, whose blood flows into a cup; over it is the dove of the Holy Spirit. Angels, who hold the instruments of the Passion, worship the Lamb. Four groups of many persons advance from the sides, these are the holy martyrs, men and women, priests and laymen. In the foreground is the fountain of life; in the distance are the towers of the heavenly Jerusalem. On the wings other groups are coming up to adore the Lamb; on the left those who have laboured for the Kingdom of the Lord by worldly deeds—the soldiers of Christ led by St George, St Sebastian, and St Michael, the patron saints of the old Flemish guilds, followed by emperors and kings—a goodly company. Beyond the soldiers and princes, on the left, are the righteous judges, also on horseback. In front of them, on a splendidly caparisoned gray, rides a mild, benevolent old man in blue velvet trimmed with fur. This is the likeness of Hubert Van Eyck, painted after his death by his brother John, and John himself is in the group, clothed in black, with a shrewd, sharp countenance. On the right are the saints who by self-renunciation have served the Lamb in the spirit, hermits and pilgrims, among them St Christopher, St Anthony, St Paul the hermit, Mary Magdalene, and St Mary of Egypt. A compartment underneath, which represented hell, finished the whole—yet only the whole on one side, for the wings when closed presented another series of finely thought-out and finished pictures—the Annunciation; figures of Micah and Zechariah; statues of the two St Johns, with the likenesses of the donors who gave to the world so great a work of art, kneeling humbly side by side, the burgomaster somewhat mean-looking in such company in spite of the proof of his liberality, but his wife noble enough in feature and expression to have been the originator of this glory of early Flemish painting. The upper part of the picture is painted on a gold ground, round the central figure of the Lamb is vivid green grass with masses of trees and flowers—indeed there is much lovely landscape no longer indicated by a rock or a bush, but betokening close observation of nature, whether in a fruitful valley, or a rocky defile, or mountain ridges with fleecy clouds overhead. The expression of the immense number of figures is as varied and characteristic as their grouping. [2]

Hubert Van Eyck died while this work was in progress, and it was finished by his brother John six years after Hubert's death. When one thinks of the intense application and devotion which such a work costs, and recalls the bronze gates of St John that occupied Lorenzo Ghiberti 49 years, and when we read, as we shall read a few chapters farther on, of large paintings which were begun and ended in so many days — even so many hours, one can better understand what is the essential difference between the works of the early and the later painters, a difference which no skill, no power even can bridge over. John Van Eyck, who had lived late enough to have departed from the painting of sacred pictures alone, so that he left portraits and an otter hunt among his works, is three times represented in our National Gallery, in three greatly esteemed portraits, one a double portrait, believed to be the likenesses of the painter and his wife, standing hand in hand with a terrier dog at their feet.

Gossaert, called **de Mabuse** from his native town of Mabeuze, sometimes signing his name Joannes Malbodius, followed in the steps of the Van Eycks, particularly in his great picture of the 'Adoration of the Kings,' which is at Castle Howard, the seat of the Earl of Carlisle. Mabuse was in England and painted the children of Henry VII, in a picture, which is at Hampton Court. There is a picture in the palace of Holyrood, Edinburgh, which has been attributed to Mabuse. It represents on the sides of a triptych or diptych (somewhat like a folding screen) James III. and his queen with attendants. The fur on the queen's dress displays already that marvellous technical skill for which Flemish painting is so celebrated.

Hans Memling belonged to Bruges. There is a tradition of him, which is to a certain extent disproven, that he was a poor soldier relieved by the hospital of St John, Bruges, and that in gratitude he executed for the hospital the well-known reliquary of St Ursula. However it might have originated, this is the most noted work of a painter, who was distinguished frequently by his minute missal-like painting (he was also an illuminator of missals), in which he would introduce fifteen hundred small figures in a picture two feet eight inches, by six feet five inches in size, and work out every detail with the utmost niceness and care. The reliquary, or 'chasse,' is a wooden coffer or shrine about four feet in length, its style and form those of a rich Gothic church, its purpose to hold an arm of the saint. The whole exterior is covered with miniatures by Memling, nearly the whole of them giving incidents in the legendary history of St Ursula, a 'virgin princess of Brittany,' or of England, who, setting out with eleven thousand virgins—her companions, her lover, and an escort of knights on a pilgrimage to Rome, was, with her whole company, met and murdered, by a horde of heathen Huns, when they had reached Cologne, on their return. My readers may be aware that the supposed bones of the virgins and St Ursula form the ghastly adornment of the church founded in her honour at Cologne. It is absolutely filled with bones, built into the walls, stowed under the pavement, ranged in glass cases about the choir. Hans Memling's is a pleasanter commemoration of St Ursula.

Quintin Matsys, the blacksmith of Antwerp, was born at Louvain about 1460. Though he worked first as a smith he is said by Kugler to have belonged to a family of painters, which somewhat takes from the romance, though it adds to the probability of his story. Another painter in Antwerp having offered the hand and dowry of his daughter—beloved by Quintin Matsys—as a prize to the painter who should paint the best picture in a competition for her hand, the doughty smith took up the art, entered the lists, and carried off the maiden and her portion from all his more experienced rivals. The vitality of the legend is indicated by the inscription on a tablet to the memory of Quintin Matsys in the Cathedral, Antwerp. The Latin inscription reads thus in English:

'´Twas love connubial taught the smith to paint,'

Quintin Matsys lived and died a respected burgher of Antwerp, a member of the great Antwerp painters' guild of St Luke. He was twice married, and had thirteen children.

Whatever might have been his source of inspiration, Quintin Matsys was an apt scholar. His 'Descent from the Cross,' now in the Museum, Antwerp, was *the* 'Descent from the Cross,' and *the* picture in the Cathedral, until superseded by Rubens´ master-piece on the same subject. Still Quintin Matsys´ version remains, and is in some respects an unsurpassed picture. There is a traditional grouping of this Divine tragedy, and Quintin Matsys has followed the tradition. The body of the Lord is supported by two venerable old men—Joseph of Arimathea and Nicodemus—while the holy women anoint the wounds of the Saviour; the Virgin swooning with grief is supported by St John. The figures are full of individuality, and their action is instinct with pathos. For this picture Quintin Matsys—popular painter as he was—got only three hundred florins, equivalent to twenty-five pounds (although, of course, the value of money was much greater in those days). The Joiners´ Company, for whom he painted the 'Descent from the Cross,' sold the picture to the City of Antwerp for five times the original amount, and it is said Queen Elizabeth offered the City nearly twenty times the first sum for it, in vain.

Quintin Matsys painted frequently half-length figures of the Virgin and Child, an example of which is in the National Gallery. He excelled in the 'figure painting' of familiar subjects, then just beginning to be established, affording a token of the direction which the future eminence of the Flemish painters would take. One of his famous pictures of this kind is 'The Misers,' in the Queen's collection at Windsor. Two figures in the Flemish costume of the time, are seated at a table; before them are a heap of money and a book, in which one is writing with his right hand, while he tells down the money with his left. The faces express craft and cupidity. The details of the ink-horn on the table, and the bird on its perch behind, have the Flemish graphic exactness.

CHAPTER III.

IN EARLY SCHOOLS OF ITALIAN ART—THE BELLINI, 1422-1512—MANTEGNA, 1431-1506—GHIRLANDAJO, 1449-1498—IL FRANCIA, 1450-1518—FRA BARTOLOMMEO, 1469-1517—ANDREA DEL SARTO, 1488-1530.

I have come to the period when Italian art is divided into many schools—Paduan, Venetian, Umbrian, Florentine, Roman, Bolognese, &c., &c. With the schools and their definitions I do not mean to meddle, except it may be to mention to which school a great painter belonged. Another difficulty meets me here. I have been trying so far as I could to give the representative painters in the order of time. I can no longer follow this rule strictly, and the grouping of this chapter is made on the principle of leading my readers up by some of the predecessors who linked the older to the later Italian painters, and by some of the contemporaries of these later painters, to that central four, Lionardo da Vinci, Michael Angelo, Raphael, and Titian, who occupy so great a place in the history of art.

In the brothers **Bellini** and their native Venice, we must first deal with that excellence of colouring for which the Venetian painters were signally noted, while they comparatively neglected and underrated drawing. A somewhat fanciful theory has been started, that as Venice, Holland, and England have been distinguished for colour in art, and as all those States are by the sea, so a sea atmosphere has something to do with a passion for colour. Within more reasonable bounds, in reference to the Venetians, is the consideration that no colouring is richer, mellower, more exquisitely tinted than that which belongs to the blue Italian sky over the blue Adriatic, with those merged shades of violet, green, and amber, and that magical soft haze which has to do with a moist climate.

The two brothers **Gentile** and **Gian** or **John Bellini,** the latter the more famous of the two, were the sons of an old Venetian painter, with regard to whom the worthy speech is preserved, that he said it was like the Tuscans for son to beat father, and he hoped, in God's name, that Giovanni or Gian would outstrip him, and Gentile, the elder, outstrip both. The brothers worked together and were true and affectionate brothers, encouraging and appreciating each other.

Gentile was sent by the Doge at the request of the Sultan—either Mahommed II, or Bajazet II., to Constantinople, where Gentile Bellini painted the portrait of the Sultan and the Sultana his mother, now in the British Museum. The painter also painted the head of John the Baptist in a charger as an offering—only too suitable—from him to the Grand Turk. The legend goes on to tell that in the course of the presentation of the gift, an incident occurred which induced Gentile Bellini to quit the Ottoman Court with all haste.

The Sultan had criticized the appearance of the neck in John the Baptist's severed head, and when Gentile ventured to defend his work, the Sultan proceeded to prove the correctness of his criticism, by drawing his scimitar and cutting off at a stroke the head of a kneeling slave, and pointing to the spouting blood and the shrinking muscle, gave the horrified painter a lesson in practical anatomy. On Gentile's return from the East, he was pensioned by his State, and lived on painting, till he was eighty years of age, dying in 1501.

Gian Bellini is said to have obtained by a piece of deceit, which is not in keeping with his manly and honourable character, the secret, naturally coveted by a Venetian, of mixing colours with resin and oil. A Venetian painter had brought the secret from Flanders, and communicated it to a friend, who, in turn, communicated it to a third painter, and was murdered by that third painter for his pains, so greedy and criminal was the craving, not only to possess, but to be as far as possible the sole possessor of, the grand discovery. Gian Bellini was much less guilty, if he were really guilty. Disguised as a Venetian nobleman, he proposed to sit for his portrait to that Antonella who first brought the secret from Flanders, and while Antonella worked with unsuspicious openness, Gian Bellini watched the process and stole the secret.

Gian Bellini lived to the age of ninety, and had among his admirers the poet Ariosto and Albrecht Dürer. The latter saw Gian Bellini in his age, and said of him, when foolish mockers had risen up to scout at the old man, and his art now become classic, 'He is very old, but he is still the best of our painters.' Gian Bellini had illustrious pupils, including in their number Titian and Giorgione.

The portraits of Gentile and Gian, which are preserved in a painting by Gian, show Gentile fair-complexioned and red-haired, and Gian with dark hair.

Gian Bellini is considered to have been less gifted with imagination than some of his great brother artists; but he has proved himself a man of high moral sense, and while he stopped short at the boundary between the seen and the unseen, it is certain he must still have painted with much of 'the divine patience' and devout consecration of all his powers, and of every part of his work, which are the attributes of the earliest Italian painters. When he and his brother began to paint, Venetian art had already taken its distinctive character for open-air effects, rich scenic details in architecture, furniture and dress (said to be conspicuous in commercial communities), and a growing tendency to portraiture. Gian went with the tide, but he guided it to noble results. His simplicity and good sense, with his purity and dignity of mind, were always present. He introduced into his pictures 'singing boys, dancing cherubs, glittering thrones, and dewy flowers,' pressing the outer world into his service and that of religious art. It is said also that his Madonnas seem 'amiable beings imbued with a lofty grace;' while his saints are 'powerful and noble forms.' But he never descended to the paltry or the vulgar. He knew from the depths of his own soul how to invest a face with moral grandeur. Especially in his representations of our Saviour Gian Bellini 'displays a perception of moral power and grandeur seldom equalled in the history of art.' The example given is that of the single figure of the Lord in the Dresden Gallery, where the Son of God, without nimbus, or glory, stands forth as the 'ideal of elevated humanity.'

The greater portion of Gian Bellini's pictures remain in the churches and galleries of Venice. But the first great work at which the two brothers in their youth worked in company—the painting of the Hall of Council in the palace of the Doge, with a series of historical and legendary pictures of the Venetian wars with the Emperor Frederick Barbarossa (1177), including the Doge Ziani's receiving from the Pope the gold ring with which the Doge espoused the Adriatic, in token of perpetual dominion over the sea — was unfortunately destroyed by fire in 1577. Giovanni Bellini's greatest work, now at St Salvatore, is Christ at Emmaus, with Venetian senators and a Turkish dragoman introduced as spectators of the risen Lord.

Of another great work at Vicenza, painted in Gian Bellini's old age, when neither his skill nor his strength was abated, 'The Baptism of Christ,' Dean Alford writes thus:

'Let us remain long and look earnestly, for there is indeed much to be seen. That central figure, standing with hands folded on His bosom, so gentle, so majestic, so perfect in blameless humanity, oh what labour of reverent thought; what toil of ceaseless meditation;

what changes of fair purpose, oscillating into clearest vision of ideal truth, must it have cost the great painter, before he put forth that which we see now! It is as impossible to find aught but love and majesty in the Divine countenance, as it is to discover a blemish on the complexion of that body, which seems to give forth light from itself, as He stands in obedience, fulfilling all righteousness.

'And even on the accessories to this figure, we see the same loving and reverent toil bestowed. The cincture, where alone the body is hidden from view, is no web of man's weaving; or, if it were, it is of hers whose heart was full of divine thoughts as she wove: so bright and clear is the tint, so exquisitely careful and delicate every fold where

light may play or colour vary. And look under the sacred feet, on the ground blessed by their pressure; no dash of hurrying brush has been there: less than a long day's light, from morn to dewy eve, did not suffice to give in individual shape and shade every minutest pebble and mote of that shore of Jordan. Every one of them was worth painting, for we are viewing them as in the light of His presence who made them all and knew them all.

'And now let us pass to the other figures: to that living and glowing angelic group in the left hand of the picture. Three of the heavenly host are present, variously affected by that which they behold. The first, next the spectator, in the corner of the picture, is standing in silent adoration, tender and gentle in expression, the hands together, but only the points of the fingers touching, his very reverence being chastened by angelic modesty; the second turns on that which he sees a look of earnest inquiry, but kneels as he looks; and indeed that which he sees is one of the things which angels

desire to look into. The third, a majestic herald-like figure, stands, as one speaking, looking to the spectator, with his right hand on his garment, and his left out as in demonstration, unmistakeably saying to us who look on, "Behold what love is here!" Then, hardly noticing what might well be much noticed, the grand dark figure of the Baptist on the right, let us observe how beautifully and accurately all the features of the landscape are given.'

Of the same work another critic records: 'The attendant angels in this work (signed by the artist) are of special interest, instinct with an indefinable purity and depth of reverential tenderness elsewhere hardly rivalled. But the picture, like that in S. Giovanni Crisostomo, with which it is nearly contemporary, is almost more interesting from the astonishing truth and beauty of its landscape portions. *These* form here a feature more important, perhaps, than in any work of that period; the stratification and form of the rocks in the fore-ground, the palms and other trees relieved against the lucid distance, and the mountain-ranges of tender blue beyond, are as much beyond praise for their beauty and their truth, as they have been beyond imitation from the solidity and transparent strength of their execution! The minute finish is Nature's, and the colouring more gem-like than gems.'

No praise can exceed that bestowed on Gian Bellini's colouring for its intensity and transparency. 'Many of his draperies are like crystal of the clearest and deepest colour,' declares an authority; and another states' his best works have a clear jewel brightness, an internal gem-like fire such as warms a summer twilight. The shadows are intense and yet transparent, like the Adriatic waves when they lie out of the sun under the palace bridges.'

Portrait-painting, just beginning, was established in Venice, its later stronghold, by Gian Bellini. His truthful portrait of the Doge Loredano, one of the earliest of that series of Doges' portraits which once hung in state in the ducal palace, is now in our National Gallery.

Of Gentile Bellini, whose work was softer, but less vigorous than his brother's, the best painting extant is that at Milan of St Mark preaching at Alexandria, in which the painter showed how he had profited by his residence at Constantinople in the introduction of much rich Turkish costume, and of an animal unknown to Europe at the time—a camelopard.

Andrea Mantegna was born near Padua. He was the son of a farmer. His early history, according to tradition, is very similar to that of Giotto. Just as Cimabue adopted Giotto, Squarcione, a painter who had travelled in Italy and Greece, and made a great collection of antiques, from which he taught in a famous school of painters, adopted Andrea Mantegna at the early age of ten years. It was long believed that Mantegna, in the end, forfeited the favour of his master by marrying Nicolosa Bellini, the sister of Gentile and Gian Bellini, whose father was the great rival of Squarcione; and farther, that Mantegna's style of painting had been considerably influenced by his connection with the Bellini. Modern researches, which have substituted another surname for that of Bellini as the surname of Andrea Mantegna's wife, contradict this story.

Andrea Mantegna, a man of much energy and fancy, entered young into the service of the Gonzaga lords of Mantua, receiving from them a salary of thirty pounds a year and a piece of land, on which the painter built a house, and painted it within and without — the latter one of the first examples of artistic waste, followed later by Tintoret and Veronese, regardless of the fact that painting could not survive in the open air of Northern Italy.

Andrea Mantegna had his home at Mantua, except when he was called to Rome to paint for the Pope, Innocent VIII. An anecdote is told by Mrs Jameson of this commission. It seems the Pope's payments were irregular; and one day when he visited his painter at work, and his Holiness asked the meaning of a certain allegorical female figure in the design, Andrea answered, with somewhat audacious point, that he was trying to represent *Patience*. The Pope, understanding the allusion, paid the painter in his own coin, by remarking in reply, 'If you would place Patience in fitting company, you would paint Discretion at her side.' Andrea took the hint, said no more, and when his work was finished not only received his money, but was munificently rewarded.

Andrea Mantegna had two sons and a daughter. One of his sons painted with his father, and, after Andrea Mantegna's death, completed some of his pictures.

Andrea Mantegna's early study of antique sculpture moulded his whole life's work. He took great delight in modelling, in perspective, of which he made himself a master, and in chiaroscuro, or light and shade. Had his powers of invention and grace not kept pace with his skill, he would have been a stiff and formal worker; as it was, he carried the austerity of sculpture into painting, and his greatest work, the 'Triumph of Julius Cæsar,' would have been better suited for the chiselled frieze of a temple than it is for the painted frieze of the hall of a palace. Yet he was a great leader and teacher in art, and the true proportions of his drawing are grand, if his colouring is harsh. I am happy to say that Mantegna's 'Triumph of Julius Cæsar' is in England at Hampton Court, having been bought from the Duke of Mantua by Charles I. These cartoons, nine in number, are sketches in water-colour or distemper on paper fixed on cloth. They are faded and dilapidated, as they well may be, considering the slightness of the materials and their age, about four hundred years. At the same time, they are, after the cartoons of Raphael (which formed part of the same art collection of Charles I.), perhaps the most valuable and interesting relic of art in England.

The series of the 'Triumph' contain the different parts, originally separated by pillars, of a long and splendid procession. There are trumpeters and standard bearers, the statues of the gods borne aloft, battering-rams and heaps of glittering armour, trophies of conquest in huge vases filled with coin, garlanded oxen, and elephants. The second last of the series, presents the ranks of captives forming part of the show, rebellious men, submissive women, and unconscious children—a moving picture. In the last of the series comes the great conqueror in his chariot, a youth in the crowd following him, carrying his banner, on which is inscribed Cæsar's notable despatch, 'Veni, vidi, vici;' 'I came, I saw, I conquered.'

Another of Mantegna's best pictures is in distemper—in which, and on fresco, Mantegna chiefly painted,—and is in the Louvre, Paris. It is the Madonna of Victory, so called from its being painted to commemorate the deliverance of Italy from the French army under Charles VIII., a name which has acquired a sardonic meaning from the ultimate destination of the picture. This picture—which represents the Virgin and Child on a throne, in an arbour of fruit and flowers, between the archangels, Michael and St Maurice, in complete armour, with the patron saints of Mantua and the infant St John in the front, and the Marquis Ludovico of Mantua and his wife, Isabella D'Este, kneeling to return thanks—was painted by Mantegna at the age of seventy years; and, as if the art of the man had mellowed with time, it is the softest and tenderest of his pictures in execution. A beautiful Madonna of Mantegna's, still later in time, is in the National Gallery.

When Mantegna was sixty years old he took up the art of engraving, and prosecuted it with zeal and success, being one of the earliest painters who engraved his own pictures, and this accomplishment spread them abroad a hundredfold.

Domenico Ghirlandajo was properly **Domenico Bicordi,** but inherited from his father, a goldsmith in Florence, 3 the by-name of **Ghirlandajo** or Garland-maker—a distinctive appellation said to have been acquired by the elder man from his skill in making silver garlands for the heads of Florentine women and children. Domenico Ghirlandajo worked at his father's craft till he was twenty-four years of age, when, having in the mean time evinced great cleverness in taking the likenesses of the frequenters of Ghirlandajo the elder's shop, the future painter abandoned the goldsmith's trade for art pure and simple. He soon vindicated the wisdom of the step which he had taken by giving proofs of something of the strength of Masaccio, united with a reflection of the feeling of Fra Angelico.

Ghirlandajo was summoned soon to Rome to paint in the Sistine Chapel, afterwards to be so glorious; but his greatest works were done in the prime of his manhood, in his native city, Florence, where he was chosen as the teacher of Michael Angelo, who was apprenticed to Ghirlandajo for three years.

While still in the flower of his age and crowned with golden opinions, being, it is said with effusion, 'the delight of his city,' Ghirlandajo died after a short illness, in Ghirlandajo's time Florence had reached her meridian, and her citizens outvied each other in the magnificence of their gifts to their fair mother city. Ghirlandajo was fitted to be their painter; himself a generous-spirited artist, in the exuberance of life and power, he wished that his fellow-citizens would give him all the walls of the city to cover with frescoes. He was content with the specified sum for his painting, desiring more the approbation of his employers than additional crowns. His genius lying largely in the direction of portrait painting, he introduced frequently the portraits of contemporaries, causing them to figure as spectators of his sacred scenes. One of these contemporaries thus presented, was Amerigo Vespucci, who was to give his name to a continent. Another was a Florentine beauty, a woman of rank, Ginevra de Benci.

Ghirlandajo was lavish in his employment of rich Florentine costumes and architecture. He even made the legends of the saints and the histories of the Bible appear as if they had happened under the shadow of Brunelleschi's duomo and Giotto's campanile, and within sound of the flow of the Arno. In the peculiar colouring used in fresco painting Ghirlandajo excelled.

He painted a chapel for a Florentine citizen, Francesco Sasetti, in the church of the Trinità, Florence, with scenes from the life of St Francis. Of these, the death of St Francis, surrounded by the sorrowing monks of his order, with the figures of Francesco Sasetti and his wife, Madonna Nera, on one side of the picture, is considered the best. As a curious illustration of the modernizing practice of Ghirlandajo, he has painted an old priest at the foot of the bier, chanting the litanies for the dying, with spectacles on his nose, the earliest known representation of these useful instruments.

Ghirlandajo painted during four years the choir of the church of Santa Maria Novella, Florence, for one of the great Florentine benefactors, Giovanni Tornabuone, and there are to be seen some of Ghirlandajo's finest frescoes from the history of John the Baptist and the Virgin.

A Madonna and Child with angels in the National Gallery is attributed to Ghirlandajo.

Francesco Francia, or **Il Francia,** was born at Bologna, and was the son of a carpenter, whose surname was Raibaloni, but Francesco assumed the name of his master, a goldsmith, and worked himself at a goldsmith's trade till he was forty years of age. Indeed he may be said never to have relinquished his connection with the trade, and certainly he was no more ashamed of it than of his calling as a painter, for he signed himself indiscriminately 'goldsmith' and 'painter,' and sometimes whimsically put 'goldsmith' to his paintings and 'painter' to his jewellery. He was a famous designer of dies for coins and medals, and it is quite probable, as a countryman of his own has sought to prove, that he was the celebrated type-cutter, known as 'Francesco da Bologna.' But it is with Francesco *pictor* that we have to do.

Though he only began to prosecute the painter's art in middle age, he rose with remarkable rapidity to eminence, was the great painter of Lombardy in his day, rivalling Squarcione, Mantegna's teacher in his school, which numbered two hundred scholars, and becoming the founder of the early Bolognese school of painters.

Francia is said to have been very handsome in person, with a kindly disposition and an agreeable manner. He was on terms of cordial friendship with Raphael, then in his youth, and thirty years Il Francia's junior. Il Francia addressed an enthusiastic sonnet to Raphael, and there is extant a letter of Raphael's to Il Francia, excusing himself for not sending his friend Raphael's portrait, and making an exchange of sketches, that of his 'Nativity' for the drawing of Il Francia's 'Judith;' while it was to Il Francia's care that Raphael committed his picture of St Cecilia, when it was first sent to Bologna. These relations between the men and their characters throw discredit on the tradition that Il Francia died from jealous grief caused by the sight of Raphael's 'St Cecilia.' As Il Francia was seventy years of age at the time of his death, one may well attribute it to physical causes. Il Francia had at least one son, and another kinsman, painters, whose paintings were so good as to be occasionally confounded with those of Il Francia.

Il Francia is thought to have united, in his works, a certain calm sedateness and frank sincerity to the dreamy imaginativeness of some of his contemporaries. His finest works are considered to be the frescoes from the life of St Cecilia in the church of St Cecilia at Bologna.

Of a Madonna and Child, by Francia, at Bologna, I shall write down another of Dean Alford's descriptions,—many of which I have given for this, among other reasons, that these descriptions are not technical or professional, but the expression of the ardent admiration and grateful comprehension of a sympathetic spectator. 'He,' speaking of the Divine Child, 'is lying in simple nakedness on a rich red carpet, and is supported by a white pillar, over which the carpet passes. Of these accessories every thread is most delicately and carefully painted; no slovenly washes of meretricious colour where He is to be served, before whom all things are open; no perfunctory sparing of toil in serving Him who has given us all that is best. On his right hand kneels the Virgin Mother in adoration, her very face a magnificat—praise, lowliness, confidence; next to her, Joseph, tell-ing by his looks the wonderful story, deeply but simply. Two beautiful angels kneel, one on either side — hereafter, perhaps, to kneel in like manner in the tomb. Their faces seemed to me notable for that which I have no doubt the painter intended to express, — the pure abstraction of reverent adoration, unmingled with human sympathies. The face and figure of the Divine Infant are full of majesty, as he holds his hands in blessing towards the spectator, who symbolizes the world which He has come to save. Close to him on the ground, on his right, two beautiful goldfinches sit on a branch in trustful repose; on his left springs a plant of the meadow-trefoil. Thus lightly and reverently has the master touched the mystery of the Blessed Trinity: the goldfinch symbolizing by its colours, the trefoil by the form of its leaf.'

In our own National Gallery is a picture by Il Francia of the enthroned Virgin and Child and her mother, St Anne, who is presenting a peach to the infant Christ; at the foot of the throne is the little St John; to the right and left are St Paul with the sword, St Sebastian bound to a pillar and pierced with arrows, and St Lawrence with the emblematical grid-iron, &c. &c. Opposite this picture hangs, what once formed part of it, a solemn, sorrowful Pietà, as the Italians call a picture representing the dead Redeemer mourned over by the Virgin and by the other holy women. These pictures were bought by our Government from the Duke of Lucca for three thousand five hundred pounds.

Fra Bartolommeo. We come to a second gentle monk, not unlike Fra Angelico in his nature, but far less happy than Fra Angelico, in having been born in stormy times. Fra Bartolommeo, called also **Baccio della Porta,** or Bartholomew of the gate, from the situation of his lodgings when a young man, but scarcely known in Italy by any other name than that of **Il Frate**, or the Friar, was born near Florence, and trained from his boyhood to be a painter. In his youth, however, a terrible public event convulsed Florence, and revolutionized Baccio della Porta's life. He had been employed to paint in that notable Dominican convent of St Mark, where Savonarola, its devoted friar, was denouncing the sins of the times, including the profligate luxury of the nobles and the degradation of the representatives of the Church. Carried away by the fervour and sincerity of the speaker, Baccio joined the enthusiasts who cast into a burning pile the instruments of pride, vanity, and godless intellect denounced by the preacher. Baccio's sacrifice to the flaming heap of splendid furniture and dress, and worldly books, was all his designs from profane subjects and studies of the undraped figure. A little later Savonarola was excommunicated by the Pope and perished as a martyr; and Baccio, timid from his natural temper, distracted by doubt, and altogether horror-stricken, took a monk's vows, and entered the same convent of St Mark, where for four years he never touched a pencil.

At the request of his superior Fra Bartolommeo painted again, and when Raphael visited Florence, and came with all his conquering sweetness and graciousness to greet the monk in his cell, something of Il Frate's old love for his art, and delight in its exercise, returned. He even visited Rome, but there his health failed him, and the great works of Lionardo, Michael Angelo, and Raphael, when he compared his own with theirs, seemed to crush and overwhelm him. But he painted better for his visit to Rome, even as he had painted better for his intimacy with Raphael. Nay, it is said Raphael himself painted better on account of his brotherly regard for, and confidence in, Fra Bartolommeo.

Fra Bartolommeo died aged forty-eight years. Among his best pupils was a nun of St Catherine's, known as Suor Plautilla.

To Il Frate, as a painter, is attributed great softness and harmony, and even majesty, though, like Fra Angelico, he was often deficient in strength. He was great in the management of draperies, for the better study of which he is said to have invented the lay figure. He indulged in the introduction into his pictures of rich architecture. He was fond of painting boy-angels—in which he excelled—playing frequently on musical instruments, or holding a canopy over the Virgin. Very few of his works are out of Italy; the most are in Florence, especially in the Pitti Palace. His two greatest works are the Madonna della Misericordia, or the Madonna of Mercy, at Lucca, where the Virgin stands with outstretched arms pleading for the suppliants, whom she shelters under the canopy, and who look to her as she looks to her Son,—and the grand single figure of St Mark, with his Gospel in his hand, in the Pitti Palace, Florence. Sir David

Wilkie said of the Madonna of Mercy, 'that it contained the merits of Raphael, of Titian, of Rembrandt, and of Rubens.'

Andrea Vanucchi, commonly called **Andrea del Sarto,** from the occupation of his father, who was a tailor (in Italian, *sarto*), was born at Florence in 1488. He was first a goldsmith, but soon turned painter, winning early the commendatory title of 'Andrea senza errori,' or 'Andrea the Faultless.' His life is a miserable and tragic history. In the early flush of his genius and industry, with its just crown of fame and success, he conceived a passion for a beautiful but worthless woman, whom, in spite of the opposition of his friends, he married. She rendered his home degraded and wretched, and his friends and scholars fell off from him. In disgust he quitted Florence, and entered the service of Francis I, of France; but his wife, for whom his regard was a desperate infatuation, imperiously summoned him back to Florence, to which he returned, bringing with him a large sum of money, entrusted to him by the king for the purchase of works of art. Instigated by his wife, Andrea del Sarto used this money for his, or rather her, purposes, and dared not return to France. Even in his native Florence he was loaded with reproach and shame. He died of the plague at the age of fifty-five years, according to tradition, plundered and abandoned in his extremity by the base woman for whom he had sacrificed principle and honour. We may read the grievous story of Andrea del Sarto, written by one of the greatest of England's modern poets.

As may be imagined, Andrea del Sarto's excellence lay in the charm of his execution. His works were deficient in earnestness and high feeling, and some will have it, that, evilly haunted as he was, he perpetually painted in his Madonnas the beautiful but base-souled face of the woman who ruined him. Andrea del Sarto's best works are in Florence, particularly in the cloisters of the convent of the Annunziata. In the court of the same convent is his famous Riposo (or rest of the Holy Family on their way to Egypt), which is known as the 'Madonna of the Sack,' from the circumstance of Joseph in the picture leaning against a sack. This picture has held a high place in art for hundreds of years.

CHAPTER IV.

LIONARDO DA VINCI, 1452-1519 — MICHAEL ANGELO, 1475-1564 — RAPHAEL, 1483-1520 — TITIAN, 1477-1566.

We have arrived at the triumph of art, not, indeed, in unconsciousness and devotion, but in fulness and completeness, as shown in the works of four of the greatest painters and men whom the world ever saw. Of the first, **Lionardo da Vinci,** born at Vinci in the neighbourhood of Florence, 1452, it may be said that the many-sidedness which characterized Italians — above all Italians of his day — reached its height in him. Not only was he a painter, a sculptor, an architect, and engineer, but also one of the boldest speculators of the generation which gave birth to Columbus, and was not less original and ingenious than he was universally accomplished — an Admirable Crichton among painters. There is a theory that this many-sidedness is a proof of the greatest men. indicating a man who might have been great in any way, who, had his destiny not found and left him a painter, would have been equally great as a philosopher, a man of science, a poet, or a statesman. It may be so; but the life of Lionardo tends also to illustrate the disadvantage of too wide a grasp and diffusion of genius. Beginning much and finishing little, not because he was idle or fickle, but because his schemes were so colossal and his aims so high, he spent his time in preparation for the attainment of perfect excellence, which eluded him. Lionardo was the pioneer, the teacher of others, rather than the complete fulfiller of his own dreams; and the life of the proud, passionate man was, to himself at least, a life of failure and mortification. This result might, in a sense, have been avoided; but Lionardo, great as he was, proved also one of those unfortunate men whose noblest efforts are met and marred by calamities which could have hardly been foreseen or prevented.

Lionardo da Vinci was the son of a notary, and early showed a taste for painting as well as for arithmetic and mathematics. He was apprenticed to a painter, but he also sedulously studied physics. He is said, indeed, to have made marvellous guesses at truth, in chemistry, botany, astronomy, and particularly, as helping him in his art, anatomy. He was, according to other accounts, a man of noble person, like Ghirlandajo. And one can scarcely doubt this who looks at

Lionardo's portrait painted by himself, or at any engraving from it, and remarks the grand presence of the man in his cap and furred cloak; his piercing wistful eyes; stately outline of nose; and sensitive mouth, unshaded by his magnificent flowing beard.

He was endowed with surprising bodily strength, and was skilled in the knightly exercises of riding, fencing, and dancing. He was a lover of social pleasure, and inclined to indulge in expensive habits. While a lad he amused himself by inventing machines for swimming, diving, and flying, as well as a compass, a hygrometer, &c. &c. In a combination from the attributes of the toads, lizards, bats, &c. &c., with which his studies in natural history had made him familiar, he painted a nondescript monster, which he showed suddenly to his father, whom it filled with horror. But the horror did not prevent the old lawyer selling the wild phantasmagoria for a large sum of money. As something beyond amusement, Lionardo planned a canal to unite Florence with Pisa (while he executed other canals in the course of his life), and suggested the daring but not impossible idea of raising *en masse*, by means of levers, the old church of San Giovanni, Florence, till it should stand several feet above its original level, and so get rid of the half-sunken appearance which destroyed the effect of the fine old building. He visited the most frequented places, carrying always with him his sketch-book, in which to note down his observations; he followed criminals to execution in order to witness the pangs of despair; he invited peasants to his house and told them laughable stories, that he might pick up from their faces the essence of comic expression. [4] A mania for truth — alike in great and little things — possessed him.

Lionardo entered young into the service of the Gonzaga family of Milan, being, according to one statement, chosen for the office which he was to fill, as the first singer in *improvisatore* of his time (among his other inventions he devised a peculiar kind of lyre). He showed no want of confidence in asserting his claims to be elected, for after declaring the various works he would undertake, he added with regard to painting — 'I can do what can be done, as well as any man, be he who he may.' He received from the Duke a salary of five hundred crowns a year. He was fourteen years at the court of Milan, where, among other works, he painted his 'Cenacolo,' or 'Last Supper,' one of the grandest pictures ever produced. He painted it, contrary to the usual practice, in oils upon the plastered walls of the refectory of the Dominican convent, Milan. The situation was damp, and the material used proved so unsuitable for work on plaster, that, even before it was exposed to the reverses which in the course of a French occupation of Milan converted the refectory into a stable, the colours had altogether faded, and the very substance of the picture was crumbling into ruin.

The equestrian statue of the old Duke of Milan by Lionardo excited so much delight in its first freshness, that it was carried in triumph through the city, and during the progress it was accidentally broken. Lionardo began another, but funds failed for its completion, and afterwards the French used the original clay model as a target for their bowmen.

Lionardo returned to Florence, and found his great rival, Michael Angelo, already in the field. Both of the men, conscious of mighty gifts, were intolerant of rivalry. To Lionardo especially, as being much the elder man, the originator and promoter of many of the new views in art which his opponent had adopted, the competition was very distasteful, and to Michael Angelo he used the bitter sarcasm which has been handed down to us, 'I was famous before you were born.'

Nevertheless Lionardo consented to compete with Michael Angelo for the painting in fresco of one side of the council-hall, by the order of the gonfaloniere for the year. Lionardo chose for his subject a victory of the Florentines over the Milanese, while Michael Angelo took a scene from the Pisan campaigns. Not only was the work never done (some say partly because Lionardo *would* delay in order to make experiments in oils) on account of political troubles, but the very cartoons of the two masters, which all the artists of the day flocked to see, have been broken up, dispersed, and lost; and of one only, that of Michael Angelo, a small copy remains, while but a fragment from Lionardo's was preserved in a copy made by Rubens.

Lionardo went to Rome in the pontificate of Leo X., but there his quarrel with Michael Angelo broke out more violently than ever. The Pope too, who loved better a gentler, more accommodating spirit, seemed to slight Lionardo, and the great painter not only quitted Rome in disgust, but withdrew his services altogether from ungrateful Italy.

At Pavia Lionardo was presented to Francis 1, of France, who, zealous in patronizing art, engaged the painter to follow Francis's fortunes at a salary of seven hundred crowns a year. Lionardo spent the remainder of his life in France. His health had long been declining before he died, aged sixty-seven years, at Cloux, near Amboise. He had risen high in the favour of Francis. From this circumstance, and the generous, chivalrous nature of the king, there doubtless arose the tradition that Francis visited Lionardo on his death-bed; and that, while in the act of gently assisting him to raise himself, the painter died in the king's arms. Court chronicles do their best to demolish this story, by proving Francis to have been at St Germain on the day when Lionardo died at Cloux.

Lionardo was never married, and he left what worldly goods he possessed to a favourite scholar. Besides his greater works, he filled many MS. volumes, some with singularly accurate studies and sketches, maps, plans for machines, scores for music (three volumes of these are in the Royal Library at Windsor), and some with writing, which is written—probably to serve as a sort of cipher—from right to left, instead of from left to right. One of his writings is a valuable 'Treatise' on painting; other writings are on scientific and philosophic subjects, and in these Lionardo is believed to have anticipated some of the discoveries which were reached by lines of close reasoning centuries later.

Lionardo's genius as a painter was expressed by his uniting, in the very highest degree, truth and imagination. He was the shrewdest observer of ordinary life, and he could also realize the higher mysteries and profounder feelings of human nature. He drew exceedingly well. Of transparent lights and shadows, or chiaroscuro, he was the greatest master; but he was not a good colourist. His works are very rare, and many which are attributed to him are the pictures of his scholars, for he founded one of the great schools of Milan or Lombardy. There is a tradition that he was, as Holbein was once believed to be, ambidextrous, or capable of using his left hand as well as his right, and that he painted with two brushes—one in each hand. Thus more than fully armed, Lionardo da Vinci looms out on us like a Titan through the mists of centuries, and he preaches to us the simple homily, that not even a Titan can command worldly success; that such men must look to higher ends as the reward of their travail, and before undertaking it they must count the cost, and be prepared to renounce the luxurious tastes which clung to Lionardo, and which were not for him or for such men as he was.

Lionardo's great painting was his 'Last Supper,' of which, happily, good copies exist, as well as the wreck of the picture itself. The original is now, after it is too late, carefully guarded and protected in its old place in the Dominican convent of the Madonna della Grazia, Milan. The assembled company sit at a long table, Christ being seated in the middle, the disciples forming two separate groups on each side of the Saviour. The gradations of age are preserved, from the tender youth of John to the grey hairs of Simon; and all the varied emotions of mind, from the deepest sorrow and anxiety to the eager desire of revenge, are here portrayed. The well-known words of Christ, 'One of you shall betray me,' have caused the liveliest emotion. The two groups to the left of Christ are full of impassioned excitement, the figures in the first turning to the Saviour, those in the second speaking to each other, — horror, astonishment, suspicion, doubt, alternating in the various expressions. On the other hand, stillness, low whispers, indirect observations, are the prevailing expressions in the groups on the right. In the middle of the first group sits the betrayer; a cunning, sharp profile, he looks up hastily to Christ, as if speaking the words, 'Master, is it I?' while, true to the Scriptural account, his left hand and Christ's right hand approach, as if unconsciously, the dish that stands before them. [5]

A sketch of the head of Christ for the original picture, which has been preserved on a torn and soiled piece of paper at Brera, expresses the most elevated seriousness, together with Divine gentleness pain on account of the faithless disciple, a full presentiment of his own death, and resignation to the will of the Father. It gives a faint idea of what the master may have accomplished in the finished picture.

During his stay at Florence Lionardo painted a portrait of that Ginevra Benci already mentioned as painted by Ghirlandajo; and a still more famous portrait by Lionardo was that of Mona Lisa, the wife of his friend Giocondo. This picture is also known as 'La Jaconde.' I wish to call attention to it because it is the first of four surpassingly beautiful portraits of women which four great painters gave in succession to the world. The others, to be spoken of afterwards, are Raphael's 'Fornarina,' Titian's 'Bella Donna,' and Rubens' 'Straw Hat.' About the original of 'La Jaconde' there never has been a mystery such as there has been about the others. At this portrait the unsatisfied painter worked at intervals for four years, and when he left it he pronounced it still unfinished. 'La Jaconde' is now in the Louvre in nearly ruined condition, yet a judge says of it that even now 'there is something in this wonderful head of the ripest southern beauty, with its airy background of a rocky landscape, which exercises a peculiar fascination over the mind.'

There is a painting of the Madonna and Child Christ said to be by Lionardo, and probably, at least, by one of his school, and which belongs, I think, to the Duke of Buccleuch, and was exhibited lately among the works of the old masters. The group has at once something touching and exalted in its treatment. The Divine Child in the Mother's arms is strangely attracted by the sight of a cross, and turns towards it with ineffable longing, while the Virgin Mother, with a pang of foreboding, clasping the child in her arms, seeks to draw him back.

The fragment of the cartoon in which Lionardo competed with Michael Angelo, may be held to survive in the fine painting by Rubens called 'the Battle of the Standard.' Of a famous Madonna and St Anne, by Lionardo, the original cartoon in black chalk is preserved under glass in our Royal Academy. [6]

Michael Angelo Buonarroti, born at Castel Caprese near Arezzo in Tuscany, 1475, is the next of these universal geniuses, a term which we are accustomed to hold in contempt, because we have only seen it exemplified in parody. After Lionardo, indeed, Michael Angelo, though he was also painter, sculptor, architect, engineer, poet, musician, might almost be regarded as restricted in his pursuits, yet still so manifold was he, that men have loved to make a play upon his name and call him 'Michael the angel,' and to speak of him as of a king among men.

Michael Angelo was of noble descent, and though his ancient house had fallen into comparative poverty, his father was mayor or podesta of Chiusi, and governor of the castle of Chiusi and Caprese. Michael Angelo was destined for the profession of the law, but so early vindicated his taste for art, that at the age of thirteen years he was apprenticed to Ghirlandajo. Lorenzo the Magnificent was then ruling Florence, and he had made a collection of antique models in his palace and gardens, and constituted it an academy for young artists. In this academy Michael Angelo developed a strong bias for sculpture, and won the direct patronage of the Medici.

To this period of his life belong two characteristic anecdotes. In a struggle with a fellow-student, Michael Angelo received a blow from a mallet in his face, which, breaking bone and cartilage, lent to his nose the rugged bend,

'The bar of Michael Angelo.'

An ill-advised member of the Medician house, while entertaining a party of guests during a snowstorm, sent out the indignant artist to make a snow man within sight of the palace windows These anecdotes bear indirectly on the ruling qualities of Michael Angelo—qualities so integral that they are wrought into his marble and painted on his canvas—proud independence and energy.

Before going farther I wish to guard against a common misapprehension of Michael Angelo—that he was a haughty, arrogant man, absolutely narrow in his half-idolatrous, half-human worship of art. Michael Angelo was severe in place of being sweet; he was impatient of contradiction; he was careless and scornful of ceremony; and in his very wrath at flattery and hypocrisy, he was liable to sin against his own honesty and sincerity. But he was a man with a lofty sense of duty and a profound reverence for God. He was, unlike Lionardo, consistently simple, frugal, and temperate, throughout his long life. If he held up a high standard to others, and enforced it on them with hardness, he held up a higher standard to himself, and enforced it on himself more hardly still. He was a thoroughly unworldly man, and actions which had their root in unworldliness have been ascribed unjustly to a kind of Lucifer pride. Greed, and the meanness of greed, were unknown to him. He worked for the last ten years of his life (under no less than five different Popes) at his designs for St Peter's, steadfastly refusing pay for the work, saying that he did it for the honour of God and his own honour. He made many enemies and suffered from their enmity, but I cannot learn that, except in one instance, he was guilty of dealing an unworthy blow at his opponents. He was generous to his scholars, and without jealousy of them, suffering them to use his designs for their own purposes. He said, 'I have no friends, I need none, I wish for none;' but that was in feeling himself 'alone before Heaven;' and of the friends whom he did possess, he loved them all the more devotedly and faithfully, because they were few in number.

One need only be told of his love for his old servant Urbino, whom he presented with two thousand crowns to render him independent of service; and when the servant was seized with his last illness Michael Angelo nursed him tenderly, sleeping in his clothes on a couch that he might be ready to attend his patient. When his cares were ended, Michael Angelo wrote to a correspondent—'My Urbino is dead—to my infinite grief and sorrow. Living, he served me truly; and in his death he taught me how to die. I have now no other hope than to rejoin him in Paradise.'

Of Michael Angelo's more equal friendship with Vittoria Colonna I hope my readers will read at leisure for themselves. No nobler, truer friendship ever existed. It began when the high-born and beautiful, gifted, and devout Marchesa de Pescara—most loyal of wives and widows, was forty-eight, and Michael Angelo sixty-four years of age. After a few years of privileged intercourse and correspondence, which were the happiest years in Michael Angelo's life, it ended for this world when he stood mourning by her lifeless clay. 'I was born a rough model, and it was for thee to reform and remake me,' the great painter had written humbly of himself to his liege lady. [7]

Italy, in Michael Angelo's time, as Germany in Albert Dürer's, was all quickened and astir with the new wave of religious thought which brought about the Reformation. Ochino and Peter Martyr, treading in the footsteps of Savonarola, had preached to eager listeners, but 'in Italy men did not adopt Lutheranism, though they approached it;' and in all the crowd of great Italian artists of the day, Michael Angelo shows deepest traces of the conflict—of its trouble, its seriousness, its nobleness. He only, among his brethren, acted out his belief that the things of the world sank into insignificance before those thoughts of God and immortality which were alone fully worthy of the soul. And it was, as to a religious work for which he was fitted, that he at last gave himself up to the raising of St Peter's. We shall have next in order the life of a man who had all the winning qualities which Michael Angelo wanted, but we shall hardly, through the whole range of history, find a nobler man than Michael Angelo.

After his first visit to Rome, 1496, Michael Angelo executed his colossal statue of David. In 1503 he entered into the competition with Lionardo for the painting of one end of the Council-hall, in Florence, which has been already mentioned. For this object he drew as his cartoon, 'Pisan soldiers surprised while bathing by a sudden trumpet call to arms.' The grand cartoon, of which only a small copy exists, was said to have been torn to pieces as an act of revenge by a fellow-sculptor, whom Michael Angelo had offended.

Michael Angelo was invited to Rome by Julius II. in 1504 to aid in erecting the unapproachable monument which the Pope projected raising for himself. Then commenced a series of contentions and struggles between the imperious and petulant Pope and the haughty, uncompromising painter, in which the latter certainly had the best of it. At one time in the course of the quarrel, Michael Angelo departed from Rome without permission or apology, and stoutly refused to return, though followed hotly by no less than five different couriers, armed with threats and promises, and urged to make the reparation by his own gonfaloniere. At last a meeting and a reconciliation between Michael Angelo and the Pope were effected at Bologna. Michael Angelo designed for Pope Julius II, not only the statue of Pope Julius at Bologna, which was finally converted into a cannon, and turned against the very man whose effigy it had originally presented, but also for that tomb which was never completed, the famous figure of Moses seated, grasping his beard with one hand.

While employed at the tomb, Michael Angelo, then in his fortieth year, was desired by the Pope to undertake the decoration of the ceiling of the Sistine Chapel. Here, again, the hand of an enemy is said to have been at work. Michael Angelo, with the first place as a sculptor, was inexperienced in fresco painting; while Raphael, who was taking the place of Lionardo as Michael Angelo's most formidable rival (yet whom it is said Michael Angelo pointed out as the fittest painter of the ceiling), and who was then engaged in painting the Vatican chambers, had already achieved the utmost renown. It was anticipated by secret hostility, so records tradition, that Michael Angelo would fail signally in the unaccustomed work, and that his merit as an artist would pale altogether before that of Raphael's. I need hardly write how entirely malice was balked in the verdict to which posterity has set its seal.

Michael Angelo brought artists from Florence to help him in his great undertaking, for over the chapel, whose walls had already been painted by older artists—among them Ghirlandajo, was an enormous vault of 150 feet in length by 50 in breadth, which Michael Angelo was required to cover with designs representing the Fall and Redemption of Man. But the painter was unable to bear what seemed to him the bungling attempts of his assistants; so dismissing them all and destroying their work, he shut himself up, and working in solitude and secrecy, set himself to evolve from his own inner consciousness the gigantic scenes of a tremendous drama. In 22 months (or, as Kugler holds, in three years, including the time spent on the designs) he finished gloriously the work, the magnitude of which one must see to comprehend. On All Saints' Day, 1512, the ceiling was uncovered, and Michael Angelo was hailed, little though he cared for such clamorous hailing, as a painter indeed. For this piece of work Michael Angelo received 3000 crowns.

Pope Julius died, and was succeeded by Leo X. of the Medician house, but, in spite of early associations as well as of mother country, Michael Angelo was no more acceptable to the Pope—a brilliantly polished, easy-tempered man of the world, who filled the chair of St Peter's, than Lionardo had been. Leo X, greatly preferred Raphael, to whom all manner of pleasantness as well as of courteous deference was natural, to the two others. At the same time, Leo employed Michael Angelo, though it was more as an architect than as a painter, and rather at Florence than at Rome. At Florence Michael Angelo executed for Pope Clement VII., another Medici, the mortuary chapel of San Lorenzo, with its six great statues, those of the cousins Lorenzo de Medici and Giuliano de Medici, the first called by the Florentines 'Il Pensièro,' or 'Pensive Thought,' with the four colossal recumbent figures named respectively the Night, the Morning, the Dawn, and the Twilight.

In 1537 Michael Angelo was employed by his fellow citizens to fortify his native city against the return of his old patrons the Medici, and the city held out for nine months.

Pope Paul III., an old man when elected to the popedom, but bent on signalizing his pontificate with as splendid works of art as those which had rendered the reigns of his predecessors illustrious, summoned another man, grown elderly, Michael Angelo, upwards of sixty years, reluctant to accept the commission, to finish the decoration of the Sistine Chapel; and Michael Angelo painted on the wall, at the upper end, his painting, 'The Last Judgment.' The picture is forty-seven feet high by forty-three wide, and it occupied the painter eight years. It was during its progress that Michael Angelo entered on his friendship with Vittoria Colonna.

For the chapel called the Paolina or Pauline Chapel Michael Angelo also painted less-known frescoes, but from that time he devoted his life to St Peter's. He had said that he would take the old Pantheon and 'suspend it in air,' and he did what he said, though he did not live to see the great cathedral completed. His sovereign, the Grand Duke of Florence, endeavoured in vain with magnificent offers to lure the painter back to his native city. Michael Angelo protested that to leave Rome then would be 'a sin and a shame, and the ruin of the greatest religious monument in Christian Europe.' Michael Angelo, like Lionardo, did not marry; he died at Rome in 1563, in his eighty-ninth year.

His nephew and principal heir, [8] by the orders of the Grand Duke of Florence, and it is believed according to Michael Angelo's own wish, removed the painter's body to Florence, where it was buried with all honours in the church of Santa Croce there

The traits which recall Michael Angelo personally to us, are the prominent arch of the nose, the shaggy brows, the tangled beard, the gaunt grandeur of a figure like that of one of his prophets.

While Michael Angelo lived, one Pope rose on his approach, and seated the painter on his right hand, and another Pope declined to sit down in his painter's presence; but the reason given for the last condescension, is that the Pope feared that the painter would follow his example. And if the Grand Duke Cosmo uncovered before Michael Angelo, and stood hat in hand while speaking to him, we may have the explanation in another assertion, that 'sovereigns asked Michael Angelo to put on his cap, because the painter would do it unasked.'

The solitary instance in which Michael Angelo is represented as taking an unfair advantage of an antagonist, is in connection with the painter's rivalry in his art with Raphael. Michael Angelo under-valued the genius of Raphael, and was disgusted by what the older man considered the immoderate admiration bestowed on the younger. A favourite pupil of Michael Angelo's was Sebastian Del Piombo, who being a Venetian by birth was an excellent colourist. For one of his pictures—the very 'Raising of Lazarus' now in the National Gallery, which the Pope had ordered at the same time that he had ordered Raphael's 'Transfiguration'—it is rumoured that Michael Angelo gave the designs and even drew the figures, leaving Sebastian the credit, and trusting that without Michael Angelo's name appearing in the work, by the help of his drawing in addition to Sebastian's superb colouring, Raphael would be eclipsed, and that by a painter comparatively obscure.

The unwarrantable inference that the whole work was that of one painter, constituted a stratagem altogether unworthy of Michael Angelo, and if it had any existence, its getting wind disappointed and foiled its authors. When the story was repeated to Raphael, his sole protest is said to have been to the effect that he was glad that Michael Angelo esteemed him so highly as to enter the lists with him.

We can judge of Michael Angelo's attainments as a poet, even without having recourse to the original Italian, by Wordsworth's translations of some of the Italian master's sonnets, and by Mr John

Edward Taylor's translations of selections from Michael Angelo's poems.

Michael Angelo was greater as an architect and a sculptor than as a painter, because his power and delight lay in the mastery of form, and in the assertion, through that mastery, of the idealism of genius. It is not necessary to speak here of the mighty harmonies and the ineffable dignity of simplicity, somewhat marred by the departure from Michael Angelo's designs, in St Peter's. It has been the fashion to praise them to the skies, and it has been a later fashion to decry them, in awarding a preference to the solemn shades and the dim rich dreaminess of Gothic architecture. Both fashions come to this, after all, that beauty, like these great men of genius of old, is many-sided.

In Michael Angelo's works of sculpture a weird charm attaches to his monuments in honour of the Medici in the chapel of San Lorenzo, Florence. Perhaps something of this weirdness has to do with the tragic history of the men, and with a certain mystery which has always shrouded the sculptor's meaning in these monuments.

Mrs Jameson quotes an account of Michael Angelo at work. 'An eye-witness has left us a very graphic description of the energy with which, even in old age, Michael Angelo handled his chisel: — "I can say that I have seen Michael Angelo at the age of sixty, and, with a body announcing weakness, make more chips of marble fly about in a quarter of an hour than would three of the strongest young sculptors in an hour, — a thing almost incredible to him who has not beheld it. He went to work with such impetuosity and fury of manner, that I feared almost every moment to see the block split into pieces. It would seem as if, inflamed by the idea of greatness which inspired him, this great man attacked with a species of fury the marble which concealed the Statue."' — *Blaise de Vigenére.*

In painting Michael Angelo regarded colouring as of secondary importance. He is not known to have executed one painting in oil, and he treated oil and easel-painting generally as work only fit for women or idle men. While he approached the sublime in his painting, it was by no means faultless. Even in form his efforts were apt to tend to heaviness and exaggeration, and the fascination which robust muscular delineation had for him, betrayed him into materialism. Fuseli's criticism of Michael Angelo's work, that Michael Angelo's women were female men, and his children diminutive giants, is judged correct. Incomparably the greatest painting of Michael Angelo's is his ceiling of the Sistine Chapel. It includes upwards of 200 figures, the greater part colossal, as they were to be looked at, in the distance, from below.

'The ceiling of the Sistine Chapel contains the most perfect works done by Michael Angelo in his long and active life. Here his great spirit appears in noblest dignity, in its highest purity; here the attention is not disturbed by that arbitrary display to which his great power not unfrequently seduced him in other works. The ceiling forms a flattened arch in its section; the central portion, which is a plain surface, contains a series of large and small pictures, representing the most important events recorded in the book of Genesis — the Creation and Fall of Man, with its immediate consequences. In the large triangular compartments at the springing of the vault are sitting figures of the Prophets and Sibyls, as the

foretellers of the coming Saviour. In the soffits of the recesses between these compartments, and in the arches underneath, immediately above the windows, are the ancestors of the Virgin, the series leading the mind directly to the Saviour. The external of these numerous representations is formed by an architectural frame-work of peculiar composition, which encloses the single subjects, tends to make the principal masses conspicuous, and gives to the whole an appearance of that solidity and support so necessary, but so seldom attended to in soffit decorations, which may be considered as if suspended. A great number of figures are also connected with the framework; those in unimportant situations are executed in the colour of stone or bronze; in the more important, in natural colours. These serve to support the architectural forms, to fill up and to connect the whole. They may be best described as the living and embodied *genii* of architecture. It required the unlimited power of an architect, sculptor, and painter, to conceive a structural whole of so much grandeur,

to design the decorative figures with the significant repose required by the sculpturesque character, and yet to preserve their subordination to the principal subjects, and to keep the latter in the

proportions and relations best adapted to the space to be filled.'—
Kugler.

The pictures from the Old Testament, beginning from the altar,
are:—

1. The Separation of Light and Darkness.
2. The Creation of the Sun and Moon.
3. The Creation of Trees and Plants.
4. The Creation of Adam.
5. The Creation of Eve.
6. The Fall and the Expulsion from Paradise.
7. The Sacrifice of Noah.
8. The Deluge.
9. The Intoxication of Noah.

'The scenes from Genesis are the most sublime representations of
these subjects;—the Creating Spirit is unveiled before us. The peculiar type which the painter has here given of the form of the Almighty

Father has been frequently imitated by his followers, and even by
Raphael, but has been surpassed by none. Michael Angelo has represented him in majestic flight, sweeping through the air, surrounded by *genii*, partly supporting, partly borne along with him, covered
by his floating drapery; they are the distinct syllables, the separate
virtues of his creating word. In the first (large) compartment we see
him with extended hands, assigning to the sun and moon their respective paths. In the second, he awakens the first man to life. Adam lies stretched on the verge of the earth in the act of raising himself; the Creator touches him with the point of his finger, and appears thus to endow him with feeling and life. This picture displays
a wonderful depth of thought in the composition, and the utmost
elevation and majesty in the general treatment and execution. The
third subject is not less important, representing the Fall of Man, and
his Expulsion from Paradise. The tree of knowledge stands in the
midst; the serpent (the upper part of the body being that of a woman) is twined around the

stem; she bends down towards the guilty pair, who are in the act
of plucking the forbidden fruit. The figures are nobly graceful, par-

ticularly that of Eve. Close to the serpent hovers the angel with the sword, ready to drive the fallen beings out of Paradise. In this double action, this union of two separate moments, there is something peculiarly poetic and significant: it is guilt and punishment in one picture. The sudden and lightning-like appearance of the avenging angel behind the demon of darkness has a most impressive effect.'—*Kugler.*

The lower portion of the ceiling is divided into triangles, occupied by the Prophets and Sibyls in solemn contemplation, accompanied by angels and genii. Beginning from the left of the entrance their order is—

1. Joel.
2. Sibylla Erythræa.
3. Ezekiel.
4. Sibylla Persica.
5. Jonah.
6. Sibylla Libyca.
7. Daniel.
8. Sibylla Cumæa.
9. Isaiah.
10. Sibylla Delphica.

'The prophets and sibyls in the triangular compartments of the curved portion of the ceiling are the largest figures in the whole work; these, too, are among the most wonderful forms that modern art has called into life. They are all represented seated, employed with books or rolled manuscripts; genii stand near or behind them. These mighty beings sit before us pensive, meditative, inquiring, or looking upwards with inspired countenances. Their forms and movements, indicated by the grand lines and masses of the drapery, are majestic and dignified. We see in them beings, who, while they feel and bear the sorrows of a corrupt and sinful world, have power to look for consolation into the secrets of the future. Yet the greatest variety prevails in the attitudes and expression: each figure is full of individuality. Zacharias is an aged man, busied in calm and circumspect investigation; Jeremiah is bowed down, absorbed in thought, the thought of deep and bitter grief; Ezekiel turns with hasty movements to the genius next to him, who points upwards with joyful

expectation, etc. The sibyls are equally characteristic: the Persian, a lofty, majestic woman, very aged; the Erythræan, full of power, like the warrior goddess of wisdom; the Delphic, like Cassandra, youthfully soft and graceful, but with strength to bear the awful seriousness of revelation.'—*Kugler*.

'The belief of the Roman Catholic Church in the testimony of the sibyl is shown by the well-known hymn, said to have been composed by Pope Innocent III, at the close of the thirteenth century, beginning with the verse—

> "Dies iræ, dies illa,
> Solvet sæclum in favilla
> Teste David cum Sibylla."

It may be inferred that this hymn, admitted into the liturgy of the Roman Church, gave sanction to the adoption of the sibyls into Christian art. They are seen from this time accompanying the prophets and apostles, in the cyclical decorations of the church.... But the highest honour that art has rendered to the sibyls has been by the hand of Michael Angelo,

on the ceiling of the Sistine Chapel. Here in the conception of a mysterious order of women, placed above and without all considerations of the graceful or the individual, the great master was peculiarly in his element. They exactly fitted his standard, of art, not always sympathetic, nor comprehensible to the average human mind, of which the grand in form and the abstract in expression were the first and last conditions. In this respect, the sibyls on the Sistine Chapel ceiling are more Michael Angelesque than their companions the prophets. For these, while types of the highest monumental treatment, are yet men, while the sibyls belong to a distinct class of beings, who convey the impression of the very obscurity in which their history is wrapt—creatures who have lived far from the abodes of men, who are alike devoid of the expression of feminine sweetness, human sympathy, or sacramental beauty; who are neither Christians nor Jewesses, Witches nor Graces, yet living, grand, beautiful, and true, according to laws revealed to the great Florentine genius only.

Thus their figures may be said to be unique, as the offspring of a peculiar sympathy between the master's mind and his subject. To this sympathy may be ascribed the prominence and size given them, both prophets and sibyls, as compared to their usual relation to the subjects they environ. They sit here on twelve throne-like niches, more like presiding deities, each wrapt in self-contemplation, than as tributary witnesses to the truth and omnipotence of Him they are intended to announce. Thus they form a gigantic frame-work round the subjects of the Creation, of which the birth of Eve, as the type of the Nativity, is the intentional centre. For some reason, the twelve figures are not prophets and sibyls alternately — there being only five sibyls to seven prophets, — so that the prophets come together at one angle. Books and scrolls are given indiscriminately to them.

'The Sibylla Persica, supposed to be the oldest of the sisterhood, holds the book close to her eyes, as if from dimness of sight, which fact, contradicted as it is

by a frame of obviously Herculean strength, gives a mysterious intentness to the action.

'The Sibylla Libyca, of equally powerful proportions, but less closely draped, is grandly wringing herself to lift a massive volume from a height above her head on to her knees.

'The Sibylla Cumana, also aged, and with her head covered, is reading with her volume at a distance from her eyes.

'The Sibylla Delphica, with waving hair escaping from her turban, is a beautiful young being, the most human of all, gazing into vacancy or futurity. She holds a scroll.

'The Sibylla Erythræa, grand, bare-headed creature, sits reading intently with crossed legs, about to turn over her book.

'The prophets are equally grand in structure, and though, as we have said, not more than men, yet they are the only men that could well bear the juxtaposition with their stupendous female colleagues. Ezekiel, between Erythræa and Persica, has a scroll in his

hand that hangs by his side, just cast down, as he turns eagerly to listen to some voice.

'Jeremiah, a magnificent figure, with elbow on knee and head on hand, wrapt in meditation appropriate to one called to utter lamentation and woe. He has neither book nor scroll.

'Jonah is also without either. His position is strained and ungraceful, looking upwards, and apparently remonstrating with the Almighty upon the destruction of the gourd, a few leaves of which are seen above him. His hands are placed together with a strange and trivial action, supposed to denote the counting on his fingers the number of days he was in the fish's belly. A formless marine monster is seen at his side.

'Daniel has a book on his lap, with one hand on it. He is young, and a piece of lion's skin seems to allude to his history.' [9]

In the recesses between the prophets and sibyls are a series of lovely family groups, representing the genealogy of the Virgin, and expressive of calm expectation of the future. The four corners of the ceiling contain groups illustrative of the power of the Lord displayed in the especial deliverances of his chosen people. Near the altar are:

Right, The Deliverance of the Israelites by the Brazen Serpent.

Left, The Execution of Haman.

Near the entrance are:

Right, Judith and Holofernes.

Left, David and Goliath. [10]

Michael Angelo was thirty-nine years of age when he painted the ceiling of the Sistine. When he began to paint the 'Day of Judgment' he was above sixty years of age, and his great rival, Raphael, had already been dead thirteen years.

The picture of the 'Day of Judgment,' with much that renders it marvellous and awful, has a certain coarseness of conception and execution. The moment chosen is that in which the Lord says, 'Depart from me, ye cursed,' and the idea and even attributes of the principal figure are taken from Orcagna's old painting in the Campo Santo. But with all Michael Angelo's advantages, he has by no means improved on the original idea. He has robbed the figure of the Lord of its transcendant majesty; he has not been able to impart to the ranks of the blessed the look of blessedness which 'Il Beato' himself might have conveyed. The chief excellence of the picture is in the ranks of the condemned, who writhe and rebel against their agonies. No wonder that the picture is sombre and dreadful.

Of the allegorical figures of 'Night' and 'Morning' in the chapel of San Lorenzo, there are casts at the Crystal Palace.

A comparison and a contrast have been instituted between Michael Angelo and Milton, and Raphael and Shakespeare. There may be something in them, but, as in the case of broken metaphors, they will not bear being pushed to a logical conclusion or picked to pieces. The very transparent comparison which matches Michael Angelo with his own countryman, Dante, is after all more felicitous and truer. Michael Angelo with Lionardo are the great chiefs of the Florentine School.

Raphael Sanzio, or **Santi of Urbino,** the head of the Roman School, was one of those very exceptional men who seem born to happiness, to inspire love and only love, to pass through the world making friends and disarming enemies, who are fully armed to confer pleasure while almost incapable of either inflicting or receiving pain. To this day his exceptional fortune stands Raphael's memory in good stead, since for one man or woman who yearns after the austere righteousness and priceless tenderness of Michael Angelo, there are ten who yield with all their hearts to the gay, sweet gentleness and generosity of Raphael. No doubt it was also in his favour as a painter, that though a man of highly cultivated tastes, 'in close intimacy and correspondence with most of the celebrated men of his time, and interested in all that was going forward,' he did not, especially in his youth, spend his strength on a variety of studies, but devoted himself to painting. While he thus vindicated his share of the breadth of genius of his country and time, by giving to the world the loveliest Madonnas and Child-Christs, the most dramatic of battle-pieces, the finest of portraits, his noble and graceful fertility of invention and matchless skill of execution were confined to and concentrated on painting. He did not diverge long or far into the sister arts of architecture and sculpture, though his classic researches in the excavations of Rome were keen and zealous (a heap of ruins having given to the world in 1504 the group of the Laocoon), so that a writer of his day could record that 'Raphael had sought and found in Rome another Rome.'

Raphael was born in the town of Urbino, and was the son of a painter of the Umbrian School, who very early destined the boy to his future career, and promoted his destination by all the efforts in Giovanni Santi's power, including the intention of sending away and apprenticing the little lad to the best master of his time, Perugino, so called from the town where he resided, Perugia. Raphael's mother died when he was only eight years of age, and his father died when he was no more than eleven years, before the plans for his education were put into action. But no stroke of outward calamity, or loss—however severe, could annul Raphael's birthright of universal favour. His step-mother, the uncles who were his guardians, his clever, perverse, unscrupulous master, all joined in a common love of Raphael and determination to promote his interests.

Raphael at the age of twelve years went to Perugia to work under Perugino, and remained with his master till he was nearly twenty years of age. In that interval he painted industriously, making constant progress, always in the somewhat hard, but finished, style of Perugino, while already showing a predilection for what was to prove Raphael's favourite subject, the Madonna and Child. At this period he painted his famous *Lo Sposalizio* or the 'Espousals,' the marriage of the Virgin Mary with Joseph, now at Milan. In 1504 he visited Florence, remaining only for a short time, but making the acquaintance of Fra Bartolommeo and Ghirlandajo, seeing the cartoons of Lionardo and Michael Angelo, and from that time displaying a marked improvement in drawing. Indeed nothing is more conspicuous in Raphael's genius in contra-distinction to Michael Angelo's, than the receptive character of Raphael's mind, his power of catching up an impression from without, and the candour and humility with which he availed himself unhesitatingly of the assistance lent him by others.

Returning soon to Florence, Raphael remained there till 1508, when he was twenty-five years, drawing closer the valuable friendships he had already formed, and advancing with rapid strides in his art, until his renown was spread all over Italy, and with reason, since already, while still young, he had painted his 'Madonna of the Goldfinch,' in the Florentine Gallery, and his 'La Belle Jardiniere,' or Madonna in a garden among flowers, now in the Louvre.

In his twenty-fifth year Raphael was summoned to Rome to paint for Pope Julius II. My readers will remember that Michael Angelo in the abrupt severity of his prime of manhood, was soon to paint the ceiling of the Sistine Chapel for the same despotic and art-loving Pope, who had brought Raphael hardly more than a stripling to paint the '*Camere*' or '*Stanze*' chambers of the Vatican.

The first of the halls which Raphael painted (though not the first in order) is called the Camera della Segnatura (in English, signature), and represents Theology, Poetry, Philosophy, with the Sciences, Arts, and Jurisprudence. The second is the 'Stanza d'Eliodoro,' or the room of Heliodorus, and contains the grandest painting of all, in the expulsion of Heliodorus from the Temple of Jerusalem (taken from Maccabees), the Miracle of Bolsena, Attila, king of the Huns, terrified by the apparition of St Peter and St Paul, and St Peter delivered from prison. The third stanza painted by Raphael is the 'Stanza dell' Incendio' (the conflagration), so called from the extinguishing of the fire in the Borgo by a supposed miracle, being the most conspicuous scene in representations of events taken from the lives of Popes Leo III, and IV.; and the fourth chamber, which was left unfinished by Raphael, and completed by his scholars, is the 'Sala di Constantino,' and contains incidents from the life of the Emperor Constantine, including the splendid battle-piece between Constantine and Maxentius. At these chambers, or at the designs for them, Raphael worked at intervals, during the popedoms of Julius II., who died in the course of the painting of the Camere, and Leo X., for a period of twelve years, till Raphael's death in 1520, after which the 'Sala di Constantino' was completed by his scholars.

Raphael has also left in the Vatican a series of small pictures from the Old Testament, known as Raphael's Bible. This series decorates the thirteen cupolas of the 'Loggie,' or open galleries, running round three sides of an open court. Another work undertaken by Raphael should have still more interest for us. Leo X., resolving to substitute woven for painted tapestry round the lower walls of the interior of the Sistine Chapel, commanded Raphael to furnish drawings to the Flemish weavers, and thence arose eleven cartoons, seven of which have been preserved, have become the property of England, and are the glory of the Kensington Museum. The subjects of the cartoons in the seven which have been saved, are 'The Death of Ananias,' 'Elymas the Sorcerer struck with Blindness,' 'The Healing of the Lame Man at the Beautiful Gate of the Temple,' 'The Miraculous Draught of Fishes,' 'Paul and Barnabas at Lystra,' 'St Paul Preaching at Athens,' and 'The Charge to St Peter.' The four cartoons which are lost, were 'The Stoning of St Stephen,' 'The Conversion of St Paul,' 'Paul in Prison,' and 'The Coronation of the Virgin.'

In those cartoons figures above life-size were drawn with chalk upon strong paper, and coloured in distemper, and Raphael received for his work four hundred and thirty gold ducats (about £650), while the Flemish weavers received for their work in wools, silk, and gold, fifty thousand gold ducats. The designs were cut up in strips for the weavers' use, and while some strips were destroyed, the rest lay in a warehouse at Arras, till Rubens became aware of their existence, and advised Charles I, to buy the set, to be employed in the tapestry manufactory established by James I. at Mortlake. Brought to this country in the slips which the weavers had copied, the fate of the cartoons was still precarious. Cromwell bought them in Charles I.'s art collection, and Louis XIV, sought, but failed, to re-buy them. They fell into farther neglect, and were well-nigh forgotten, when Sir Godfrey Kneller recalled them to notice, and induced William III, to have the slips pasted together, and stretched upon linen, and put in a room set apart for them at Hampton Court, whence they were transferred, within the last ten years, for the greater advantage of artists and the public, to Kensington Museum.

The woven tapestries for which the cartoons were designed had quite as chequered a career. In the two sacks of Rome by French soldiers, the tapestries were seized, carried off, and two of them burnt for the bullion in the thread. At last they were restored to the Vatican, where they hang in their faded magnificence, a monument of Leo X, and of Raphael. An additional set of ten tapestry cartoons were supplied to the Vatican by Raphael's scholars.

Raphael painted for the Chigi family in their palace, which is now the Villa Farnesina, scenes from the history of Cupid and Psyche, and the Triumph of Galatea, subjects which show how the passion for classical mythology that distinguishes the next generation, was beginning to work. To these last years belong his 'Madonna di San Sisto,' so named from its having been painted for the convent of St Sixtus at Piacenza, and his last picture, the 'Transfiguration,' with which he was still engaged when death met him unexpectedly.

Raphael, as the Italians say, lived more like a *'principe'* (prince) than a *'pittore'* (painter). He had a house in Rome, and a villa in the neighbourhood, and on his death left a considerable fortune to his heirs. There has not been wanting a rumour that his life of a principe was a dissipated and prodigal life; but this ugly rumour, even if it had more evidence to support it, is abundantly disproven by the nature of Raphael's work, and by the enormous amount of that work, granting him the utmost assistance from his crowd of scholars. He had innumerable commissions, and retained an immense school from all parts of Italy, the members of which adored their master. Raphael had the additional advantage of having many of his pictures well engraved by a contemporary engraver named Raimondi.

Like Giotto, Raphael was the friend of the most distinguished Italians of his day, including Count Castiglione, and the poet Ariosto. He was notably the warm friend of his fellow-painters both at home and abroad, with the exception of Michael Angelo. A drawing of his own, which Raphael sent, in his kindly interchange of such sketches, to Albert Dürer, is, I think, preserved at Nüremberg. The sovereign princes of Italy, above all Leo X., were not contented with being munificent patrons to Raphael, they treated him with the most marked consideration. The Cardinal Bibbiena proposed the painter's marriage with his niece, ensuring her a dowry of three thousand gold crowns, but Maria di Bibbiena died young, ere the marriage could be accomplished; and Raphael, who was said to be little disposed to the match, did not long survive her. He caught cold, as some report, from his engrossing personal superintendence of the Roman excavations; and, as others declare, from his courtly assiduity in keeping an appointment with the Pope, was attacked by fever, and died on his birth-day, April 6th, 1520, having completed his thirty-seventh year.

All Rome and Italy mourned for him. When his body lay in state, to be looked at and wept over by multitudes, his great unfinished picture of the 'Transfiguration' was hung above the bed. He was buried in a spot chosen by himself in his lifetime, and, as it happened, not far from the resting-place of his promised bride. Doubts having been raised as to Raphael's grave, search was made, and his body was exhumed in 1833, and re-buried with great pomp. Raphael's life and that of Rubens form the ideal painter's life — bountiful, splendid, unclouded, and terminating ere it sees eclipse or decay — to all in whom the artistic temperament is united to a genial, sensuous, pleasure-loving nature.

Raphael was not above the middle height, and slightly made. He was sallow in colour, with brown eyes, and a full yet delicate mouth; but his beautiful face, like that of our English Shakespeare, is familiar to most of us. With regard to Raphael's face, the amount of womanliness in it is a striking characteristic. One hears sometimes that no man's character is complete without its share of womanliness: surely Raphael had a double share, for womanliness is the most distinctive quality in his face, along with that vague shade of pensiveness which we find not infrequently, but strangely enough, in those faces which have been associated with the happiest spirits and the brightest fortunes.

Raphael and his scholars painted and drew about nine hundred pictures and sketches, including a hundred and twenty Madonnas, eight of which are in private collections in England. Of Raphael's greatness, Kugler writes that 'it is not so much in kind as in degree. No master left behind *so many* really excellent works as he, whose days were so early numbered; in none has there been observed so little that is unpleasant.' All authorities agree in ascribing much of Raphael's power to his purely unselfish nature and aim. His excellence seems to lie in the nearly perfect expression of material beauty and harmony, together with grandeur of design and noble working out of thought. We shall see that this devotion to material beauty has been made something of a reproach to Raphael, as it certainly degenerated into a snare in the hands of his followers, while unquestionably the universal appreciation of Raphael's work, distinguished from the partial appreciation bestowed on the great works of others, proceeds from this evident material beauty which is open to all.

Then, again, Raphael, far more than Andrea del Sarto, deserved to be called 'faultless;' and this general absence of defects and equality of excellence is a great element of Raphael's wide popularity; for, as one can observe for one's self, in regarding a work of art, there is always a large proportion of the spectators who will seize on an error, dwell on it, and be incapable of shaking off its influence, and rising into the higher rank of critics, who discover and ponder over beauties. I would have it considered also, that this equality of excellence does not necessarily proceed always from a higher aim, but may arise rather from an unconsciously lower aim.

The single reproach brought against Raphael as a painter is that — according to some witnesses only, for most deny the implication — Raphael so delighted in material beauty that he became enslaved by it, till it diminished his spiritual insight. It is an incontestable truth that in Raphael, as in all the great Italian painters of his century, there was a falling away from the simple earnestness, the exceeding reverence, the endless patience, the self-abstraction, and self-devotion of the earliest Italian and Flemish painters. Therefore there has been within the last fifty or sixty years that movement in modern art, which is called Pre-raphaelitism, and which is, in fact, a revolt against subjection to Raphael, and his supposed undue exaltation of material beauty, and subjection of truth to beauty — so called. But we must not fall into the grave mistake of imagining that there was any want of vigour and variety in Raphael's grace and tenderness, or that he could not in his greatest works rise into a grandeur in keeping with his subject. Tire as we may of hearing Raphael called the king of painters, as the Greeks tired of hearing Aristides called 'the just,' this fact remains: no painter has left behind him such a mass of surpassingly good work; in no other work is there the same charm of greatest beauty and harmony.

It is hard for me to give you an idea in so short a space of Raphael's work. I must content myself with quoting descriptions of two of his Stanze, those of the Heliodorus and the Segnatura. 'Heliodorus driven out of the Temple (2 Maccabees iii.). In the background Onias the priest is represented praying for Divine interposition;—in the foreground Heliodorus, pursued by two avenging angels, is endeavouring to bear away the treasures of the temple. Amid the group on the left is seen Julius II., in his chair of state, attended by his secretaries. One of the bearers in front is Marc-Antonio Raimondi, the engraver of Raphael's designs. The man with the inscription, "Jo Petro de Folicariis Cremonen," was secretary of briefs to Pope Julius. Here you may fancy you hear the thundering approach of the heavenly warrior, and the neighing of his steed; while in the different groups who are plundering the treasures of the temple, and in those who gaze intently on the sudden consternation of Heliodorus, without being able to divine its cause, we see the expression of terror, amazement, joy, humility, and every passion to which human nature is exposed.' [11]

'The Stanza della Segnatura is so called from a judicial assembly once held here. The frescoes in this chamber are illustrative of the Virtues of Theology, Philosophy, Poetry, and Jurisprudence, who are represented on the ceiling by Raphael, in the midst of arabesques by *Sodoma*. The square pictures by Raphael refer:—the Fall of Man to Theology; the Study of the Globe to Philosophy; the Flaying of Marsyas to Poetry; and the Judgment of Solomon to Jurisprudence.

'*Entrance Wall.*—"The School of Athens." Raphael consulted Ariosto as to the arrangement of its 52 figures. In the centre, on the steps of a portico, are seen Plato and Aristotle, Plato pointing to heaven and Aristotle to earth. On the left is Socrates conversing with his pupils, amongst whom is a young warrior, probably Alcibiades. Lying upon the steps in front is Diogenes. To his left, Pythagoras is writing on his knee, and near him, with ink and pen, is Empedocles. The youth in the white mantle is Francesco Maria della Rovere, nephew of Julius II. On the right is Archimedes drawing a geometrical problem upon the floor. The young man near him with uplifted hands is Federigo II., Duke of Mantua. Behind these are Zoroaster, Ptolemy, one with a terrestrial, the other with a celestial globe, addressing two figures, which represent Raphael and his master Perugino. The drawing in brown upon the socle beneath this fresco, is by *Pierino del Vaga*, and represents the death of Archimedes.

'*Right Wall.*—"Parnassus." Apollo surrounded by the Muses; on his right, Homer, Virgil, and Dante. Below on the right, Sappho, supposed to be addressing Corinna, Petrarch, Propertius, and Anacreon; on the left Pindar and Horace, Sannazzaro, Boccaccio, and others. Beneath this, in grisaille, are,—Alexander placing the poems of Homer in the tomb of Achilles, and Augustus preventing the burning of Virgil's Æneid.

'*Left Wall.*—Above the window are Prudence, Fortitude, and Temperance. On the left, Justinian delivers the Pandects to Tribonian. On the right, Gregory IX. (with the features of Julius II.) delivers the Decretals to a jurist;—Cardinal de' Medici, afterwards Leo X., Cardinal Farnese, afterwards Paul III., and Cardinal del Monte, are represented near the Pope. In the socle beneath is Solon addressing the people of Athens.

'*Wall of Egress.*—"The Disputa." So called from an impression that it represents a Dispute upon the Sacrament. In the upper part of the composition the heavenly host are present; Christ between the Virgin and St John the Baptist; on the left, St Peter, Adam, St John, David, St Stephen, and another; and on the right, St Paul, Abraham, St James, Moses, St Lawrence, and St George. Below is an altar surrounded by the Latin fathers, Gregory, Jerome, Ambrose, and Augustine. Near St Augustine stand St Thomas Aquinas, St Anacletus, with the palm of a martyr, and Cardinal Buenaventura reading. Those in front are Innocent III., and in the background, Dante, near whom a monk in a black hood is pointed out as Savonarola. The Dominican on the extreme left is supposed to be Fra Angelico. The other figures are uncertain.' ...

'Raphael commenced his work in the Vatican by painting the ceiling and the four walls in the room called *della Segnatura*, on the surface of which he had to represent four great compositions, which embraced the principal divisions of the encyclopedia of that period; namely, Theology, Philosophy, Poetry, and Jurisprudence.

'It will be conceived, that to an artist imbued with the traditions of the Umbrian School, the first of these subjects was an unparalleled piece of good fortune: and Raphael, long familiar with the allegorical treatment of religious compositions, turned it here to the most admirable account; and, not content with the suggestions of his own genius, he availed himself of all the instruction he could derive from the intelligence of others. From these combined inspirations resulted, to the eternal glory of the Catholic faith and of Christian art, a composition without a rival in the history of painting, and, we may also add, without a name; for to call it lyric or epic is not enough, unless, indeed, we mean, by using these expressions, to compare it with the allegorical epic of Dante, alone worthy to be ranked with this marvellous production of the pencil of Raphael.

'Let no one consider this praise as idle and groundless, for it is Raphael himself who forces the comparison upon us, by placing the figure of Dante among the favourite sons of the Muses; and, what is still more striking, by draping the allegorical figure of Theology in the very colours in which Dante has represented Beatrice; namely, the white veil, the red tunic, and the green mantle, while on her head he has placed the olive crown.

'Of the four allegorical figures which occupy the compartments of the ceiling, and which were all painted immediately after Raphael's arrival in Rome, Theology and Poetry are incontestably the most remarkable. The latter would be easily distinguished by the calm inspiration of her glance, even were she without her wings, her starry crown, and her azure robe, all having allusion to the elevated region towards which it is her privilege to soar. The figure of Theology is quite as admirably suited to the subject she personifies; she points to the upper part of the grand composition, which takes its name from her, and in which the artist has provided inexhaustible food for the sagacity and enthusiasm of the spectator.

'This work consists of two grand divisions,—Heaven and Earth—which are united to one another by that mystical bond, the Sacrament of the Eucharist. The personages whom the Church has most honoured for learning and holiness, are ranged in picturesque and animated groups on either side of the altar, on which the consecrated wafer is exposed. St Augustine dictates his thoughts to one of his disciples; St Gregory, in his pontifical robes, seems absorbed in contemplation of celestial glory; St Ambrose, in a slightly different attitude, appears to be chanting the Te Deum; while St Jerome, seated, rests his hands on a large book, which he holds on his knees. Pietro Lombardo, Duns Scotus, St Thomas Aquinas, Pope Anacletus, St Buenaventura, and Innocent III., are no less happily characterized; while, behind all these illustrious men, whom the Church and succeeding generations have agreed to honour, Raphael has ventured to introduce Dante with his laurel crown, and, with still greater boldness, the monk Savonarola, publicly burnt ten years before as a heretic.

'In the glory, which forms the upper part of the picture, the Three Persons of the Trinity are represented, surrounded by patriarchs, apostles, and saints: it may, in fact, be considered in some sort as a *resumé* of all the favourite compositions produced during the last hundred years by the Umbrian School. A great number of the types, and particularly those of Christ and the Virgin, are to be found in the earlier works of Raphael himself. The Umbrian artists, from having so long exclusively employed themselves on mystical subjects, had certainly attained to a marvellous perfection in the representation of celestial beatitude, and of those ineffable things of which it has been said that the heart of man cannot conceive them, far less, therefore, the pencil of man portray; and Raphael, surpassing them in all, and even in this instance, while surpassing himself, appears to have fixed the limits, beyond which Christian art, properly so called, has never since been able to advance.' [12]

Of Raphael's Madonnas, I should like to speak of three. The Madonna di San Sisto: 'It represents the Virgin standing in a majestic attitude; the infant Saviour *enthroned* in her arms; and around her head a glory of innumerable cherubs melting into light. Kneeling before her we see on one side St Sixtus, on the other St Barbara, and beneath her feet two heavenly cherubs gaze up in adoration. In execution, as in design, this is probably the most perfect picture in the world. It is painted throughout by Raphael's own hand; and as no sketch or study of any part of it was ever known to exist, and as the execution must have been, from the thinness and delicacy of the colours, wonderfully rapid, it is supposed that he painted it at once on the canvas—a *creation* rather than a picture. In the beginning of the last century the Elector of Saxony, Augustus III., purchased this picture from the monks of the convent for the sum of sixty thousand

florins (about £6000), and it now forms the chief boast and ornament of the Dresden Gallery' [13]

The Madonna del Cardellino (our Lady of the Goldfinch): 'The
Virgin is sitting on a rock, in a flowery meadow. Behind are the
usual light and feathery trees, growing on the bank of a stream,
which passes off to the left in a rocky bend, and is crossed by a
bridge of a single arch. To the right, the opposite bank slopes upward in a gentle glade, across which is a village, backed by two
distant mountain-peaks.

'In front of the sitting matronly figure of the Virgin are the holy
children, our Lord and the Baptist, one on either side of her right
knee. She has been reading, and the approach of St John has caused
her to look off her book (which is open in her left hand) at the new
comer, which she does with a look of holy love and gentleness, at
the same time caressingly drawing him to her with her right hand,
which touches his little body under the right arm. In both hands,
which rest across the Virgin's knee, he holds a captive goldfinch,
which he has brought, with childish glee, as an offering to the Holy
Child. The infant Jesus, standing between his mother's knees, with
one foot placed on her foot, and her hand, with the open book, close
above his shoulder, regards the Baptist with an upward look of
gentle solemnity, at the same time that he holds his bent hand over
the head of the bird.

'So much for mere description. The inner feeling of the picture,
the motive which has prompted it, has surely hardly ever been surpassed. The Blessed Virgin, in casting her arm round the infant St
John, looks down on him with a holy complacency for the testimony
which he is to bear to her Son. Notice the human boyish glee with
which the Baptist presents the captured goldfinch, and, on the other
hand, the divine look, even of majesty and creative love, with which
the infant Jesus, laying his hand on the head of the bird, half re-
proves St John, as it were saying, "Love them and hurt them not."
Notice, too, the unfrightened calm of the bird itself, passive under
the hand of its loving Creator. All these are features of the very
highest power of human art.

'Again, in accompaniments, all is as it should be. The Virgin,
modestly and beautifully draped; St John, girt about the loins, not

only in accord with his well-known prophetic costume, but also as partaking of sinful humanity, and therefore needing such cincture: the Child Redeemer, with a slight cincture, just to suggest motherly care, but not over the part usually concealed, as indeed it never ought to be, seeing that in Him was no sin, and that it is this spotless purity which is ever the leading idea in representations of Him as an infant. Notice, too, his foot, beautifully resting on that of his mother; the unity between them being thus wonderfully though slightly kept up. Her eye has just been dwelling on the book of the Prophecies open in her hand; and thus the spectator's thought is ruled in accordance with the high mission of the Holy One of God, and thrown forward into the grand and blessed future. It is a holy and wonderful picture; I had not seen any in Italy which had struck or refreshed me more.' [14]

And allow me to write two or three words with regard to the 'Madonna della Sedia,' or our Lady of the Chair, an engraving of which used to charm me when a child. The Virgin, very young and simple-looking in her loveliness, is seated on a low chair, clasping the Divine Child, who is leaning in weariness on her breast. In the original picture, St John with his cross is standing — a boy at the Virgin's knee, but he is absent from the old engraving. The meek adoring tenderness in the face of the mother, the holy ingenuousness in that of the child, are expressions to be long studied.

Of Raphael's cartoons, which, so many of us can see for ourselves, I cannot trust myself to do more than to repeat what strikes me as a singularly apt phrase of Hazlitt's, given by Mrs Jameson, that the cartoons are instances in which 'the corruptible has put on incorruption.' That from the very slightness of the materials employed, and the very injuries which the cartoons have sustained, we have the greatest triumph of art, where 'the sense of power supersedes the appearance of effort,' and where the result is the more majestic for being in ruins. 'All other pictures look like oil and varnish, we are stopped and attracted by the colouring, the penciling, the finishing, the instrumentality of art; but the painter seems to have flung his mind on the canvas.... There is nothing between us and the subject; we look through a frame and see Scripture histories, and amidst the wreck of colour and the mouldering of material beauty, nothing is left but a universe of thought, or the broad imminent shadows of calm contemplation and majestic pains.'

And that Raphael did not neglect the minutest details in these sketches, will be seen by the accompanying note: 'The foreground of Raphael's two cartoons, "The Miraculous Draught of Fishes," and "The Charge to Peter," are covered with plants of the common sea cole-wort, of which the sinuated leaves and clustered blossoms would have exhausted the patience of any other artist; but have appeared worthy of prolonged and thoughtful labour to the great mind of Raphael.' — *Ruskin*.

Whole clusters of anecdotes gather round the cartoons, which, as they have to do with the work and not the worker, I leave untouched, with regret. But I must forewarn my readers by mentioning some of the refuted criticisms which have been applied to the cartoons. Reading the criticisms and their answers ought to render us modest and wary in 'picking holes' in great pictures, as forward and flippant critics, old and young, are tempted to pick them. With regard to the 'Miraculous Draught of Fishes,' a great outcry was once set up that Raphael had made the boat too little to hold the figures he has placed in it. But Raphael made the boat little advisedly; if he had not done so, the picture would have been 'all boat,' a contingency scarcely to be desired; on the other hand, if Raphael had diminished the figures to suit the size of the boat, these figures would not have suited those of the other cartoons, and the cartoon would have lost greatly in dignity and effect.

In the cartoon of the 'Death of Ananias,' carping objectors were ready to suggest that Raphael had committed an error in time by introducing Sapphira in the background counting her ill-gotten gains, at the moment when her no less guilty husband has fallen down in the agonies of death. It was hours afterwards that Sapphira entered into the presence of the apostles. But we must know that time and space do not exist for painters, who have to tell their story at one stroke, as it were.

In the treating of the 'Lame Man at the Beautiful Gate of the Temple,' some authorities have found fault with Raphael for breaking the composition into parts by the introduction of pillars, and, farther, that the shafts are not straight. Yet by this treatment Raphael has concentrated the principal action in a sort of frame, and thus has been enabled to give more freedom of action to the remaining figures in the other divisions of the picture. 'It is evident, moreover, that had the shafts been perfectly straight, according to the severest law of good taste in architecture, the effect would have been extremely disagreeable to the eye; by their winding form they harmonize with the manifold forms of the moving figures around, and they illustrate, by their elaborate elegance, the Scripture phrase, "the gate which is called Beautiful."' — *Mrs Jameson.*

Of Raphael's portraits I must mention that wonderful portrait of Leo X., often reckoned the best portrait in the world for truth of likeness and excellence of painting, and those of the so-called 'Fornarina,' or 'baker'. Two Fornarinas are at Rome and one at Florence. There is a story that the original of the first two pictures was a girl of the people to whom Raphael was attached; and there is this to be said for the tradition, that there is an acknowledged coarseness in the very beauty of the half-draped Fornarina of the Barberini Palace. The 'Fornarina' of Florence is the portrait of a noble woman, holding the fur-trimming of her mantle with her right hand, and it is said that the picture can hardly represent the same individual as that twice represented in Rome. According to one guess the last 'Fornarina' is Vittoria Colonna, the Marchesa de Pescara, painted by Sebastian del Piombo, instead of by Raphael; and according to another, the Roman 'Fornarina' is no Fornarina beloved by Raphael, but Beatrice Pio, a celebrated improvisatrice of the time.

An 'innovation of modern times is to spell Raphael's name in England as the modern Italians spelt it, *Raffaelle*, a word of four syllables, and yet to pronounce this Italian word as if it were English, as *Raphael*. Vasari wrote Raffaello; he himself wrote Raphael on his pictures, and has signed the only autograph letter we have of his, Raphaello.' [15]

Titian, or **Tiziano Vecelli,** the greatest painter of the Venetian School, reckoned worthy to be named with Lionardo, Michael Angelo and Raphael, was born of good family at Capo del Cadore in the Venetian State, in 1477. There is a tradition that while other painters made their first essays in art with chalk or charcoal, the boy Titian, who lived to be a glorious colourist, made his earliest trials in painting with the juice of flowers. Titian studied in Venice under the Bellini, and had Giorgione, who was born in the same year, for his fellow-scholar, at first his friend, later his rival. When a young man Titian spent some time in Ferrara; there he painted his 'Bacchus and Ariadne,' and a portrait of Lucrezia Borgia. In 1512, when Titian was thirty-five years of age, he was commissioned by the Venetians to continue the works in the great council-hall, which the advanced age of Gian Bellini kept him from finishing. Along with this commission Titian was appointed in 1516 to the office of la Sanseria, which gave him the duty and privilege of painting the portraits of the Doges as long as he held the office; coupled with the office was a salary of one hundred and twenty crowns a year. Titian lived to paint five Doges; two others, his age, equal to that of Gian Bellini, prevented him from painting.

In 1516, Titian painted his greatest sacred picture, the 'Assumption of the Virgin.' In the same year he painted the poet Ariosto, who mentions the painter with high honour in his verse.

In 1530, Titian, a man of fifty-three years, was at Bologna, where there was a meeting between Charles V, and Pope Clement VII., when he was presented to both princes.

Charles V, and Philip II, became afterwards great patrons and admirers of Titian, and it is of Charles V. and Titian that a legend, to which I have already referred, is told. The Emperor, visiting the painter while he was at work, stooped down and picked up a pencil, which Titian had let fall, to the confusion and distress of the painter, when Charles paid the princely compliment, 'Titian is worthy of being served by Cæsar.' Titian painted many portraits of Charles V., and of the members of his house. As Maximilian had created Albrecht Dürer a noble of the Empire, Charles V, created Titian a Count Palatine, and a Knight of the Order of St Iago, with a pension, which was continued by Philip II., of four hundred crowns a year. It is doubtful whether Titian ever visited the Spain of his patrons, but Madrid possesses forty-three of his pictures, among them some of his finest works.

Titian went to Rome in his later years, but declined to abandon for Rome the painter's native Venice, which had lavished her favours on her son. He lived in great splendour, paying annual summer visits to his birth-place of Cadore, and occasionally dwelling again for a time at Ferrara, Urbino, Bologna. In two instances he joined the Emperor at Augsburgh. When Henry III, of France landed at Venice, he was entertained *en grand seigneur* by Titian, then a very old man; and when the king asked the price of some pictures which pleased him, Titian at once presented them as a gift to his royal guest.

Titian married, as has been recently ascertained, and had three children, — two sons, the elder a worthless and scandalous priest; the second a good son and accomplished painter; and a daughter, the beautiful Lavinia, so often painted by her father, and whose name will live with his. Titian survived his wife thirty-six years; and his daughter, who had married, and was the mother of several children, six years. His second son and fellow-painter died of the same plague which struck down Titian, in 1566, at the ripe age of eighty-nine years.

Titian is said to have been a man of irritable and passionate temper. The hatred between him and the painter, Pordenone, was so bitter, that the latter thought his life in danger, and painted with his shield and poniard lying ready to his hand. Titian grasped with imperious tenacity his supremacy as a painter, sedulously kept the secrets of his skill, and was most unmagnanimously jealous of the attainments of his scholars. No defect of temper, however, kept Titian from having two inseparable convivial companions — one of them the architect, Sansovino, and the other the profligate wit, Aretino, who was pleased to style himself the 'friend of Titian and the scourge of princes.' Though Titian is said, in the panic of the great plague, to have died not only neglected, but plundered before his eyes, still Venice prized him so highly, that she made in his favour the single exception of a public funeral, during the appalling devastation wrought by the pestilence.

From an engraving of a portrait of Titian by himself, which is before me, I can give the best idea of his person. He looks like one of the merchant princes, whom he painted so often and so well, in richly furred gown, massive chain, and small cap, far off his broad forehead: a stately figure, with a face — in its aquiline nose and keen eyes, full of sagacity and fire, which no years could tame.

Towards the close of Titian's life, there was none who even approached the old Venetian painter in the art which he practised freely to the last. Painting in Italy was everywhere losing its pre-eminence. It had become, even when it was not so nominally, thoroughly secularized;—and with reason, for the painters by their art-creed and by their lives were fitter to represent gods and goddesses, in whom no man believed, than to give earnest expression to a living faith. Even Titian, great as he was, proved a better painter of heathen mythology than of sacred subjects.

But within certain limits and in certain directions, Titian stands unequalled. He has a high place for composition and for drawing, and his colouring was, beyond comparison, grand and true. He was great as a landscape painter, and he was the best portrait painter whom the world ever saw. In his painting is seen, not, indeed, the life of the spirit, but the life of the senses 'in its fullest power,' and in Titian there was such large mastery of this life, that in his freedom there was no violence, but the calmness of supreme strength, the serenity of perfect satisfaction. His painting was a reflection of the old Greek idea of the life of humanity as a joyous existence, so long as the sun of youth, maturity, health, and good fortune shone, without even that strain of foreboding pain, and desperate closing with fate, which troubled the bliss of ancient poet or sculptor. A large proportion of Titian's principal pictures are at Venice and Madrid.

Among Titian's finest sacred pictures, are his 'Assumption of the Virgin,' now in the Academy, Venice, where 'the Madonna, a powerful figure, is borne rapidly upwards, as if divinely impelled; .., fascinating groups of infant angels surround her, beneath stand the apostles, looking up with solemn gestures;' and his 'Entombment of Christ,' a picture which is also in Venice. Titian's Madonnas were not so numerous as his Venuses, many of which are judged excellent examples of the master. His 'Bacchus and Ariadne,' in the National Gallery, is described by Mrs Jameson, 'as presenting, on a small scale, an epitome of all the beauties which characterize Titian, in the rich, picturesque, animated composition, in the ardour of Bacchus, who flings himself from his car to pursue Ariadne; the dancing bacchanals, the frantic grace of the bacchante, and the little joyous satyr in front, trailing the head of the sacrifice.'

Titian's landscapes are the noble backgrounds to many of his pictures. These landscapes were not only free, but full. 'The great masters of Italy, almost without exception, and Titian, perhaps, more than any other (for he had the highest knowledge of landscape), are in the constant habit of rendering every detail of their foregrounds with the most laborious botanical fidelity; witness the Bacchus and Ariadne, in which the foreground is occupied by the common blue iris, the aquilegia, and the wild rose; *every stamen* of which latter is given, while the blossoms and leaves of the columbine (a difficult flower to draw) have been studied with the most exquisite accuracy.' — *Ruskin.*

In portraits, Titian conveyed to the sitters and transferred to his canvas, not only a life-likeness, but a positively noble dignity in that likeness. What in Van Dyck and Sir Joshua Reynolds was the bestowing of high breeding and dainty refinement, became under Titian's brush dignity, pure and simple, very quiet, and wonderfully real. There is this peculiarity in connection with the number of portraits which Titian executed, that many of them have descended to us without further titles than those of 'A Venetian Senator,' 'A Lady,' &c., &c., yet of the individual life of the originals no one can doubt. With regard to Titian's portraits of women, I have already referred to those of his beautiful daughter, Lavinia. In one portrait, in the Berlin Museum, she is holding a plate of fruit; in another, in England, the plate of fruit is changed into a casket of jewels; in a third, at Madrid, Lavinia is Herodias, and bears a charger with the head of John the Baptist. A 'Violante' — as some say, the daughter of Titian's scholar, Palma, though dates disprove this — sat frequently to Titian, and is said to have been loved by him.

I have written, in connection with Lionardo's 'Jaconde' and Raphael's 'Fornarina,' of Titian's 'Bella Donna.' He has various 'Bellas,' but, as far as I know, this is *the* 'Bella Donna,' — 'a splendid, serious beauty, in a red and blue silk dress,' in the Sciarra Gallery, Rome.

I have read that critics were at one time puzzled by the singular yellow, almost straw colour, appearing profusely in the hair of the women of the Venetian painters of this time, and that it was only by consulting contemporary records that it was learnt that the Venetian women indulged in the weak and false vanity of dyeing their black hair a pale yellow—a process, in the course of which the women drew the hair through the crown of a broad-brimmed hat, and spreading it over the brim, submitted patiently to bleaching the hair in a southern sun.

Among Titian's portraits of men, those of the 'Emperor Charles V.' and the 'Duke of Alva' are among the most famous.

Titian painted, and painted wonderfully, to the very last. He was eighty-one when he painted the 'Martyrdom of St Lawrence,' one of his largest and grandest compositions, and in the last year of his life he painted—leaving it not quite completed,—a 'Pietà;' showing that his hand owned the weight of years, [16] but the conception of the subject is still animated and striking, the colours still glowing; while, Titian-like, the light still flows around the mighty group in every gradation of tone.

CHAPTER V.

GERMAN ART—ALBRECHT DÜRER, 1471-1528.

Albrecht Dürer carries us to a different country and a different race. And he who has been called the father of German painting is thoroughly German, not only in his Saxon honesty, sedateness, and strength, but in the curious mixture of simplicity, subtlety, homeliness, and fantasticalness, which are still found side by side in German genius.

Albrecht Dürer was born at that fittest birth-place for the great German painter, quaint old Nuremberg, in 1471. He was the son of a goldsmith, and one of a family of eighteen children; a home school in which he may have learnt early the noble, manly lessons of self-denial and endurance, which he practised long and well. He was trained to his father's trade until the lad's bent became so unmistakable that he was wisely transferred to the studio of a painter to serve his apprenticeship to art.

When the Nuremberg apprenticeship was completed, Albrecht followed the German custom, very valuable to him, of serving another and a 'wandering apprenticeship,' which carried him betimes through Germany, the Netherlands, and Italy, painting and studying as he went. He painted his own portrait about this time, showing himself a comely, pleasant, and pleased young fellow, in a curious holiday suit of plaited low-bodied shirt, jerkin, and mantle across the shoulder, with a profusion of long fair curls, of which he was said to have been vain, arranged elaborately on each side, the blue eyes looking with frank confidence out of the blonde face. He painted himself a little later with the brave kindly face grown mature, and the wisdom of the spirit shining in the eyes, and weighing on the brows.

On his return from his travels, Albrecht Dürer's father arranged his son's marriage with the daughter of a musician in Nuremberg. The inducement to the marriage seems to have been, on the father's part, the dowry, and on the son's the beauty of the bride. How unhappy the union proved, without any fault of Albrecht's, has been the theme of so many stories, that I am half inclined to think that some of us must be more familiar with Albrecht Dürer's wedded life than with any other part of his history. It seems to me, that there is considerable exaggeration in these stories, for granted that Agnes Dürer was a shrew and a miser, was Albrecht Dürer the man to be entirely, or greatly, at such a woman's mercy? Taking matters at their worst, dishonour and disgrace did not come near the great painter. He was esteemed, as he deserved to be; he had a true friend in his comrade Pirkheimer; he had his art; he had the peace of a good conscience; he had the highest of all consolations in his faith in Heaven. Certainly it is not from Albrecht himself that the tale of his domestic wretchedness has come. He was as manfully patient and silent as one might have expected in a man upright, firm, and self-reliant as he was tender. I do not think it is good for men, and especially for women, to indulge in egotistical sentimentality, and to believe that such a woman as Agnes Dürer could utterly thwart and wreck the life of a man like Albrecht. It is not true to life, in the first place; and it is dishonouring to the man, in the second; for although, doubtless, there are men who are driven to destruction or heartbroken by even the follies of women, these men have not the stout hearts, the loyal spirits, the manly mould of Albrecht Dürer.

But making every allowance for the high colours with which a tale that has grown stale is apt to be daubed, I am forced to admit the inference that a mean, sordid, contentious woman probably did as much as was in her power to harass and fret one of the best men in Germany, or in the world. Luckily for himself, Albrecht was a severe student, had much engrossing work which carried him abroad, and travelled once at least far away from the harassing and galling home discipline. For anything further, I believe that Albrecht loved his greedy, scolding wife, whose fair face he painted frequently in his pictures, and whom he left at last well and carefully provided for, as he bore with her to the end.

In 1506 Albrecht Dürer re-visited Italy alone, making a stay of eight months in Venice, where he formed his friendship with the old Gian Bellini, and where Albrecht had the misfortune to show the proofs and plans of his engravings to the Italian engraver, Raimondi, who engraved Raphael's paintings, and who proved himself base enough to steal and make use of Albrecht Dürer's designs to the German's serious loss and inconvenience.

A little later Albrecht Dürer, accompanied by his wife, visited the Netherlands. The Emperor Maximilian treated the painter with great favour, and a legend survives of their relations:—Dürer was painting so large a subject that he required steps to reach it. The Emperor, who was present, required a nobleman of his suite to steady the steps for the painter, an employment which the nobleman declined as unworthy of his rank, when the Emperor himself stepped forward and supplied the necessary aid, remarking, 'Sir, understand that I can make Albrecht a noble like and above you' (Maximilian had just raised Albrecht Dürer to the rank of noble of the empire), 'but neither I nor any one else can make an artist like him.' We may compare this story with a similar and later story of Holbein and Henry VIII., and with another earlier story, having a slight variation, of Titian and Charles V. The universality of the story shakes one's belief in its individual application, but at least the legend, with different names, remains as an indication of popular homage to genius.

While executing a large amount of work for the great towns and sovereign princes of Germany, some of whom were said to consult the painter on their military operations, relying on his knowledge of mathematics, and his being able to apply it to military engineering and fortification, Albrecht Dürer was constantly improving and advancing in his art, laying down his prejudices, and acquiring fresh ideas, as well as fresh information, according to the slow but sure process of the true German mind, till his last work was incomparably his best.

Germany was then in the terrible throes of the Reformation, and Albrecht Dürer, who has left us the portraits of several of the great Reformers, is believed to have been no uninterested spectator of the struggle, and to have held, like his fellow-painter, Lucas Cranach — though in Albrecht Dürer's case the change was never openly professed — the doctrines of the Reformation.

There is a portrait of Albrecht Dürer, painted by himself, in his later years. (By the way, Albrecht was not averse to painting his own portrait as well as that of his friend Pirkheimer, and of making the fullest claim to his work by introducing into his religious and historical pictures his own figure holding a flag or tablet, inscribed with his name in the quiet self-assertion of a man who was neither ashamed of himself, nor of anything he did.) In that last portrait, Albrecht is a thoughtful, care-worn man, with his fair locks shorn. Some will attribute the change to Agnes Dürer, but I imagine it proceeds simply from the noble scars of work and time; and that when Albrecht Dürer died in his fifty-seventh year, if it were in sourness and bitterness of spirit, as some of his biographers have stated, that sourness and bitterness were quite as much owing to the grievous troubles of his time and country, which so large-minded a man was sure to lay to heart, as to any domestic trouble. Albrecht Dürer was greatly beloved by his own city of Nuremberg, where his memory continues to be cherished. His quaint house still stands, and his tomb bears the motto 'Emigravit,'

'For the great painter never dies.'

Albrecht Dürer's name ranks with the names of the first painters of any time or country, though his work as a painter was, as in the case of William Hogarth, subservient to his work as an engraver. With the knowledge of a later generation to that of the earliest Italian and Flemish painters, Albrecht Dürer had much of their singleness of purpose, assiduity of application, and profound feeling. He had to labour against a tendency to uncouthness in stiff lines and angular figures; to petty elaboration of details; and to that grotesqueness which, while it suited in some respects his allegorical engravings, marred his historical paintings, so that he was known to regret the wasted fantastic crowding and confusion of his earlier work. From the Italians and Flemings he learnt simplicity, and a more correct sense of material beauty. The purity, truth, and depth of the man's spirit, from which ideal beauty proceeds, no man could add to.

Among Albrecht Dürer's greatest paintings are his 'Adoration of the Trinity' at Vienna, his 'Adam and Eve' at Florence, and that last picture of 'The Apostles,' presented by Albrecht Dürer to his native city, 'in remembrance of his career as an artist, and at the same time as conveying to his fellow-citizens an earnest and lasting exhortation suited to that stormy period.' The prominence given to the Bible in the picture, points to it as the last appeal in the great spiritual struggle. With regard to this noble masterly picture, Kugler has written, 'Well might the artist now close his eyes. He had in this picture attained the summit of art; here he stands side by side with the greatest masters known in history.'

But I prefer to say something of Albrecht Dürer's engravings, which are more characteristic of him and far more widely known than his paintings; and to speak first of those two wonderful and beautiful allegories, 'Knight, Death, and the Devil,' and 'Melancolia.' In the first, which is an embodiment of weird German romance as well as of high Christian faith, the solitary Knight, with his furrowed face and battered armour, rides steadfastly on through the dark glen, unmoved by his grisly companions, skeleton Death on the lame horse, and the foul Fiend in person. Contrast this sketch and its thoughtful touching meaning with the hollow ghastliness of Holbein's 'Dance of Death.'

In 'Melancolia' a grand winged woman sits absorbed in sorrowful thought, while surrounded by all the appliances of philosophy, science, art, mechanics, all the discoveries made before and in Albrecht Dürer's day, in the book, the chart, the lever, the crystal, the crucible, the plane, the hammer. The intention of this picture has been disputed, but the best explanation of it is that which regards the woman as pondering on the humanly unsolved and insoluble mystery of the sin and sorrow of life.

In three large series of woodcuts, known as the Greater and the Lesser Passion of the Lord, and the Life of the Virgin, and taken partly from sacred history and partly from tradition, Albrecht Dürer exceeded himself in true beauty, simple majesty, and pathos. Photographs have spread widely these fine woodcuts, and there is, at least, one which I think my readers may have seen, 'The Bearing of the Cross,' in which the blessed Saviour sinks under his burden. In the series of the Life of the Virgin there is a 'Repose in Egypt,' which has a naïve homeliness in its grace and serenity. The woodcut represents a courtyard with a dwelling built in the ruins of an ancient palace. The Virgin sits spinning with a distaff and spindle beside the Holy Child's cradle, by which beautiful angels worship. Joseph is busy at his carpenter's work, and a number of little angels, in merry sport, assist him with his labours. [17]

I shall mention only one more work of Albrecht Dürer's, that which is known as the Emperor Maximilian's Prayer Book. This is pen-and-ink sketches for the borders of a book (as the old missals were illuminated), which are now preserved in the Royal Library, Munich. In these little drawings the fancy of the great artist held high revel, by no means confining itself to serious subjects, such as apostles, monks, or even men in armour, but indulging in the most whimsical vagaries, with regard to little German old women, imps, piping squirrels, with cocks and hens hurrying to listen to the melody.

CHAPTER VI.

LATER ITALIAN ART — GIORGIONE, 1477-1511 — CORREGGIO. ABOUT 1493-1534 — TINTORETTO, 1512-1574 — VERONESE, 1530-1588.

Giorgio Barbarelli, known as **'Giorgione,** — in Italian, 'big,' or, as I have heard it better translated, 'strapping George' — was born at Castelfranco, in Treviso, about 1477, the same year in which Titian was born. Nothing is known of his youth before he came to Venice and studied in the school of Gian Bellini along with Titian.

The two men were friends in those days, but soon quarrelled, and Giorgione's early death completed their separation. Titian was impatient and arrogant; Giorgione seems to have been one of those proud, shy, sensitive men—possibly morbidly sensitive, with whom it is always difficult to deal; but it is recorded of him, as it is not recorded of his great compeer, that Giorgione was frank and friendly as an artist, however moody and fitful he might be as a man.

Giorgione soon became known. According to one account, he painted the façade of the house which he dwelt in, for an advertisement of his abilities as a painter, a device which was entirely successful in procuring him commissions; but unfortunately for posterity, these were frequently to paint other façades, sometimes in company with Titian; grand work, which has inevitably perished, if not by fire, by time and by the sea-damp of Venice, for to Venice Giorgione belonged, and there is no sign that he ever left it.

He had no school, and his love of music and society—the last taste found not seldom, an apparent anomaly, in silent, brooding natures—might tend to withdraw him from his art. He has left a trace of his love for music in his pictures of 'Concerts' and of 'Pastorals,' in which musical performances are made prominent. In Giorgione, with his romantic, idealizing temperament, genre [18] pictures took this form, while he is known to have painted from Ovid and from the Italian tales of his time. He was employed frequently to paint scenes on panels, for the richly ornamented Venetian furniture. Giorgione was not without a bent to realism in his very idealism, and is said to have been the first Italian painter who 'imitated the real texture of stuffs and painted draperies from the actual material.'

Giorgione died at the early age of thirty-three years, in 1511. One account represents him as dying of the plague, others attribute his death to a sadder cause. He is said to have had a friend and fellow-painter who betrayed their friendship, and carried off the girl whom Giorgione loved. Stung to the quick by the double falsehood, the tradition goes on to state that Giorgione fell into despair with life and all it held, and so died.

A portrait of Giorgione is in the Munich Gallery; it is that of a very handsome beardless lad, 'with a peculiar melancholy in the dark glowing eyes.'

Giorgione was, like Titian, grand and free in drawing and composition, and superb in colour. [19] Mrs Jameson has drawn a nice distinction between the two painters as colourists. That the colours of Giorgione 'appear as if lighted from within, and those of Titian from without;' that 'the epithet glowing applies best to Giorgione, that of golden to Titian.'

Giorgione's historic pictures are rare, his sacred pictures rarer still; among the last is a 'Finding of Moses,' now in Milan, thus described by Mrs Jameson: 'In the centre sits the princess under a tree; she looks with surprise and tenderness on the child, which is brought to her by one of her attendants; the squire, or seneschal, of the princess, with knights and ladies, stand around; on one side two lovers are seated on the grass; on the other are musicians and singers, pages with dogs. All the figures are in the Venetian costume; the colouring is splendid, and the grace and harmony of the whole composition is even the more enchanting from the naïveté of the conception. This picture, like many others of the same age and style, reminds us of those poems and tales of the middle ages, in which David and Jonathan figure as *preux chevaliers*, and Sir Alexander of Macedon and Sir Paris of Troy fight tournaments in honour of ladies' eyes and the "blessed Virgin." They must be tried by their own aim and standard, not by the severity of antiquarian criticism.'

In portraits Giorgione has only been exceeded by Titian. In the National Gallery there is an unimportant 'St Peter the Martyr,' and a finer 'Maestro di Capella giving a music lesson,' which Kugler assigns to Giorgione, though it has been given elsewhere to Titian. The 'refined voluptuousness and impassioned sombreness' of Giorgione's painting have instituted a comparison between him and Lord Byron as a poet.

Correggio's real name was **Antonio Allegri,** and he has his popular name from his birth-place of Correggio, now called Reggio; although at one time there existed an impression that Correggio meant 'correct,' from the painter's exceedingly clever feats of foreshortening.

His father is believed to have been a well-to-do tradesman, and the lad is said to have had an uncle a painter, who probably influenced his nephew. But Correggio had a greater master, though but for a very short time, in Andrea Mantegna, who died when Correggio was still a young boy. Mantegna's son kept on his father's school, and from him Correggio might have received more regular instruction. He early attained excellence, and in the teeth of the legends which lingered in Parma for a full century, his genius received prompt notice and patronage. He married young, and from records which have come to light, he received a considerable portion with his wife.

The year after his marriage, when he was no more than six-and-twenty, Correggio was appointed to paint in fresco the cupola of the church of San Giovanni at Parma, and chose for his subject the 'Ascension of Christ;' for this work and that of the 'Coronation of the Virgin,' painted over the high altar, Correggio got five hundred gold crowns, equivalent to £1500. He was invited to Mantua, where he painted from the mythology for the Duke of Mantua. Indeed, so far and wide had the preference for mythological subjects penetrated, that one of Correggio's earliest works was 'Diana returning from the Chase;' painted for the decoration of the parlour of the Abbess of the convent of San Paulo, Parma.

Correggio was a second time called upon to paint a great religious work in Parma—this time in the cathedral, for which he selected 'The Assumption of the Virgin.' A few of the cartoons for these frescoes were discovered thirty or forty years ago, rolled up and lying forgotten in a garret in Parma; they, are now in the British Museum.

In 1533, Correggio, then residing in his native town, was one of the witnesses to the marriage of his sovereign, the Lord of Correggio. In the following year the painter had engaged to paint an altar-piece for an employer, who paid Correggio in advance twenty-five gold crowns, but the latter dying very soon afterwards, in the forty-first year of his age, 1534, his father, who was still alive, was in circumstances to repay the advance on the picture, which had not been painted.

Correggio is said to have been modest and retiring in disposition, and this, together with the fact that, like Giorgione, he did not have a school, has been suggested as the source of the traditions which prevailed so long in Italy. These traditions described the painter as a man born in indigent circumstances, living obscurely in spite of his genius (there is a picture of Correggio's in England, which was said to have been given in payment for his entertainment at an inn), and leading to the end a life of such ill-requited labour, that having been paid for his last picture in copper money, and being under the necessity of carrying it home in order to relieve the destitution of his family, he broke down under the burden, and overcome by heat and weariness, drank a rash draught of water, which caused fever and death.

The story, disproven as it is, is often alluded to still, and remains as a foil to those flattering and courtly anecdotes which I have been repeating of royal and imperial homage paid to Dürer, Titian, and Holbein. I fancy the last-mentioned stories may have grown from small beginnings, and circulated purely in the artist world; but that the former is an utterance of the engrained persuasion of the great world without, that art as a means of livelihood is essentially non-remunerative in the sense of money-getting.

Modest as Correggio may have been, he was not without pride in his art. After looking for the first time on the St Cecilia of Raphael, Correggio is reported to have exclaimed with exultation, 'And I too am a painter.'

He left behind him on his death a son and a daughter, the former living to be a painter of no great name. In the picture of Correggio in the attitude of painting, painted by himself, we see him a handsome spare man with something of a romantic cavalier air, engaged in his chosen art.

Correggio's pictures go to prove that under his seemingly quiet exterior he was a man of the liveliest sensibilities and the keenest perceptions, His pictures, unlike Titian's in their repose, are full of motion and excitement. Correggio is spoken of as a painter who delighted 'in the buoyance of childish glee, the bliss of earthly, the fervour of heavenly love,' whose radiant sphere of art sorrow rarely clouded; but when sorrow did enter, it borrowed from the painter's own quivering heart the very sharpness of anguish. The same authority tells us of Correggio, that he has painted 'the very heartthrobs of humanity.' But it seems as if such a nature, with its self-conscious veil of forced stillness, must have had a tendency to vehemence and excess; and so we hear that Correggio's foreshortening was sometimes violent, and the energy of his actors spasmodic; thus the cruelly smart contemporary criticism was pronounced on his frescoes of the 'Assumption of the Virgin,' in which legs and arms in wild play are chiefly conspicuous from below, that Correggio had prepared for the Parmese 'a fricassée of frogs.' In addition, the great modern critic, Mr Ruskin, has boldly accused Correggio 'both of weakness and meretriciousness,' and there is this to be said of a nature so highly strung as Correggio's was strung, that it was not a healthily balanced nature.

But if the painter were really inferior in his sense of form and expression to his great predecessors, he was so great in one department, that in it he was held worthy, not only to found the school of Parma, but to be classed with the first four painters of Italy.

That chiarascuro, or treatment of light and shade, in which Lionardo and Andrea Mantegna were no mean proficients, was brought to such perfection by Correggio, that, as Mrs Jameson has sought to illustrate technical expressions, 'you seem to look through. Correggio's shadows, and to see beyond them the genuine texture of the flesh.' In undulating grace of motion, in melting softness of outline, fixed on a canvas, he surpassed all rivals, including Raphael; and this widely attractive quality ('luscious refinement,' Mr Ruskin terms it) in connection with Correggio's ardent, if undisciplined sensibility, has rendered him one of the most valued of painters; his best paintings being highly prized and costly as the easel pictures attributed to Raphael. Sir W. Stirling Maxwell writes that an old Duke of Modena was suspected of having caused Correggio's 'Notte' to be stolen from a church at Reggio, and that the princes of Este were wont to carry 'The Magdalene Reading' with them on their journeys, while the king of Poland kept it under lock and key in a frame of jewelled silver.

Among Correggio's master-pieces, besides his frescoes, there is at Parma his picture called 'Day,' from the broad flood of daylight in the picture (and doubtless in contrast to his famous 'Notte' or 'Night,' in the Dresden Gallery). Here is a Virgin and Child, with St Jerome presenting to them his translation of the Scriptures, and the Magdalene bending to kiss in adoration the feet of the infant Saviour.

In the Dresden Gallery in addition to the 'Notte' are five pictures, one of the marriage of St Catherine as the Church—the bride, espoused with a ring to the infant Saviour, a favourite subject of Italian painters, and a specially favourite subject with Correggio; and another, the Magdalene reading, half shrouded with her flowing hair, so well known by engravings. I must say a few more words of the 'Notte,'—it is a nativity illuminated entirely by the unearthly glory shining from the Child Christ. Virgin and Child are bathed and half lost in the fair radiance, which falls softly on a shepherd and maiden, leaving the rest of the figures, the stalled beasts, and the surroundings of the stable, in dim shadow.

In our National Gallery there are fine specimens of Correggio. There is an 'Ecce Homo': Christ crowned with thorns, holding out his bound hands, with a Roman soldier softening into pity, Pilate hardening in indifference, and the Virgin fainting with sorrow. There are also 'the Virgin with the Basket,' so named from the little basket in front of the picture; and 'a Holy Family;' and there is a highly-esteemed picture from a mythological subject, 'Mercury teaching Cupid to read in the presence of Venus.'

We must return to the Venice of Titian, and see how his successors, with much more of the true painter in them than the fast degenerating scholars of other Italian schools, were mere men, if great men, matched with Titian.

Tintoretto is only Tintoretto or Tintoret because his father was a dyer, and 'Il Tintoretto' is in Italian, 'the little dyer.' Tintoretto's real name was one more in keeping with his pretensions, **Jacopo Robusti.** He was born in Venice, in 1512, and early fore-shadowed his future career by drawing all kinds of objects on the walls of his father's dye-house, an exercise which did not offend or dismay the elder Robusti, but, on the contrary, induced him to put the boy into the school of Titian, where Tintoretto only remained a short time. Titian did not choose to impart what could be imparted of his art to his scholars, and, in all probability, Tintoretto was no deferential and submissive scholar. There is a tradition that Titian expelled this scholar from his academy, saying of the dyer's son, that 'he would never be anything but a dauber.'

Tintoret was not to be daunted. He lived to be a bold-tempered, dashing man, and he must have been defiant, even in his boyhood, as he was swaggering in his youth, when he set up an academy of his own, and inscribed above the door, 'The drawing of Michael Angelo and the colouring of Titian.' He had studied and taught himself from casts and theories since he left the school of Titian, and then, with worldly wisdom equal to his daring, he commenced his artistic career by accepting every commission, good or bad, and taking what pay he could get for his work; but, unfortunately for him and for the world, he executed his work, as might have been expected, in the same headlong, indiscriminate spirit, acquiring the name of 'Il Furioso' from the rapidity and recklessness of his manner of painting. Often he did not even give himself the trouble of making any sketch or design of his pictures beforehand, but composed as he painted.

Self-confident to presumption, he took for his inspirations the merest impulses, and considerably marred the effect of his unquestionably grand genius by gross haste and carelessness. He was a successful man in his day, as so energetic and unscrupulous a man was likely enough to be, and his fellow-citizens, who saw principally on the surface, [20] were charmed beyond measure by his tremendous capacity for invention, his dramatic vigour, his gorgeous, rampant richness and glare; or, by contrast, his dead dulness of ornament and colouring; and were not too greatly offended by his occasional untruthfulness in drawing and colouring, and the inequality of his careless, slovenly, powerful achievements. Yet even Tintoret's fascinated contemporaries said of him that he 'used three pencils: one gold, one silver, one lead.'

Naturally Tintoretto painted an immense number of pictures, to only three of which, however, he appended his name. These were, 'The Crucifixion,' and 'The Miracle of the Slave,' two of fifty-seven pictures which he painted for the school of St Roch alone, in Venice;

the other was the 'Marriage at Cana,' in the church of Santa Maria della Saluto, Venice.

There is an authentic story told of Tintoretto in his age, which is in touching contrast to what is otherwise known of the man. Besides a son, Dominico, who was a painter, Tintoret had a daughter, Marietta, very dear to him, who was also a painter — indeed, so gifted a portrait painter, as to have been repeatedly invited to foreign courts to practise her art, invitations which she declined, because she would not be parted from her father. To Tintoret's great grief, this daughter died as she was thirty years of age, and her father was in his seventy-eighth year. When her end was unmistakably near, the old man took brush and canvas and struggled desperately to preserve a last impression of the beloved child's face, over which death was casting its shadow.

Tintoretto died four years later, in 1594. His portrait is that of a man who holds his head high and resolutely; he has, strange to say, a somewhat commonplace face, with its massive nose, full eye, short curly beard and hail. The forehead is not very broad, but the head is 'long,' as Scotch people say, and they count long-headedness not only an indication of self-esteem, but of practical shrewdness. Tintoret's power was native, and had received little training; it is a proof of the strength of that power that he could not quench it. His faults, as a painter, I have already had to chronicle in the sketch of the man. He was greatest on large canvases, where his recklessness was lost in his strength; and in portraits, where his quickness in seizing striking traits more than equalled that rapidity of conclusion in realizing, and still more notably in classifying, character, which, to say the least, is liable to error.

Even before Tintoretto lived sacred subjects and! art had entirely changed places. In the days of Fra Angelico and the Van Eycks, art was the means by which painters brought before men sacred subjects, to whose design painters looked with more or less of conviction and feeling. By the time that Tintoret painted, sacred subjects were the means by which painters showed their art; means, the design of which was largely lost sight of, and which might be freely tortured and twisted, falsified, well-nigh burlesqued, if, by so doing, painters could better display their originality, skill, and mastery of technicalities. Sacred subjects had become more and more human in the lower sense, and less and less divine. A man who had so little reverence as Tintoret showed for his own higher self, his fellow-men, and his art, would scarcely seem well qualified to take up sacred subjects. But criticism is entirely and hopelessly divided on the question, for while some authorities hold that he made of the awful scene of the Crucifixion a merely historical and decidedly theatrical procession, other authorities maintain that he preserved in that 'great composition' 'repose and dignity, solemnity and reverence.'

Here is M. Charles Blanc, the French art critic's opinion of Tintoret's largest work, seventy-four feet in length and thirty feet in height: The Glory of Paradise, in the great hall or throne-room of the Doge's Palace: —

'If the shadows had not become so black, such a picture would have had something of sublimity; but that sky, without transparency, the lights of which, even, are of a burnt and baked colour, has rather the air of a lit-up Erebus than of a Paradise. Four hundred figures are in motion in this vast enclosure, some naked, others draped, but draped uniformly in a staring red or a hard blue, which form as many spots, in some sort symmetrical. The manner is quick; a little loose, but confident. The models are neither taken from nature nor from the ideal, they are drawn from practice, and are in general only turns of the head, without beauty and without delicacy. The angels are agitated like demons; and the whole—coarse enough in execution as in thought, is imposing nevertheless by mass, movement, and number. It is the striking image of a multitude in the air, a rout in the heavens, or rather in purgatory.'

Here, again, is Mr Ruskin's unequalled estimate of Tintoret's works: 'I should exhaust the patience of the reader if I were to dwell at length on the various stupendous developments of the imagination of Tintoret in the Scuola di San Rocco alone. I would fain join awhile in that solemn pause of the journey into Egypt, where the silver boughs of the shadowy trees lace with their tremulous lines the alternate folds of fair cloud, flushed by faint crimson light, and lie across the streams of blue between those rosy islands like the white wakes of wandering ships; or watch beside the sleep of the disciples among those mossy leaves that lie so heavily on the dead of the night beneath the descent of the angel of the agony, and toss fearfully above the motion of the torches as the troop of the betrayer emerges out of the hollows of the olives; or wait through the hour of accusing beside the judgment-seat of Pilate, where all is unseen, unfelt, except the one figure that stands with its head bowed down, pale like the pillar of moonlight, half bathed in the glory of the Godhead, half wrapt in the whiteness of the shroud. Of these and all other thoughts of indescribable power that are now fading from the walls of those neglected chambers, I may perhaps endeavour at a future time to preserve some image and shadow more faithfully than by words; but I shall at present terminate our series of illustrations by reference to a work of less touching, but more tremendous appeal; the Last Judgment in the church of Santa Maria dell' Orto.'

'By Tintoret only has this unimaginable event been grappled with in its verity; not typically, nor symbolically, but as they may see it who shall not sleep, but be changed. Only one traditional circumstance he has received with Dante and Michael Angelo, the Boat of the Condemned; but the impetuosity of his mind bursts out even in the adoption of this image; he has not stopped at the scowling ferryman of the one, nor at the sweeping blow and demon-dragging of the other; but, seized Hylas-like by the limbs, and tearing up the earth in his agony, the victim is dashed into his destruction; nor is it the sluggish Lethe, nor the fiery lake, that bears the cursed vessel, but the oceans of the earth and the waters of the firmament gathered into one white, ghastly cataract; the river of the wrath of God, roaring down into the gulf where the world has melted with its fervent heat, choked with the ruin of nations, and the limbs of its corpses tossed out of its whirling like water-wheels. Bat-like, out of the holes, and caverns, and shadows of the earth, the bones gather, and the clay-heaps heave, rattling and adhering into half-kneaded anatomies, that crawl, and startle, and struggle up among the putrid weeds, with the clay clinging to their clotted hair, and their heavy eyes sealed by the earth darkness yet, like his of old who went his way unseeing to the Siloam pool; shaking off one by one the dreams of the prison-house, hardly hearing the clangour of the trumpets of the armies of God; blinded yet more, as they awake, by the white light of the new heaven, until the great vortex of the four winds bears up their bodies to the judgment-seat; the Firmament is all full of them, a very dust of human souls, that drifts, and floats, and falls in the interminable, inevitable light; the bright clouds are darkened with them as with thick snow; currents of atom life in the arteries of heaven, now soaring up slowly, and higher and higher still, till the eye and thought can follow no farther, borne up, wingless, by their inward faith, and by the angel powers invisible, now hurled in countless drifts of horror before the breath of their condemnation.'

There is only one little work, of small consequence, by Tintoretto in the National Gallery, but there are nearly a dozen in the Royal Galleries, as Charles I. was an admirer and buyer of 'Tintorettos.' Two Tintorettos which belonged to King Charles I, are at Hampton Court; the one is 'Esther fainting before Ahasuerus,' and the other the 'Nine Muses.' With another 'Esther' I have been familiar from childhood by an old engraving. I think the subject must have been in some respects congenial to Tintoret, and he has certainly revelled in the sumptuousness of the mighty Eastern tyrant, in royal mantle and ermine tippet, seated on his throne, and stretching his jewelled sceptre to Esther, who is in the rich costume of a Venetian lady of the period, and sinking into the arms of her watchful maids, with a fair baby face, and little helpless hands, having dainty frills round the wrists, which scarcely answer to our notion of the attributes of the magnanimous, if meek, Jewish heroine.

Paul Cágliari of Verona is far better known as **Paul Veronese.** He was born in Verona in 1530, and was the son of a sculptor. He was taught by his father to draw and model, but abandoned sculpture for the sister art of painting, which was more akin to his tastes, and which he followed in the studio of an uncle who was a fair painter.

Quitting Verona, Paul Veronese repaired to Venice, studying the works of Titian and Tintoret, and settling in their city, finding no want of patronage even in a field so fully appropriated before he came to take his place there. His first great work was the painting of the church of St Sebastian, with scenes from the history of Esther. Whether he chose the subject or whether it was assigned to him, it belonged even more to him than to Tintoret, for Veronese was the most magnificent of the magnificent Venetian painters. From that date he was kept in constant employment by the wealthy and luxurious Venetians. He visited Rome in the suite of the Venetian ambassador in 1563, when he was in his thirty-fourth year, and he was invited to Spain to assist in the decoration of the Escurial by Philip II., but refused the invitation.

Veronese is said to have been a man of kindly spirit, generous and devout. In painting for churches and convents, he would consent to receive the smallest remuneration, sometimes not more than the price of his colours and canvas. For his fine picture now in the Louvre, the 'Marriage of Cana,' he is believed not to have had more than forty pounds in our money. He died when he was but fifty-eight years of age, in 1588. He had married and left sons who were painters, and worked with their father. He had a brother, Benedotto, who was also a painter, and who is thought to have painted many of the architectural backgrounds to Veronese's pictures.

Veronese's portrait, which he has left us, gives the idea of a more earnest and impressionable man than Tintoret. A man in middle age, bald-headed, with a furrowed brow, cheeks a little hollowed, head slightly thrown back, and a somewhat anxious as well as intent expression of face; what of the dress is seen, being a plain doublet with turned-over collar, and a cloak arranged in a fold across the breast, and hanging over the right shoulder like a shepherd's 'maud' or plaid. Looking at the engraving, and hearing of Paul Veronese's amiability and piety, one has little difficulty in thinking of the magnificent painter, as a single-hearted, simple-minded man, neither vain nor boastful, nor masterful save by the gift of genius.

I have called Paul Veronese a magnificent painter, and magnificence is the great attribute of his style; but before going farther into his merits and defects, I should like to quote to you a passage from Mr Ruskin, the most eloquent and dogmatic of art critics, prefacing the passage with the statement that the true lesson which it teaches is particularly needful for women, who, if they love art at all, are apt to regard it chiefly for its sentiment, and to undervalue such proper painter's work, such breadth and affluence and glory of handling, as are to be met with on the canvases of painters like Veronese and Rubens. 'But I perceive a tendency among some of the more thoughtful critics of the day to forget the business of a painter is *to paint*, and so altogether to despise those men, Veronese and Rubens for instance, who were painters, *par excellence*, and in whom the expressional qualities are subordinate. Now it is well, when we have strong moral or poetical feeling manifested in painting, to mark this as the best part of the work; but it is not well to consider as a thing of small account the painter's language in which that feeling is conveyed; for if that language be not good and lovely, the man may indeed be a just moralist or a great poet, but he is not a *painter*, and it was wrong of him to paint.'

It was said of Paul Veronese, that while he had not 'the brilliance and depth of Titian' or the 'prodigious facility' of Tintoret, yet, in some respects, Veronese surpassed both. But he was certainly deficient in a sense of suitability and probability. He, of all painters, carried to an outrageous extent the practice, which I have defended in some degree, of painting sacred and historical subjects as if they had happened in his own day and city. He violated taste and even reason in painting every scene, lofty or humble, sacred or profane, alike, with the pomp of splendour and richness of ornament which were the fashion of the time; but he had a vivid perception of character, and a certain greatness of mind which redeemed his plethora of gorgeousness from monotony or vulgarity.

Veronese is reported to have been far more correct and careful in drawing than was Tintoret, while Veronese's prodigality of colour was a mellowed version of Tintoret's glare or deadness. One of Veronese's best pictures is the 'Marriage of Cana,' painted originally for the refectory of the convent of San Giorgio, Venice, and now in the Louvre. 'It is not less than thirty feet long and twenty feet high, and contains about one hundred and thirty figures, life size. The Marriage Feast of the Galilean citizen is represented with a pomp worthy of "Ormuz or of Ind." A sumptuous hall of the richest architecture; lofty columns, long lines of marble balustrades rising against the sky; a crowd of guests splendidly attired, some wearing orders of knighthood, are seated at tables covered with gorgeous vases of gold and silver, attended by slaves, jesters, pages, and musicians. In the midst of all this dazzling pomp, this display of festive enjoyment, these moving figures, these lavish colours in glowing approximation, we begin after a while to distinguish the principal personages, our Saviour, the Virgin Mary, the twelve Apostles, mingled with Venetian senators and ladies, clothed in the rich costume of the sixteenth century; monks, friars, poets, artists, all portraits of personages existing in his own time; while in a group of musicians he has introduced himself and Tintoretto playing the violoncello, while Titian plays the bass. The bride in this picture is said to be the portrait of Eleanor of Austria, the sister of Charles V, and second wife of Francis I.' [21]

Though Veronese is not greatly esteemed as a portrait painter, it so happens that the highly-prized picture of his in our National Gallery, called 'The Family of Darius before Alexander,' is understood to be family portraits of the Pisani family in the characters of Alexander, the Persian queen, &c., &c. Another of Veronese's pictures in the National Gallery is 'The Consecration of St Nicholas, Bishop of Myra.'

CHAPTER VII.

CARRACCI, 1555-1609—GUIDO RENI, 1575-1642—DOMENICHINO, 1581-1641—SALVATOR ROSA, 1615-1673.

In the falling away of the schools of Italy, and especially of the followers of Michael Angelo and Raphael, into mannerism and exaggeration, fitly expressed in delineation of heathen gods and goddesses, there arose a cluster of painters in the North of Italy who had considerable influence on art.

The **Carracci** included a group of painters, the founders of the later Bolognese School. Lodovico, the elder of the three, was born at Bologna, 1555. He was educated as a painter, and was so slow in his education, that he received from his fellow-scholars the nickname of 'Il Bue' (the ox). But his perseverance surmounted every obstacle. He visited the different Italian towns, and studied the works of art which they contained, arriving at the conclusion that he might acquire and combine the excellences of each. This combination, which could only be a splendid patch-work without unity, was the great aim of his life, and was the origin of the term *eclectic* applied to his school. Its whole tendency was to technical excellence, and in this tendency, however it might achieve its end, painting showed a marked decline. As an example of the motives and objects supplied by the school, I must borrow some lines from a sonnet of the period written by Agostino Carracci:

'Let him, who a good painter would be,
Acquire the drawing of Rome,
Venetian action, and Venetian shadow,
And the dignified colouring of Lombardy,
The terrible manner of Michael Angelo,
Titian's truth and nature,
The sovereign purity of Correggio's style,
And the true symmetry of Raphael;

And a little of Parmegiano'a grace,
But without so much study and toil,
Let him only apply himself to imitate the works
Which our Niccolino has left us here.'

Lodovico opened a school of painting at Bologna, in which he was for a time largely assisted by his cousins. He died 1619.

Agostino Carracci, cousin of Lodovico, was born at Bologna in 1559. His father was a tailor, and Agostino himself began life as a jeweller. He became a painter and an engraver in turn, devoting himself chiefly to engraving. Towards the beginning of the seventeenth century he was with his more famous brother, Annibale, at Rome, where he assisted in painting the Farnese Gallery, designing and executing the two frescoes of Galatea and Aurora with such success, according to his contemporaries, that it was popularly said that 'the engraver had surpassed the painter in the Farnese.' Jealousy arose between the brothers in consequence, and they separated, not before Annibale had perpetrated upon Agostino a small, but malicious, practical joke, which has been handed down to us. Agostino was fond of the society of people of rank, and Annibale, aware of his brother's weakness, took the opportunity, when Agostino was surrounded by some of his aristocratic friends, to present him with a caricature of the two brothers' father and mother, engaged in their tailoring work.

Agostino died at Parma when he was a little over forty, and was buried in the cathedral there, in 1602.

Annibale, Agostino's younger brother, was born in 1560. It was intended by his parents that he should follow their trade and be a tailor, but he was persuaded by his cousin Lodovico to become a painter. After visiting Parma, Venice, and Bologna, he worked with his cousin and teacher for ten years. Annibale was invited to Rome by the Cardinal Odoardo Farnese, to decorate the great hall of his palace in the Piazza Farnese, with scenes from the heathen mythology, for which work he received a monthly salary of ten scudi, about two guineas, with maintenance for himself and two servants, and a farther gift of five hundred scudi. It was a parsimonious payment, and the parsimony is said to have preyed on the mind and affected the health of Annibale, and a visit to Naples, where he, in common with not a few artists, suffered from the jealous persecutions of the Neapolitan painters, completed the breaking up of his constitution. He painted, with the assistance of Albani, the frescoes in the chapel of San Diego in San Giacomo degli Spagnole, and pressed upon his assistant more than half of his pay. Annibale's health had already given way, and after a long illness he died, when forty-nine years of age, at Rome, 1609, and was buried near Raphael in the Pantheon.

The merit of the Carracci lay in their power of execution, and in a certain 'bold naturalism, or rather animalism,' which they added to their able imitations, for their pictures are not so much their own, as 'After Titian,' 'After Correggio,' &c. In this intent regard to style, and this perfecting of means to an end, thought and its expression were in a manner neglected. Yet to the Carracci, and their school, is owing a certain studied air of solemnity and sadness in 'Ecce Homos,' and 'Pietás,' which, in proportion to its art, has a powerful effect on many beholders, who prefer conventionality to freedom; or rather, who fail to distinguish conventionality in its traces. Annibale was the most original while the least learned of the Carracci; yet, even of Annibale, it could be said that he lacked enthusiasm in his subjects. His best productions are his mythological subjects in the Farnese Palace. A celebrated picture of his, that of the 'Three Marys' (a dead Christ, the Madonna, and the two other Marys), is at Castle Howard, and has been exhibited at Manchester, and I think also at Leeds.

At Manchester it attracted the greatest attention and admiration. I believe this was not only because Annibale Carracci in the 'Three Marys' does attain to a most piteous mournfulness of sentiment, but because such work as that of the Carracci finds readiest acceptance from a general public, which delights in striking, superficial effects. The same reason, in conjunction with the decline of Italian art, may account for the great number of the Carracci school and followers.

Annibale Carracci was one of the first who practised landscape painting and genre pictures, such as 'The Greedy Eater,' as separate branches of art. Two of Annibale's landscapes are in the National Gallery.

Guido Reni, commonly called **'Guido,'** was born at Bologna, 1575. His father was a musician, and Guido was intended for the same calling, but finally became a painter and student in the school of the Carracci. He followed Annibale Carracci to Rome, and dwelt there for twenty years. He obtained great repute and favour, but taking offence at some supposed injustice, he left Rome, and settled at last in Bologna, where he established a large school. Though he made great sums of money, which might have enabled him to live in the splendour which he coveted, on account of his addiction to gambling and his grossly extravagant habits, he was constantly in debt, and driven to tax his genius to the utmost, and to sell its fruits for what they would bring, irrespective of what he owed to himself, his art, and to the giver of all good gifts. He died at Bologna, and was buried with much pomp in the church of San Dominico, 1642.

Of Guido we hear that he had three styles: the first, after the vigorous manner of Michael Angelo; the second, in the prevailing ornamental taste of the Rome of his day and the Carracci. This is considered Guido's best style, and is distinguished by its subtle management of light and shade. His third, which is called his 'silvery style,' from its greys, degenerated into insipidity, with little wonder, seeing that at this stage he sold his time at so much per hour to picture-dealers, who stood over him, watch in hand, to see that he fulfilled his bargain, and carried away the saints he manufactured wet from the easel. Such manufactory took him only three hours, sometimes less. His charges had risen from five guineas for a head, and twenty guineas for a whole figure, to twenty times that amount.

He painted few portraits, but many 'fancy' heads of saints. Nearly three hundred pictures by Guido are believed to be in existence. Guido's individual distinction was his refined sense of beauty, but it was over-ruled by 'cold calculation,' and developed into a mere abstract conception of 'empty grace' without heart or soul.

His finest work is the large painting of 'Phœbus and Aurora' in a pavilion of the Rospigliosi Palace at Rome. In our National Gallery there are nine specimens of Guido's works, including one of his best 'Ecce Homos,' which belonged to the collection of Samuel Rogers.

Domenico Zampieri, commonly called **Domenichino,** was another Bolognese painter, and another eminent scholar of the Carracci. He was born in 1581, and, after studying under a Flemish painter, passed into the school of the Carracci. While yet a very young man, Domenichino was invited to Rome, where he soon earned a high reputation, competing successfully with his former fellow-scholar, Guido. Domenichino's 'Flagellation of St Andrew,' and 'Communion of St Jerome,' in payment of which he only received about five guineas; his 'Martyrdom of St Sebastian,' and his 'Four Evangelists,' which are among his masterpieces, were all painted in Rome, and remain in Rome.

Domenichino is said to have excited the extreme hostility of rival painters, and to have suffered especially from the malice of the Neapolitans, when he was invited to work among them. After a cruel struggle Domenichino died in Naples, not without a horrible suspicion of having being poisoned, at the age of sixty, in 1641. One of his enemies—a Roman on this occasion—destroyed what was left of Domenichino's work in Naples.

The painter's fate was a miserable one, and by a coincidence between his fortune and his taste in subjects, he has identified his name with terrible representations of martyrdoms. Kugler writes that martyrdom as a subject for painting, which had been sparingly used by Raphael and his scholars, had come into fashion in Domenichino's time, for 'painters and poets sought for passionate emotion, and these subjects (martyrdoms) supplied them with plentiful food.' Sensationalism is the florid hectic of art's decay, whether in painting or in literature.

Domenichino is accredited with more taste than fancy. He made free use of the compositions of even contemporary artists, while he individualized these compositions. His good and bad qualities are those of his school, already quoted, and perhaps it is in keeping with these qualities that the excellence of Domenichino's works lies in subordinate parts and subordinate characters. There are examples of Domenichino in the National Gallery.

I shall close my long list of the great Italian painters of the past with one who was quite apart from and opposed to the Carracci school, and whose triumphs and failures were essentially his own. **Salvator Rosa,** born in 1615 near Naples, was the son of an architect. In opposition to his father Salvator Rosa became a painter. Having succeeded in selling his sketches to a celebrated buyer, the bold young Neapolitan started for Rome at the age of twenty years; and Rome, 'the Jerusalem of Painters,' became thenceforth Salvator Rosa's head-quarters, though the character of the man was such as to force him to change his quarters not once or twice only in his life, and thus he stayed some time, in turn, at Naples, Viterbo, Volterra, and Florence. At Volterra the aggressive nature of the painter broke forth in a series of written satires on a medley of subjects—music, poetry (both of which Salvator himself cultivated), painting, war, Babylon, and envy. These incongruous satires excited the violent indignation of the individuals against whom Salvator's wit was aimed, and their efforts at revenge, together with his own turbulent spirit, drove him from place to place.

Salvator Rosa was at Naples 1647, and took part in the riots, so famous in song and story, which made Masaniello, the young fisherman, for a time Captain-General and Master of Naples, when it was, according to law, a Spanish dependency governed by a viceroy. Salvator was in the Compagnia della Morte commanded by Falcone, a battle painter, during the troubles, a wild enough post to please the wild painter, even had he not been in addition a personal adherent of the ruling spirit Masaniello, whom Salvator Rosa painted more than once. After so eventful a life, the painter died peaceably enough in his fifty-ninth year, of dropsy, at Rome, and left a considerable fortune to his only son.

Salvator Rosa was the incarnation of the arrogant, fickle, fierce Neapolitan spirit, and he carried it out sufficiently in an undisciplined, stormy life, without the addition of the popular legend that he had at one time joined a troop of banditti, and indulged in their excesses. The legend seems to have arisen from Salvator Rosa's familiarity with mountain passes, and his love of peopling them appropriately with banditti in action. Salvator Rosa was a dashing battle painter, a mediocre historical painter, and an excellent portrait painter as well as landscape painter. But it is chiefly by the savage grandeur of his mountain or forest landscapes, with their fitting *dramatis personæ*, that he has won his renown. Mr Ruskin, while he allows Salvator's gift of imagination, denounces him for the reckless carelessness and untruthfulness to nature of his painting. Many of Salvator Rosa's pictures are in the Pitti Palace in Florence, and many are in England.

CHAPTER VIII.

RUBENS, 1577-1640—REMBRANDT, 1606 OR 1608-1669—TENIERS, FATHER AND SON, 1582-1694—WOUVERMAN, 1620-1668—CUYP, 1605; STILL LIVING, 1638—PAUL POTTER, 1625-1654—CORNELIUS DE HEEM, 1630.

A long interval elapsed between the Van Eycks and Quintin Matsys, and Rubens; but if Flemish art was slow of growth and was only developed after long pauses, it made up for its slowness and delays by the burst of triumph into which Flemish and Dutch art broke forth in Rubens and his school, in Rembrandt and Cuyp and Ruysdael.

Peter Paul Rubens was born at Siegen in Westphalia, on the day of St Peter and St Paul, 1577. But though Rubens was born out of Antwerp, he was a citizen of Antwerp by descent as well as by so many later associations. His father, John Rubens, a lawyer, an imprudent, thriftless man in character and habits, had been compelled to leave Antwerp in consequence of religious disturbances which broke out there about the time that the northern provinces, more at one and more decided in their union than the southern provinces, established their independence. Rubens spent his early boyhood at Cologne, but on the death of his father when he was ten years of age, his mother, a good and 'discreet' woman, to whom the painter owed much, and confessed his debt, returned with her family to Antwerp. His mother had destined him for his father's profession, but did not oppose her son's preference for art.

After studying under two different artists, and becoming a master in the guild of St Luke, Rubens went to Italy in 1600, when he was a young man of three-and-twenty years of age. He was eight years absent, entering the service of the ducal sovereign of Mantua, being sent by him on a diplomatic mission to Madrid to Philip III, of Spain, visiting on his own account Rome, where he found the Carracci and Guido [22] at the height of their fame, Venice and Genoa, 'leaving portraits where he went.'

With Genoa, its architecture, and its situation, Rubens was specially charmed, but he quitted it in haste, being summoned home to attend the death-bed of his mother, from whom he had parted eight years before; and arriving too late to see her in life. A man of strong feelings in sorrow as in joy, he withdrew into retirement, and resided for his season of mourning in a religious house.

Loving Italy with a painter's enthusiasm, so that to the latest day of his life he generally wrote in Italian, and loved to sign his name 'Pietro Paolo Rubens,' he had intended to return and settle in Mantua, but having been named court painter to the Governess of the Netherlands, Clara Eugenia, and her husband Albert, Rubens had sufficient patriotism and sufficient worldly foresight to induce him to relinquish his idea, and establish himself in his native Antwerp. He was already a man of eminence in his profession, and a man of mark out of it. Go where he would he made friends, and he so recommended himself to his royal patrons by his natural suavity, tact, and sagacity, that he was not only in the utmost favour with them as a right courtly painter, but was employed by them, once and again, on delicate, difficult, private embassies. But it was not only to his patrons that Rubens was endeared, he was emphatically what men call 'a good fellow,' alike to superiors, equals, and inferiors; a frank, honest, bountiful, and generous man. His love of courts and their splendour was the chivalrous homage which a man of his cast of mind paid to the dignity and picturesqueness of high estate.

He married a year after his mother's death, when he was in his thirty-third year. His first wife, Isabella Brant, was a connection of his own (and so was his second wife). He built and painted, in fresco, a fine house in Antwerp, and laid out a pleasant garden, which contained a rotunda, filled with his collection of pictures by the Italian masters, antique gems, &c. &c., already gathered abroad. He set himself to keep house in a liberal fashion, to dispense benefits, and to entertain friends — above all, to paint with might and main in company with his great school, the members of which, like those of Raphael's school where Raphael was concerned, were, for the most part, Rubens' devoted comrades. Counting his work not only as the great object, but the great zest of his life, never did painter receive such sweeping and accumulating commissions, and never, even by Tintoret, were commissions executed with such undaunted, unhesitating expedition.

Withal Rubens frequently left his studio and went abroad, either to act as an unofficial ambassador, or to paint at the special request of some foreign sovereign. Thus he was residing in Paris in 1620, planning for Marie de Medici the series of remarkable pictures which commemorated her marriage with Henry IV. (When I was a little girl, I went occasionally to a country house, the show place of the neighbourhood, where there were copies of this series of Rubens' pictures. I can remember yet looking at them with utter bewilderment, caused by the dubious taste that impelled Rubens to indulge in the oddest mixture of royal personages, high church dignitaries, patron saints, and gods and goddesses.) In 1628 Rubens was in Spain on a mission from his sovereign to her kinsman, Philip IV.; in the following year he was in England, on a service of a similar description to Charles I., from whom, even as Rubens had already received it from King Philip, the painter had the honour of knighthood.

In the mean time Rubens' first wife died, after a union of seventeen years, in 1626; and four years later, in 1630, the painter, when he was a man of fifty years, re-married another connection of his own, Helena Fourment, a girl only in her sixteenth year. Both of his wives were handsome, fair, full-formed Flemish beauties. Elizabeth (in Spanish, Isabella) Brant's beauty was of a finer order than that of her successor, expressing larger capacity of affection and intellect.

But on Helena Fourment Rubens doted, while to both women he seems to have been affectionately attached. He has painted them so often, that the face of no painter's wife is so familiar to the art world, and even to the greater world without, as are the faces of these two women, and above all, that of Helena Fourment. He had seven children, who frequently figure in their mothers' portraits. He has left notable portraits of his two sons by his first wife, of his eldest daughter, Clara Eugenia, when eight years of age, and of his daughter Elizabeth, a buxom baby, dressed in velvet and point lace, playing with toys.

After a life of unbroken success and the highest honours, the last distinction conferred on Rubens was, that he was chosen to arrange the gala, and to be the right-hand man who should conduct the Cardinal Infant, the successor of Clara Eugenia, on his first entrance into Antwerp. But the hand of premature disease and death, which not even he could resist, was already on the great painter; his constitution had been undermined by repeated attacks of gout, and he died at the age of sixty years, in 1640. He was the possessor of great wealth at the time of his death, and only a part of his collection, which was then sold, brought so large a sum in those days, as twenty thousand pounds. Rubens' second wife, Helena Fourment, to whom he had been married ten years, survived him, a widow at twenty-six years of age, and married again.

Rubens' portrait is even better known than those of his wives, for, as I have said of Raphael in his popularity, Rubens in his life is the beau-ideal of a painter to the many. The portrait is worthy of the man, with something gallant in the manliness, and with thought tempering what might have been too much of bravado and too much of débonnaireté in the traits. His features are handsome in their Flemish fulness, and match well with hazel eyes, chestnut hair, and a ruddy complexion; his long moustache is turned up, and he wears the pointed beard which we see so often in the portraits by Rubens' scholar, Van Dyck. The great flapping hat, worn alike by men and women, slightly cocked to one side, is the perfection of picturesque head gear. Equally picturesque, and not in the slightest degree effeminate on a man like Rubens, is the falling collar of pointed mechlin, just seen above the cloak draped in large folds.

In his own day Rubens was without a rival as a painter. In a much later day Sir Joshua Reynolds pronounced Rubens 'perhaps the greatest master in the mechanical part of the art, *the best workman with his tools* that ever exercised a pencil.' His consummate excellence lay in his execution and colouring. It is brought as a reproach against his painting, that his noblest characters, even his sacred characters, were but big, brawny, red and white Flemings. His imagination only reached a certain height, and yet, if it were a very earthly Flemish imagination, it could be grandly, as it was always vigorously, earthly and Flemish. At the same time he could be deficient where proportion, and even where all the laws of art, are concerned.

It is right that I should, with regret and shame, say this of Rubens, whose geniality bordered on joviality, and whose age was a grosser age than our own, that he debased his genius by some foul and revolting pictures.

Of the general distinction between Rubens and some of his predecessors I should like to quote Mr Ruskin's passage in his defence:

'A man long trained to love the monk's vision of Fra Angelico, turns in proud and ineffable disgust from the first work of Rubens, which he encounters on his return across the Alps. But is he right in his indignation? He has forgotten that, while Angelico prayed and wept in his *olive shade,* there was different work doing in the dank fields of Flanders: — wild seas to be banked out; endless canals to be dug, and boundless marshes to be drained; hard ploughing and harrowing of the frosty clay; careful breeding of the stout horses and cattle; close setting of brick-walls against cold winds and snow; much hardening of hands, and gross stoutening of bodies in all this; gross jovialities of harvest homes, and Christmas feasts, which were to be the reward of it; rough affections, and sluggish

imaginations; fleshy, substantial, iron-shod humanities, but humanities still, — humanities which God had his eye upon, and which won perhaps, here and there, as much favour in His sight as the wasted aspects of the whispering monks of Florence (Heaven forbid that it should not be so, since the most of us cannot be monks, but must be ploughmen and reapers still). And are we to suppose there is no nobility in Rubens' masculine and universal sympathy with all this, and with his large human rendering of it, gentleman though he was by birth, and feeling, and education, and place, and, when he chose, lordly in conception also? He had his faults—perhaps great and lamentable faults,—though more those of his time and his country than his own; he has neither cloister-breeding nor boudoir-breeding, and is very unfit to paint either in missals or annuals; but he has an open sky and wide-world breeding in him that we may not be offended with, fit alike for king's court, knight's camp, or peasants cottage.'

Rubens' works are very many, nearly four thousand pictures and sketches being attributed to him and his scholars. Many are still at Antwerp, many at Madrid, but most are at Munich, where, in one great saloon and cabinet, there are ninety-five pictures by Rubens. In England, at Blenheim, there are fifteen pictures by Rubens, as the great Duchess of Marlborough would give any price for his works. I can only indicate a very few examples in the different branches of art which he made his own.

First, of his 'Descent from the Cross:' it is a single large group, distinguished by luminous colouring and correct drawing, and with regard to which the mass of white sheet against which the body of Christ is in relief in the picture, has been regarded as a bold artistic venture. An enthusiastic admirer has called it 'a most wonderful monument of the daring genius of the painter. The grandest picture in the world for composition, drawing, and colouring.' Its defects are held to be 'the bustle of the incidents and the dreadfully true delineation of merely physical agony—too terrible, real, picturesque, but not sublime—- an earthly tragedy, not a divine mystery.'

> 'Remit the anguish of that lighted stare;
> Close those wan lips! let that thorn-wounded brow
> Stream not with blood.'

There is a tradition that an accident happened to the picture while Rubens was painting it, and that Van Dyck remedied the accident by re-painting the cheek and chin of the Virgin and the arm of the Magdalene.

With regard to another picture of Rubens at Antwerp, 'The Assumption of the Virgin,' it is said that he painted it in sixteen days, for sixteen hundred florins, his usual terms being a hundred florins a-day.

'The Virgin and Serpent' (from the 12th chapter of Revelation) in the Munich gallery is very splendid. The Virgin with the new-born Saviour in her arms is mounting on the wings of an eagle, surrounded by a flood of light. The serpent, encircling the moon on which she stands, is writhing beneath her feet. God the Father is extending his protecting sceptre over her from above. The archangel, clothed in armour, is in fearful combat with the seven-headed dragon, which is endeavouring to devour the child. Although struck by lightning, the dragon is striving to twist his tail round the legs of the angel, and seizes the cloak of the Virgin with one of his hands. Other infernal monsters are writhing with impotent rage, and falling with the dragon into the abyss.'

'Nothing was more characteristic of Rubens than his choice of subjects from the mythology of the Greeks and the works of the ancient poets; and in nothing did he display more freedom, originality, and poetry.' Among his most famous mythological pictures is the 'Battle of the Amazons,' now at Munich. 'The women are driven back by the Greeks over the river Thermodon; two horses are in savage combat on the bridge; one Amazon is torn from her horse; a second is dragged along by a sable steed, and falling headlong into the river, where others are swimming and struggling. No other battle-piece, save that of the Amazons, can compare with Raphael's "Battle of Constantine."'

Another great picture is The 'Carrying off of Proserpine.' 'Pluto in his car is driven by fiery brown steeds, and is bearing away the goddess, resisting and struggling. The picture absolutely glows with genial fire. The forms in it are more slender than is general with Rubens. Among the companions of Proserpine the figure of Diana is conspicuous for grace and beauty. The victorious god of love hovers before the chariot, and the blue ocean, warmly tinted with the sunbeams, forms a splendid back-ground.' [23]

Rubens was famous for the loveliness and grace of his paintings of children. Perhaps the most beautiful is that of 'The Infant Jesus and John playing with a Lamb.'

Rubens was a great animal painter. One of his celebrated animal pictures is 'Daniel in the Lions' Den,' now at Hamilton Palace, in which each lion is a king of beasts checked in his fiercest wrath. It is said to have been painted by Rubens in a fit of pique at a false report which had been circulated that he could not paint animals, and that those in his pictures were supplied by the animal-painter, his friend and scholar, Schneyders.

Rubens' landscapes are not the least renowned of his pictures. He gave to his own rich but prosaic Flanders, all the breadth and breeziness and matchless aërial effects of a master of painting, and a true lover of nature under every aspect, who can indeed distinguish, under the most ordinary aspect, those hidden treasures which all but a lover and a man of genius would pass by. His 'Prairie of Laacken,' 'with the sun of Flanders piercing the dense yellow clouds with the force of fire,' is of great repute.

Among his famous portraits I shall mention that called 'The Four Philosophers' (Justus Lepsius, Hugo Grotius, Rubens, and his brother), with peaked beards and moustaches, in turned-over collars, ruffs and fur-trimmed robes, having books and pens, a dog, and a classic bust as accessories. The open pillared door is wreathed with a spray from without, and there is a landscape in the background. This portrait is full of power, freedom, and splendid painting.

Another portrait contains that sweetest of Rubens' not often sweet faces, called 'the Lady in the Straw Hat.' Rubens himself did not name the picture otherwise in his catalogue. Tradition says the original was Mdlle Lundens, the beauty of the seventeen provinces, and that she died young and unmarried. Connoisseurs value the picture because of the triumph of skill by which Rubens has painted brilliantly a face so much in the shade; to those who are not connoisseurs I imagine the picture must speak for itself, in its graceful, tender beauty. Forming part of the collection of the late Sir Robert Peel (I think he gave three thousand pounds for 'the Lady in the Straw

Hat'), which has been bought for the country, this beautiful portrait is now in the National Gallery.

And now I must speak of the picture of the Arundel Family. But first, a word about Thomas, Earl of Arundel. It is impossible to write an English work on art and omit a brief account of one of England's greatest art benefactors. Thomas, Earl of Arundel, representing in his day the great house of Howard, had a love of art which approached to a mania; and without being so outrageously vain as Sir Kenelm Digby, there is no doubt that the Earl counted on his art collection as a source of personal distinction. James I., himself an art collector, so far humoured the Earl in his taste as to present him with Lord Somerset's forfeited collection, valued at a thousand pounds. But Charles I, and the Earl became rival collectors, and little love was lost between them. The Earl of Arundel impairing even his great revenues in the pursuit, employed agents and ambassadors—notably Petty and Evelyn—all over Europe, to obtain for him drawings, pictures, ancient marbles, gems, &c. &c. When the civil wars broke out, Lord Arundel conveyed his priceless collection for safety to Antwerp and Padua. Eventually it was divided among his sons and scattered far and wide. The only portion of it which fell to the nation, in the course of another generation, was the Greek Marbles, known as the Arundel Marbles, which were finally presented to the University of Oxford. But in Rubens' day all this grand collection was intact, and displayed in galleries at Arundel House, which the mob thought fit to nickname 'Tart Hall;' and through these galleries Rubens was conducted by the Earl.

Lord Arundel desired to have an Arundel family portrait painted for him by Rubens. The Earl was rather given to having Arundel family portraits, for there are no less than three in which he figures. One by Van Somer, in which the hero is pointing somewhat comically with his truncheon to the statues of his collection in the background, and the last one projected by Van Dyck, but executed by an inferior artist, in which various family pieces of armour, swords, and shields, worn at Flodden, or belonging to the poet Earl of Surrey, are introduced in the hands of the sons of the family.

But it is with Rubens' 'Arundel Family,' which, we must remember, ranks second in English family pictures, that we have to do.

Thomas, Earl of Arundel, and the Lady Alathea. [24] are under a portico with twisted columns, like those in Raphael's cartoons; a rich curtain, and a landscape with a large mansion are seen beyond. The Countess is seated in a chair of state, with one hand on the head of a white greyhound; she wears a black satin gown, laced ruff, gold bracelets, and pearl necklace. Her hair is light, and decked with pearls and plumes. The Earl stands behind with a hand on her chair. His head is uncovered, the short hair inclining to grey; the whiskers and beard pointed. His vest is olive-coloured, and he has a brown mantle lined with crimson over the shoulders beneath his ruff. There is a little boy — Earl Thomas's grandson, Philip Howard, afterwards Cardinal Howard, in crimson velvet, trimmed with gold lace, and a dwarf on the other side of the dog, with one hand on its back.

Among other master-pieces of Rubens, including the 'Straw Hat,' which are in the National Gallery, there are the 'Rape of the Sabines,' and the landscape 'Autumn,' which has a view of his country château, de Stein, near Mechlin. In Dulwich Gallery there is an interesting portrait by Rubens of an elderly lady in a great Spanish ruff, which is believed to be the portrait of his mother.

Rembrandt Van Rhyn is said to have been born near Leyden about 1606 or 1608, for there is a doubt as to the exact date. His father was a miller or maltster, and there is a theory that Rembrandt acquired some of his effects of light and shade from the impressions made upon him during his life in the mill. He was a pupil at the Latin school of Leyden, and a scholar in studios both at Leyden and Amsterdam.

In 1630, when Rembrandt was a mere lad, he seems to have settled in Amsterdam, and married there in 1634, when he was six or eight and twenty years of age, a young Dutchwoman possessed of a considerable fortune, which, in case of her death and of Rembrandt's re-marriage, was to pass to her children, a provision that in the end wrought Rembrandt's ruin. The troubles of his country in the painter's time rendered his prices comparatively small and precarious, and Rembrandt, like Rubens, without Rubens' wealth, was eager in making an art collection and surrounding himself with those very forms of beauty in the great Italian masters' works, in the appreciation of which the Dutch master—judged by his own works—might have been reckoned deficient.

Rembrandt's wife died after eight years of marriage, and left him with one surviving son, Titus, and Rembrandt, having re-married, was called upon to give up the lad's inheritance. This call, together with the expenditure of the sums which Rembrandt had lavished on his collection, was too heavy upon funds never very ample, and the painter, after struggling with his difficulties, became a bankrupt in 1656. His son took possession of Rembrandt's house, and from the sale of the painter's art collection and other resources eventually recovered his mother's fortune, but Rembrandt himself never rose above the misery, degradation, and poverty of this period. He lived thirteen years longer, but it was in obscurity—out of which the only records which reach us, are stories of miserly habits acquired too late to serve their purpose, a desperate resort to low company dating from his first wife's death, and his gradual downfall.

Rubens and Rembrandt have been sometimes contrasted as the painters of light and of darkness; the contrast extended to their lives.

It will read like a humorous anti-climax after so sad a history, when I add that no other painter painted his own likeness so often as Rembrandt painted his. In the engraving before me the face is heavy and stolid-seeming enough to be that of a typical Dutchman. The eye-brows are slightly knit over the broad nose; the full lips are scantily shaded by a moustache; there is no hair on the well-fleshed cheeks and double chin. Rembrandt wears a flat cap and ear-rings. He has two rows of a chain across his doublet, and one hand thrust beneath the cloak hanging across his breast.

Rembrandt's great merits were his strong truthfulness, and his almost equally powerful sense of a peculiar kind of picturesqueness. It seems as if the German weirdness perceptible in Albrecht Dürer had in Rembrandt taken a homelier, but a more comprehensible and effective Dutch form. Kugler argues, that the long winter, with its short dark days, of Northern Europe produces in its inhabitants instinctive delight in hearth-warmth and light, and that the pleasure in looking at Rembrandt's pictures is traceable to this influence. It is in scenes by fire-light, camp-light, torch-light, that he triumphs, and his somewhat grim but very real romance owes its origin to the endless suggestions of the deep black shadows which belong to these artificial lights. There is this objection to be urged to the theory, that Rembrandt was also a good painter of his own flat Dutch landscape, painting it, however, rather under the sombre dimness of clouds and tempests than in the brightness of sunshine. But whatever its source, there is a charm so widely felt in that wonderfully perfect surrounding of uncertainty, suspicion, and alarm, with which Rembrandt has encompassed so many of his otherwise prosaic, coarse, and sometimes vulgar Dutch men and women, that we have coined a new word to express the charm, and speak of groups and incidents being *Rembrandtesque,* as we speak of their being picturesque.

Rembrandt did not always leave the vague thrill of doubt, terror, or even horror, which he sought to produce, to imagination working in the mysterious depths of his shadows. A very famous picture of his is 'Dr Deeman (an anatomist) demonstrating from a dead subject.' In another picture a man stealing from the gloom is in the act of stabbing in the back the unconscious man in the foreground. [25] Rembrandt's originality is as undoubted as his ability, and he was as great in etching as in painting. His defect as a painter was the frequent absence of any evidence in his work of a sense of refinement, grace, or even beauty; this can be said of him who spent means not his own on gathering together images of beauty and grace produced by the pencils and brushes of others. Many of Rembrandt's pictures are in the galleries of Amsterdam and the Hague, and we have many in London. The National Gallery has several examples, including two of Rembrandt's portraits.

Passing over Van Dyck, whom I reserve, as I have reserved Holbein, to class among the foreign painters resident in or closely connected with England, I come to the **Teniers** — father and son. David the elder was born at Antwerp in 1582, and David the younger also at Antwerp, in 1610. David the younger is decidedly the more eminent painter, though the works of the father are often mistaken for those of the son. The two Teniers' class of subjects was the same, being ordinarily 'fairs, markets, peasants' merry-makings, beerhouses, guard rooms.'

David the younger had great popularity, was court painter to the Archduke of Austria, and earned such an independence, that he bought for himself a château at the village of Perck, not very far from the Château de Stein of Rubens, with whom David Teniers was on terms of friendly intimacy. There Teniers, like his great associate, lived in the utmost state and bounty, entertaining the noblest of the land. David Teniers married twice, his first wife being the daughter of one of a family of Flemish painters, who were known, according to their respective proclivities in art, by the names of Peasant Breughel, Velvet Breughel, and Hell Breughel. Teniers had many children.

The elder Teniers died at Antwerp in 1649; the younger died at Brussels, and was buried at Perck, in 1694.

The distinction of the Teniers was the extreme fidelity and cleverness with which they copied (but did not explain) the life they knew — the homeliest, humblest aspect of life. They brought out with marvellous accuracy all its traits, except, indeed, the underlying strain of poetry, which, while it redeems plainness, sordidness, and even coarseness, is as true to life as is its veriest prose. With those who ask a literal copy of life, whether high or low, and ask no more, the Teniers and their school must always be in the highest favour; and to those who are wearied and sceptical of blunders and failures in seeking that underlying strain of life, the mere rugged genuineness of the Teniers' work recommends itself, and is not without its own pathos; while to very many superficial observers the simple homeliness of the life which the Teniers chose to represent, prevents the observers from missing what should be present in every life. Men and women are only conscious of the defect when the painters wander, now and then, into higher spheres and into sacred subjects, and there is the unavoidable recoil from gross blindness. I have taken the Teniers as the representatives of a numerous school of Flemish and Dutch artists, whose works abound in this country. David Teniers the younger appears at his best, several times, in Dulwich Gallery and the National Gallery.

Philip Wouverman was born at Haarlem in 1620. He was the son of a painter, able, but unrecognized in his own day. Philip Wouverman found few patrons, disposed of his pictures by hard bargains to dealers, was tempted by his want of success to abjure his art, and even went so far, according to tradition, as to burn his studies and sketches, in order to prevent his son pursuing the career which had been to him a career of bitter disappointment. He died at Haarlem, 1668, when he was no more than forty-eight years of age. Yet some nine hundred paintings bear (many of them falsely) Wouverman's name.

With all the truth and excellent execution of his contemporaries and countrymen', Philip Wouverman, who had, as he thought, missed his mark, had something which those successful men lacked—he had not only a feeling for grace, but a touch of sentiment. His scenes are commonly 'road-side inns, hunts, fights;' but along with an inclination to adopt a higher class of actors—knights and ladies, instead of peasants—there is a more refined treatment and a dash of tenderness and melancholy—the last possibly born of his own disastrous fortunes. In his love of horses and dogs, as adjuncts to his groups, he had as great a fondness for a special white horse, as Paul Potter had for black and white cattle.

Albert Cuyp was born at Dort in 1605. He was a brewer by trade, and only painted as an amateur. In spite of this, he was a great landscape painter, and has given delight to thousands by his power of expressing his own love of nature. Little is known of Cuyp's life, and the date of his death is uncertain, farther than it was later than 1638.

In affected enthusiasm, Cuyp has been called the Dutch Claude, but in reality, Cuyp surpassed, Claude in some respects. The distinction, which Mr Ruskin draws between them, is that, while Claude, in the sense of beauty, is the superior to Cuyp, in the sense of truth Claude is the inferior. Besides Cuyp's landscapes, he painted portraits, and what is called 'still life' (dead game, fruit or flower pieces, &c.), but Cuyp's triumph was found in his skies, with their 'clearness and coolness,' and in 'expressions of yellow sunlight.' Mr Ruskin admits, while he is proceeding to censure Cuyp, parts might be chosen out of the good pictures of Cuyp which have never been equalled in art.' On another occasion, Mr Ruskin has this passage full of dry humour in reference to Cuyp:

'Again, look at the large Cuyp in Dulwich Gallery, which Mr Hazlitt considers "finest in the world," and of which he very complimentarily says, "the tender green of the valleys, the gleaming lake, the purple light of the hills" have an effect like *down* on an unripe nectarine!" I ought to have apologized before now for not having studied sufficiently in Covent Garden to be provided with terms of correct and classical criticism. One of my friends begged me to observe, the other day, that Claude was "pulpy;" another added the yet more gratifying information that he was "juicy;" and it is now happily discovered that Cuyp is "downy." Now I dare say that the sky of this first-rate Cuyp is very like an unripe nectarine: all that I have to say about it is, that it is exceedingly unlike a sky. We may see for ourselves Cuyp's lovely landscapes both in the National Gallery and at Dulwich.

Paul Potter was born at Enkhuysen, in North Holland, in 1625, and was the son of a painter. Paul Potter settled, while still very young, at the Hague as an animal painter, and died in his thirtieth year, in 1654. His career, which was thus brief, had promised to be very successful, and he had established his fame, while no more than twenty-two years of age, by painting for Prince Maurice of Nassau that which continues his most renowned, though probably not his best picture, his 'Young Bull,' for some time in the Louvre, now restored to the painter's native country, and placed in the Museum at the Hague. This picture is considered nearly faultless as a vigorous, if somewhat coarse, representation of animal life in the main figure; but Paul Potter's later pictures, especially his smaller pictures of pastures with cattle feeding, having fine colouring and fine treatment of light, are now regarded as equally good in their essential excellences, and of wider scope. Paul Potter etched as well as painted. There is no example of Paul Potter in the National Gallery.

Jan David de Heem [26] and his son Cornelius, the father born in 1603, the son in 1630, and Maria Von Oesterwyck, the elder man's pupil, were eminent Flemish and Dutch flower and fruit painters. The gorgeous bloom and mellow ripeness in some of the flower and fruit pieces of Flemish and Dutch painters, like those I have mentioned, are beyond description. I would have you look at them for yourselves, where they are well represented, in the Dulwich Gallery; I would have you notice also how, as travellers declare of the splendour of tropical flowers, that they are deficient in the tender sweetness and grace of our more sober-tinted and less lavishly-blossoming English flowers; so these Flemish and Dutch full blown flower pieces have not a trace of the sentiment which modern flower painters cannot help seeking, with good result or bad result, to introduce into every tuft of primroses or of violets, if not into every cluster of grapes and bunch of cherries.

From a fact which I have already mentioned, that so many Flemish and Dutch pictures, which we may often come across, are in England, I am sorry that my space will not suffer me to give a few special words to other famous painters of these schools or school, for they merge into one, to Snyders, Jan Steen, Gerard Dow, Ruysdael, Hobbema, Van de Velde, &c., &c.

CHAPTER IX.

SPANISH ART—VELASQUEZ, 1599-1660—MURILLO. 1618-1682.

Spanish art, from its dawn to the time of Velasquez, had been of a 'severely devotional character,' austere and formal; and although one man did not work a revolution by his independent example, he did something to humanize and widen art. In the rich city of Seville in 1599, **Diego Rodriguez, de Silva y Velasquez,**—and not, as he is incorrectly called, **Diego Velasquez de Silva**, was born, and, according to an Andalusian fashion, took his mother's name of Velasquez, while his father was of the Portuguese house de Silva. Velasquez was gently born, though his father was in no higher position than that of a lawyer in Seville.

The painter was well educated, though, according to his English biographer (Sir W. Stirling Maxwell), 'he was still more diligent in drawing on his grammars and copybooks than in turning them to their legitimate use.' The lad's evident bent induced his father to make him a painter. He studied in two different Spanish studios, and married the daughter of his second master, whom the talents, assiduity, and good qualities of Velasquez had already strongly attached to the young painter.

From the first, Velasquez struck out what was then a new line in Spanish art. He gave himself up to the materialistic studies, to which the Flemish and Dutch painters were prone, painting diligently 'still life' in every form, taking his living subjects from the streets and way-sides, and keeping a peasant lad as an apprentice, 'who served him for a study in different actions and postures (sometimes crying, sometimes laughing), till Velasquez had grappled with every variety of expression.' The result of those studies was Velasquez's famous picture of the 'Aguador,' or water-carrier of Seville, which was carried off by Joseph Buonaparte in his flight from Spain, taken in his carriage at Vittoria, and finally presented by Ferdinand VII, of Spain, as a grateful offering to the Duke of Wellington, in whose gallery at Apsley House the picture remains. 'It is a composition of three figures,' Sir W. Stirling Maxwell writes; 'a sunburnt way-worn seller of water, dressed in a tattered brown jerkin, with his huge earthen jars, and two lads, one of whom receives a sparkling glass of the pure element, whilst his companion quenches his thirst from a pipkin. The execution of the heads and all the details is perfect; and the ragged trader dispensing a few maravidi's worth of his simple stock, maintains, during the transaction, a grave dignity of deportment, highly Spanish and characteristic, and worthy of an emperor pledging a great vassal in Tokay.'

Just such a group may still be seen, or was to be seen till very lately, in the quaint streets of Seville. I have read an anecdote of Velasquez and this picture, which is quite probable, though I cannot vouch for its accuracy. It is said that, while painting the water-carrier day after day, when he had been engaged with his work for several hours, Velasquez found himself vexed by perceiving, as it were, the effect of a shadow cast by some of the drapery. Small flaw as it might have been, it appeared to him to interfere with and spoil the picture. Again and again, in endeavouring to do away with this 'shadow,' Velasquez undid portions of his work, and had to repeat them next day, but always, towards the end of his task, the invidious shadow stole upon his vision. At last a friend, who was present and full of admiration for the picture, heard Velasquez exclaim, 'That shadow again!' and saw him seize a brush and prepare to dash it across the canvas. The friend remonstrated, besought, and by main force held back the painter, and at last induced him to leave the picture untouched till next day, when Velasquez discovered, to his great relief, that the shadow had been in his own wearied young eyes, and not in his admirable representation of the 'Water-carrier.'

Velasquez was in Madrid in 1623, when he was in his twenty-fifth year, and having been introduced by the Prime Minister, Olivares, to the King of Spain, Philip IV., a king who was only known to smile once or twice in his life-time, whose government was careless and blundering, but who had the reputation of being a man of some intelligence and very considerable taste, — Velasquez was received into the king's service with a monthly salary of twenty ducats, and employed to paint the royal portrait.

From the time that he became court painter, Velasquez was largely occupied in painting portraits of members of the royal family, with special repetitions of the likeness of his most Catholic Majesty. With Velasquez's first portrait of Philip in armour, mounted on an Andalusian charger, the king was so pleased, that he permitted the picture to be publicly exhibited, amidst the plaudits of the spectators, in front of the church of San Felipe el Real in Madrid. Nor was the exhibition a barren honour to the painter, for the king not only 'talked of collecting and cancelling his existing portraits,' and 'resolved that in future Velasquez should have the monopoly of the royal countenance,' he paid three hundred ducats for the picture.

About this time our own Charles I., then Prince of Wales, went in his incognito of Charles Smith to Madrid on his romantic adventure of seeking to woo and win, personally, the Infanta of Spain, and Velasquez is said to have gained Charles's notice, and to have at least begun a portrait of him. If it were ever completed it has been lost, a misfortune which has caused spurious pictures, purporting to be the real work, to be offered to the public. Sir W. Stirling Maxwell holds, with great show of truth, that this visit of Charles to Madrid, when its altars were 'glowing' with the pictures of Titian, confirmed the unhappy king's taste for art.

In 1628 Rubens came to Madrid as an envoy from the governess of the Netherlands, and the two painters, who had many points in common, and who had already corresponded, became fast friends. By the advice of Rubens, Velasquez was induced to put into execution his cherished desire of visiting Italy, the king granting his favourite painter leave of absence, the continuance of his salary, and a special sum for his expenses.

Velasquez went to Venice first, and afterwards to Rome, where he was offered, and declined, a suite of apartments in the Vatican, asking only free access to the papal galleries. There he copied many portions of Michael Angelo's 'Last Judgment'—not a hundred years old, and 'yet undimmed by the morning and evening incense of centuries,' and portions of the frescoes of Raphael. At Rome Velasquez found there before him, Domenichino, Guido Reni, alternating 'between the excitements of the gaming table and the sweet creations of his smooth flowing pencil;' 'Nicolas Poussin, an adventurer fresh from his Norman village; and Claude Gelée, a pastrycook's runaway apprentice from Lorraine.' [27] Velasquez remained a year in Rome. Besides his studies he painted three original pictures, one of them, 'Joseph's Coat,' well known among the painter's comparatively rare religious works, and now in the Escurial. In this picture his biographer acknowledges, that 'choosing rather to display his unrivalled skill in delineating vulgar forms than to risk his reputation in the pursuit of a more refined and idealized style,' Velasquez's 'Hebrew patriarchs are swineherds of Estramadura or shepherds of the Sierra Morena.'

From Rome Velasquez proceeded to Naples, where he was enabled by his prudence and forbearance to face without injury the disgraceful 'reign of terror' which the Neapolitan artists had established in the south of Italy. The Neapolitan artists more than any other Italian artists are believed to have influenced Velasquez's style.

In 1639 Velasquez painted his principal religious work, 'The Crucifixion,' for the nunnery of San Placido in Madrid, a painting in which his power has triumphed successfully over his halting imagination.

With regard to the many court groups which Velasquez was constantly taking, I may quote Sir W. Stirling Maxwell's amusing paragraph about a curious variety of human beings in the Court Gallery. 'The Alcazar of Madrid abounded with dwarfs in the days of Philip IV., who was very fond of having them about him, and collected curious specimens of the race, like other rarities. The Queen of

Spain's gallery is, in consequence, rich in portraits of these little monsters, executed by Velasquez. They are, for the most part, very ugly, displaying, sometimes in an extreme degree, the deformities peculiar to their stunted growth. Maria Barbola, immortalized by a place in one of Velasquez's most celebrated pictures, was a little dame about three feet and a half in height, with the head and shoulders of a large woman, and a countenance much underjawed, and almost ferocious in expression. Her companion, Nicolasito Pertusano, although better proportioned than the lady, and of a more amicable aspect, was very inferior in elegance as a royal plaything to his contemporary, the valiant Sir Geoffrey Hudson; or his successor in the next reign, the pretty Luisillo of Queen Louisa of Orleans. Velasquez painted many portraits of these little creatures, generally seated on the ground; and there is a large picture in the Louvre representing two of them leading by a cord a great spotted hound, to which they bear the same proportion that men of the usual size bear to a horse.'

In 1648 Velasquez again visited Italy, sent by the king this time to collect works of art for the royal galleries and the academy about to be founded. Velasquez went by Genoa, Milan, Venice (buying there chiefly the works of Tintoret), and Parma, to Rome and Naples, returning to Rome. At Rome Velasquez painted his splendidly characteristic portrait of the Pope Innocent X., 'a man of coarse features and surly expression, and perhaps the ugliest of all the successors of St Peter.'

Back at Madrid, Philip continued to load Velasquez and his family with favours, appointing the painter Quarter-Master-General of the king's household with a salary of three thousand ducats a year, and the right of carrying at his girdle a key which opened every lock in the palace.

Philip is said to have raised Velasquez to knighthood in a manner as gracious as the manner of Charles V, when he lifted up Titian's pencil. In painting one of his most renowned pictures, to which I shall refer again, 'The Maids of Honour,' Velasquez included himself at work on a large picture of the royal family. The painter represented himself with the key of his office at his girdle, and on his breast the red cross of the Order of Santiago. Philip, who came every day to see the progress of this picture, remarked in reference to the figure of the artist, that 'one thing was yet wanting, and taking up the brush painted the knightly insignia with his own royal fingers, thus conferring the accolade with a weapon not recognized in chivalry.'

As it is believed, Velasquez's court office, with all its prestige and influence, helped in causing his death. King Philip went in June, 1660, to the Isle of Pheasants in the river Bidassa, where, on ground which was neither Spanish nor French, the Spanish and French courts were to meet and celebrate with the greatest magnificence the marriage of the Grand Monarque and the Infanta Maria Teresa. One of Velasquez's official duties was to prepare lodgings for the king on his journeys, and in this instance the lodging included not only the decoration of the castle of Fuenterrabia, but the erection of a sumptuous pavilion in which the interviews of the assembled kings and queens and their revelries were to be held. Velasquez did his part of the preparations, and doubtless shared in the royal festivities, but returned to Madrid so worn out by his undertaking, and by constant attendance on his master, that he was seized with tertian fever, of which he died a few days later, while but in his sixty-first year, to the great grief of his countrymen, and above all of his king. Velasquez's wife, Doña Juana, died eight days after her husband, and was buried in his grave. The couple left one surviving child, a daughter, married to a painter.

In one picture, now at Vienna, Velasquez gives a glimpse of his family life at a time when it would seem that he had four sons and two daughters, so that the fortunate painter's home had not been free from one shadow—that of death, which must have robbed him of five of his children. In this pleasant picture, 'his wife dressed in a brown tunic over a red petticoat, sits in the foreground of a large room, with a pretty little girl leaning on her knees, and the rest of her children grouped around her; behind are the men in deep shadow, one of them, perhaps, being Mazo, the lover or the husband of the eldest daughter, and a nurse with a child; and in an alcove Velasquez himself appears, standing before his easel, at work on a portrait of Philip IV. This is one of the most important works of the master out of the Peninsula; the faces of the family sparkle on the sober background like gems. As a piece of easy actual life, the composition has never been surpassed, and perhaps it excels even "The Meninas," inasmuch as the hoops and dwarfs of the palace have not intruded upon the domestic privacy of the painter's home, in the northern gallery.' [28]

Velasquez seems to have been a man of honour and amiability. He filled a difficult office at the most jealous court in Europe with credit. He was true to his friends, and helpful to his brother artists. His biographer writes of Velasquez as handsome in person, and describes his costume when he appeared for the last time with his king in the galas at Pheasants' Isle: — 'over a dress richly laced with silver he wore the usual Castilian ruff, and a short cloak embroidered with the red cross of Santiago; the badge of the order, sparkling with brilliants, was suspended from his neck by a gold chain; and the scabbard and hilt of his sword were of silver, exquisitely chased, and of Italian workmanship.' In the likeness of Velasquez, which is the frontispiece of Sir W. Stirling Maxwell's 'Life,' the painter appears as a man of swarthy complexion, with a long compressed upper lip, unconcealed by his long, elaborately trimmed moustache; his hair, or wig, is arranged in two large frizzed bunches on each side of a face which is inclined to be lantern-jawed. He wears a dark doublet with a 'standing white collar.'

Velasquez's excellence as a painter was to be found, like that of Rembrandt, in his truth to nature; but the field of truth presented to the stately Spaniard, while it had its own ample share of humour, was a widely different field from that which offered itself to the Dutch burgher. Together with absolute truth, Velasquez had the ease and facility in expressing truth which are only acquired by a great master. Like Rubens, Velasquez made essays in many branches of painting. In sacred art, if we except his 'Crucifixion,' he did not attain a high place. With regard to his landscapes, Sir David Wilkie bore witness: — 'Titian seems his model, but he has also the breadth and picturesque effect for which Claude and Salvator Rosa are remarkable;' and Sir David added of those landscapes, 'they have the very same sun we see, and the air we breathe, the very soul and spirit of nature.'

Velasquez's *genre* pictures, to which I shall refer by and by, are excellent, but the fate was kind which confined him largely to portrait painting. It was brought as a reproach against Velasquez in his lifetime, that he could paint a head and nothing else, to which he replied with mingled spirit, sense, and good nature, that his detractors flattered him, 'for he knew nobody of whom it could be said that he painted a head thoroughly well.'

Sir W. Stirling Maxwell asserts of Velasquez's portrait painting, that no artist 'ever followed nature with more catholic fidelity; his cavaliers are as natural as his boors; he neither refined the vulgar, nor vulgarized the refined,' and goes on to quote this among other criticism: — 'his portraits baffle description and praise; he drew the minds of men; they live, breathe, and are ready to walk out of the frames.' Sir William winds up with the enthusiastic declaration, 'Such pictures as these are real history; we know the persons of Philip IV, and Olivares, as familiarly as if we had paced the avenues of the Pardo with Digby and Howell, and perhaps we think more favourably of their characters.'

I shall borrow still further from Sir W. Stirling Maxwell's graphic and entertaining book, descriptions of two of Velasquez's *genre* pictures, 'The Maids of Honour,' and the more celebrated 'Spinners,' both at Madrid. 'The scene (of the first) is a long room in a quarter of the old palace which was called the prince's quarter, and the subject, Velasquez at work on a large picture of the royal family. To the extreme right of the composition is seen the back of the easel and the canvas on which he is engaged; and beyond it stands the painter, with his pencils and palette, pausing to converse, and to observe the effect of his performance. In the centre stands the little Infanta Maria Margarita, taking a cup of water from a salver which Doña Maria Augustina Sarmiento, maid of honour to the queen, presents kneeling. To the left, Doña Isabel de Velasco, another meniña, seems to be dropping a courtesy; and the dwarfs, Maria Barbolo and Nicolas Pertusano, stand in the foreground, the little man putting his foot on the quarters of a great tawny hound, which despises the aggression, and continues in a state of solemn repose. Some paces behind these figures, Doña Marcela de Ulloa, a lady of honour in nun-like weeds, and a *guardadimas,* are seen in conversation; at the far end of the room an open door gives a view of a staircase, up which Don Josef Nieto, queen's apasentador, is retiring; and near this door there hangs on the wall a mirror, which, reflecting the countenance of the king and queen, shows that they form part of the principal group, although placed beyond the bounds of the picture. The room is hung with paintings which Palomino assures us are works of Rubens; and it is lighted by three windows in the left wall, and by the open door at the end, an arrangement of which an artist will at once comprehend the difficulties. The perfection of art which conceals art, was never better attained than in this picture. Velasquez seems to have anticipated the discovery of Daguerre, and taking a real room, and real chance grouped people, to have fixed them, as it were by magic, for all time on his canvas. The little fair-haired Infanta is a pleasing study of childhood; with the hanging-lip and full cheek of the Austrian family, she has a fresh complexion and lovely blue eyes, and gives a promise of beauty which as empress she never fulfilled. Her young attendants, girls of thirteen or fourteen, contrast agreeably with the ill-favoured dwarf beside them; they are very pretty, especially Doña Isabel de Velasco, who died a reigning beauty, and their hands are painted with peculiar delicacy. Their dresses are highly absurd, their figures being concealed by long stiff corsets and prodigious hoops; for these were the days when the mode was—

"Supporters, pooters, fardingales, above the loynes to weare;"

and the *guardainfante*, the oval hoop peculiar to Spain, was in full blow; and the robes of a dowager might have curtained the tun of Heidelberg, and the powers of Velasquez were baffled by the perverse fancy of "Fribble, the woman's tailor." The gentle and majestic hound, stretching himself and winking drowsily, is admirably painted, and seems a descendant of the royal breed immortalized by Titian in portraits of the Emperor Charles and his son.'

'The Spinners:' 'The scene is a large weaving-room, in which an old woman and young one sit, the first at her spinning-wheel, and the second winding yarn, with three girls beside them, one of whom plays with a cat. In the background, standing within an alcove filled with the light from an unseen window, are two other women displaying a large piece of tapestry to a lady customer, whose graceful figure recalls that which has given its name to Terburg's picture of

"The Satin Gown." Of the composition, the painter Mengs observed, "it seemed as if the hand had no part in it, and it had been the work of pure thought."' Velasquez, who must have seen many a bull fight, has left the world a fine example of field sports in 'The Boar Hunt,' in our National Gallery, a picture which was bought for two thousand two hundred pounds from Lord Cowley. When ambassador at the Court of Spain, it was given to him by Ferdinand VII. In a circular pen in the Pardo, 'Philip IV. and a party of cavaliers display their skill in slaying boars, to a few ladies, who sit secure in heavy old-fashioned blue coaches,' while motley groups of courtiers and peasants, huntsmen and hounds, postilions and their mules fill the foreground. Sir Edwin Landseer remarked of this picture that he had never before seen 'so much large art on so small a scale.'

Bartolomé Estévan Murillo was born at Seville in 1618, and was therefore nearly twenty years younger than his great countryman Velasquez. Murillo seems to have been of obscure origin, and to have begun his life in humble circumstances. There are traditions of his being self-taught, of his studying ragged boys, himself little more than a boy, in the gypsy quarter of Triana in Seville; of his painting in the marketplace, where he probably found the originals of the heads of saints and Madonnas (by which he made a little money in selling them for South America) in the peasants who came to Seville with their fruit and vegetables. In 1642, Murillo, then twenty-four years of age, visited Madrid, and was kindly received, and aided in his art by his senior and fellow artist, the court painter, Velasquez. It had been Murillo's intention to proceed to England to study under Van Dyck, but the death of the latter put a stop to the project. Murillo was prevented from making the painter's pilgrimage to Italy by want of means, but the loss of culture was so far supplied by the instructions given to him by Velasquez.

In 1645, when Murillo was twenty-seven years of age, he returned to Seville, and settled there, becoming as successful as he deserved; and being acknowledged as the head of the school of Seville, where he established the Academy of Art, and was its first president. Murillo married, in 1648, a lady of some fortune, and was accustomed to entertain at his house the most exclusive society of Seville.

In 1682, Murillo was at Cadiz painting a picture of the marriage of St Catherine in the church of the Capuchins there, when, in consequence of the accidental fall of the scaffolding, he received so severe an injury, that he was forced to leave his work incomplete, and to return to Seville, where he died within a few weeks, aged sixty-four years. He had two sons, and an only daughter, who was a nun, having taken the veil eight years before her father's death.

Murillo appears to have been in character a gentle, enthusiastic man, not without a touch of fun and frolic. He would remain for hours in the sacristy of the cathedral of Seville before 'the solemn awful picture of the 'Deposition from the Cross,' by Pedro de Campana. When Murillo was asked by the sacristan why he stood thus gazing there, the painter answered, 'I am waiting till these holy men have finished their work.' By his own desire, Murillo was buried before this picture. Before another 'too truthful picture of Las dos Cadaveres' in the small church of the hospital of the Caridad, Murillo used to hold his nose. One of Murillo's pictures has the odd name of 'La Virgen Sarvilleta,' or the Virgin of the Napkin. Murillo was working at the Convento de la Merced, which is almost filled with his works, when the cook of the convent begged a memorial of him, offering as the canvas a napkin, on which Murillo at once painted a 'brilliant glowing Madonna,' with a child, 'which seems quite to bound forward out of the picture.' [29]

Murillo's portrait by himself represents him in a dark doublet having wide sleeves and a square collar closed in front. His thumb is in his pallet, and the other hand, with fingers taper and delicate as those of a hand by Van Dyck, holds one of his brushes. The smooth face, with regular features, is pale and thoughtful, and with the womanliness of the aspect increased from the dark hair, which is divided slightly to one side, being allowed to fall down in long wavy curls on the shoulders.

In spite of the naturalistic studies of his early youth, and even of the naturalistic treatment which he gave to his first religious work, Murillo was possessed of greater and higher imagination than Velasquez could claim, and the longer Murillo lived and worked the more refined and exalted his ideas became. Unlike Velasquez, Murillo was a great religious painter, and during the last years of his life he painted sacred subjects almost exclusively. But, like Velasquez, Murillo was eminently a Spanish painter—his virgins are dark-eyed, olive-complexioned maidens, and even his Holy Child is a Spanish babe.

Without the elevation and the training of the best Italian painters, Murillo has left abundant proofs of great original genius. The painter's works are widely circulated, but the chief are still in Seville. Six are in the church of the Caridad, and these six include his famous 'Moses striking the Rock,' and his 'Miracle of the Loaves and Fishes;' seven 'Murillos' are in the Convento de la Merced, among them Murillo's own favourite picture, which he called 'Mi Cicadro' of 'St Thomas of Villaneuva.' 'St Thomas was the favourite preacher of Charles V., and was created Archbishop of Valencia, where he seemed to spend the whole of his revenues in charity, yet never contracted any debt, so that his people used to believe that angels must minister to his temporal wants. He is represented at his cathedral door, distributing alms, robed in black, with a white mitre. A poor cripple kneels at his feet, and other mendicants are grouped around.'

In the cathedral, Seville, is Murillo's 'Angel de la Guarda,' 'in which a glorious seraph, with spreading wings, leads a little trustful child by the hand, and directs him to look beyond earth into the heavenly light;' and his 'St Antonio.' 'The saint is represented kneeling in a cell, of which all the poor details are faithfully given, while the long arcade of the cloister can be seen through the half-open door. Above, in a transparent light, which grows from himself, the Child Jesus appears, and descends, floating through wreaths of angels, drawn down by the power of prayer.' [30]

Another of Murillo's renowned pictures is that of the patron saints of Seville, 'Santa Rufina and Santa Justina,' who were stoned to death for refusing to bow down to the image of Venus.

With regard to Murillo's pictures of flower-girls and beggar-boys, I think my readers are sure to have seen an engraving of one of the former, '*The* flower-Girl,' as it is called, with a face as fresh and radiant as her flowers. In the National Gallery there is a large Holy Family of Murillo's, and in Dulwich Gallery there is a laughing boy, an irresistible specimen of brown-cheeked, white-teethed drollery.

CHAPTER X.

ART — NICOLAS POUSSIN, 1594-1665 — CLAUDE [31] LORRAINE, 1600-1682 — CHARLES LE BRUN, 1619-1690 — WATTEAU, 1684-1721 — GREUZE, 1726-1805.

Nicolas Poussin was born at Andely in Normandy in 1594. Of his parentage little seems to have been ascertained, but it is believed that he was well educated, and his classical learning in after life was reckoned great. He was regularly trained to be a painter under a master in his native town, and afterwards in Paris.

Dissatisfied with the patronage which he received in Paris, Poussin went to Rome when he was about thirty years of age. In Rome he is said to have lived on familiar terms with a sculptor whose devotion to antique art influenced his taste, and lent it the strong classical bent which it retained. Poussin studied regularly in the school of Domenichino. After some delay in attracting public notice, 'The Death of Germanicus,' and 'The Capture of Jerusalem,' which Poussin painted for Cardinal Barberini, won general approval. In 1629, when Nicolas Poussin was in his thirty-fifth year, he married the sister of his pupil, Gaspar Dughet, who took Poussin's name, and is known as a painter, inferior to his master, by the name of Gaspar Poussin.

Nicolas Poussin returned to Paris when he was a middle-aged man, was presented to the king, Louis XIII., by Cardinal Richelieu, and offered apartments in the Tuileries, with the title of painter in ordinary, and a salary of a hundred and twenty pounds a year. Poussin agreed to settle in Paris, but on his going back to Rome to fetch his wife, and on the King of France's dying, the attractions of the Eternal City proved too great for the painter, and in place of removing his household and studio to his native country, he lived for the rest of his years in Rome, and died there in 1665, when he was seventy-one years of age. Except what can be judged of him from his work, I do not know that much has been gathered of the private character and life of Nicolas Poussin, notwithstanding that there was a biography written of him fifty years ago by Lady Calcott, and that his letters have been published in Paris. In the absence of conclusive testimony one may conclude with some probability that he was 'quiet,' like his best paintings; a man who minded his own business, and did not trouble the world by astonishing actions, good or bad. [32]

In painting his own picture, from which an engraving has been taken, Poussin's classical preferences seem to have passed into the likeness, for in the dress of the seventeenth century, the cloak (not unlike a toga), the massive hand with the heavy signet-ring resting on what looks like a closed portfolio, the painter has something of the severe air and haughty expression of an old Roman; still more, perhaps, of the French-Romans, if I may call them so, of whom revolutionary times nearly two centuries later, afforded so many examples. This is a handsome, dignified face, with austerity in its pride. The slightly curled hair is thrown back with a certain consciousness from the knit brow, and from the shoulders. There is only the faintest shadow of a moustache over the cleanly cut, firmly closed mouth.

Poussin painted largely, and his pictures have been often engraved. With harmonious composition, good drawing and colouring, his pictures alike profited and suffered from the classical atmosphere in which they had their being. They gained in that correctness which in its highest form becomes noble truthfulness, but they lost in freedom. The figures in the pictures had frequently the statuesqueness which in sculpture suits the material, but in painting is stiffness.

Nicolas Poussin had an exceptional reputation for a historical painter in his day. As a landscape painter, Mr Ruskin, while waging war with Nicolas Poussin's brother-in-law and assumed namesake, Gaspar, notably excepts Nicolas from his severest strictures, and treats his efforts in landscape painting with marked respect. At the same time, however, the critic censures the painter for a want of thorough acquaintance with nature, and the laws of nature, ignorance not uncommon in any day, and nearly universal in Nicolas Poussin's day. 'The great master of elevated ideal landscape,' Mr Ruskin calls Nicolas Poussin, and illustrates his excellence in one respect, after contrasting it with the slovenliness of Sir Joshua Reynolds, by describing the vine in Poussin's 'Nursing of Jupiter,' in the Dulwich Gallery, thus: —

'Every vine-leaf, drawn with consummate skill and untiring diligence, produces not only a true group of the most perfect grace and beauty, but one which in its pure and simple truth belongs to every age of nature, and adapts itself to the history of all time.' 'One of the finest landscapes that ancient art has produced, the work of a really great mind,' Mr Ruskin distinguishes the 'Phocian' of Nicolas Poussin in the National Gallery, before proceeding to point out its faults.

Again, Mr Ruskin, writing of the street in the centre of another landscape by Nicolas Poussin, indicates it with emphasis: — 'the street in the centre of the really great landscape of Poussin (great in feeling, at least) marked 260 in the Dulwich Gallery,' The criticism with which Mr Ruskin follows up this praise is so perfect a bit of word-painting, that I cannot refrain from writing it down here. 'The houses are dead square masses, with a light side and a dark side, and black touches for windows. There is no suggestion of anything in any of the spaces, the light wall is dead grey, the dark wall dead grey, and the windows dead black. How differently would nature have treated us. She would have let us see the Indian corn hanging on the walls, and the image of the Virgin at the angles; and the sharp, broken, broad shadows of the tiled eaves, and the deep ribbed tiles with the doves upon them, and the carved Roman capital built into the wall, and the white and blue stripes of the mattresses stuffed out of the windows, and the flapping corners of the neat blinds. All would have been there; not as such, not like the corn, nor blinds, n or tiles, not to be comprehended nor understood, but a confusion of yellow and black spots and strokes, carried far too fine for the eye to follow; microscopic in its minuteness, and filling every atom and space with mystery, out of which would have arranged itself the general impression of truth and life.' Once more, Mr Ruskin freely admits that 'all the landscape of Nicolas Poussin is imagination.'

Mr Ruskin's first definition of ideal landscape is in this manner. Every different tree and leaf, every bud, has a perfect form, which, were it not for disease or accident, it would have attained; just as every individual human face has an ideal form, which but for sin and suffering it would present: and the ideal landscape-painter has realized the perfect form, and offers it to the world, and that in a sense quite distinct from the fallacy of improving nature.

But I wish to take my readers further into imaginative landscape, and to show it to them, if possible, under additional lights. I despair of succeeding if I cannot do it by one or two simple examples. In passing through a gallery we may stop before a picture to be struck, almost startled, by the exact copy which it presents of some scene in nature; how like the clouds in the sky, the leaves on the trees, the very plumage of the birds! But pass on to another picture which may or may not have the same exact likeness, and we are possessed with quite another feeling; instead of being merely surprised by the cleverness of the imitation, we feel a thrill of delight at a reproduction of nature. In this picture there are not only the clouds we remember, but we can almost feel the shadows which they cast, and the air which stirs them. These tree-leaves are not only green, or yellow, or russet, they are tender, or crisp living leaves. One half expects to see the birds' throats swell, and hear the sweetness or the shrillness of their songs.

The first picture, with all its correctness, brightness, richness, or delicacy it may be, remains bare, hard, and barren, compared to the second. I cannot explain to my readers the cause of the difference, I can Only show it to them as they may see it for themselves, and say that I suppose it proceeds from this—that the second painter has seen farther into the heart of nature than the first, and has been able by subtler touches to make us see with his eyes.

But imaginative landscape is much more than this vivid feeling and expression of nature; there is not a cloud, or leaf, or bird too many or out of keeping with the place and the hour. The clouds are the very clouds of sunset, or sunrise, or high noon—clouds differing widely from each other, as you have no doubt observed. The trees are the beeches, or chestnuts, or pines, which would grow on the conformation of rocks, in the sheltered nook, or on the breezy upland; the birds are the linnets or the larks, the thrushes or the lapwings, which frequent these special trees, and may be seen and heard at this particular hour.

Again, landscape often tells a story, and tells it inimitably. My readers have heard of the ballad of the 'Twa Corbies,' which the writer of the ballad has made to meet and tell gruesomely where and on what carrion their feast has been. Suppose the writer of the ballad had been a painter, he might have painted the story as intelligibly by the lone hill-side, the bleaching bones of the faithful hound and gallant grey, the two loathly blue-black birds satiated with their prey. There is a significant old Scotch song with a ballad ring, by Lady Nairne, two verses of which form each a complete picture not only of different seasons, but of different phases of feeling — happiness and misery.

> 'Bonnie ran the burnie down,
> Wandering and winding;
> Sweetly sang the birds aboon,
> Care never minding.
>
> 'But now the burn comes down apace,
> Roaring and reaming,
> And for the wee birdies' sang
> Wild howlets screaming.'

Imagine these two verses painted, and the painter, from a lack of comprehension, introducing the 'wild howlets screaming' beside the burnie, 'wandering and winding,' and the 'wee birdies' foolishly and inconsequently singing with their feeble song drowned in the rush of the burn (no longer a burnie), 'roaring and reaming,' when the 'spate' is spreading desolation on every side. Don't you see how the picture would be spoilt, and the story of complete contrast left untold? I have taken advisedly an extreme and, therefore an unlikely case of halting imagination. But in imaginative landscape every 'white flower with its purple stain,' every crushed butterfly, is made to play its part in the whole, and at the same time due proportion is never lost sight of, and the less is always kept subordinate to the greater.

I have already had occasion to mention examples of Nicolas Poussin in the National Gallery and in Dulwich Gallery.

Claude Gelée, better known as **Claude Lorraine,** was a native of Lorraine, and was born at Chateau de Chamagne in the Vosges, in 1600. His parents were in humble life, and apprenticed Claude to a baker and pastry-cook. According to some biographers the cooks of Lorraine were in such request that they occasionally repaired to Rome with their apprentices in their train to serve the successor of St Peter, and Claude was thus carried, in the way of trade, to the city which might well have been the goal of his ambition. According to other writers of art histories, Claude abandoned the kneading-trough and the oven; and it was as a runaway apprentice that by some occult means he reached Rome. And when he had arrived he entered into the service of a landscape painter of good repute, to whom he was colour-boy as well as cook. The last is the account, so far, which Claude gave of himself to a friend, and it is hardly likely either that he misrepresented his history, or that his friend invented such details, though lately French authorities have questioned the authenticity of the narrative. Claude remained for nearly the entire remainder of a long life in Rome. He only once re-visited France, while he was yet a young man, under thirty years of age, in 1625 or 1627. He is supposed to have painted his earliest pictures and exe-cuted his etchings about this time, 1630 and to have painted his best pictures fifteen years later, when he was in the maturity of his life and powers. He was counted successful during his life time, as a landscape painter, but did not amass a larger fortune than about two thousand pounds. [33] He was a slow and careful painter (work-ing a fortnight at a picture with little apparent progress); his pains-taking work, and his custom of keeping a book, in which he verified his pictures, are about the most that I can tell you of the habits of one of the foreign painters, who has been most fully represented in England, and was long in the highest favour with English lovers of art. Claude Lorraine died at Rome in the eighty-third year of his age, in 1682.

Claude Lorraine's name has become a very vexed name with art critics. There was a time when he had an unsurpassed reputation as a landscape painter. The possession of a Claude was enough to confer art glory on a country-house, and possibly for this reason England, in public and private collections, has more 'Claudes' than are held by any other country. But Claude's admirers, among whom Sir George Beaumont, the great art critic of his generation, took the lead, have had their day, and, if they have not by any means passed away, are on the wane.

The wrathful indignation of the English landscape painter, Turner, at the praise which was so glibly lavished on Claude—an indignation that caused Turner to bequeath two of his own landscape paintings to the trustees of the National Gallery, on the caustic condition that they should always be placed between the two celebrated 'Claudes,' known as 'The Marriage of Isaac and Rebecca' and 'The Embarkation of the Queen of Sheba'—helped to shake the English art world's faith in its former idol. Mr Ruskin's adoption and proclamation of Turner's opinion shook the old faith still further. This reversal of a verdict with regard to Claude is peculiar; it is by no means uncommon for the decision of contemporaries to be set aside, and we shall hear of an instance presently, in the case of the painter Le Brun. In fact, it is often ominous with regard to a man's future fame, when he is 'cried up to the skies' in his own day. The probability may be that his easy success has been won by something superficial and fleeting. But Claude's great popularity has been in another generation, and with another nation. English taste may have been in fault; or another explanation seems preferable—that Claude's sense of beauty was great, with all its faults of expression, and he gave such glimpses of a beautiful world as the gazers on his pictures were capable of receiving, which to them proved irresistible.

While Claude adopted an original style as a landscape painter, so far as his contemporaries were concerned, he was to such a degree self taught, and only partially taught, that it is said he never learnt to paint figures—those in his pictures were painted by other painters, and that Claude even painted animals badly.

Mr Ruskin has been hard on Claude, whether justly or unjustly, I cannot pretend to say.

The critic denies the painter not only a sense of truth in art, but all imagination as a landscape painter 'Of men of name,' Mr Ruskin writes, 'Perhaps Claude is the best instance of a want of imagination, nearly total, borne out by painful but untaught study of nature, and much feeling for abstract beauty of form, with none whatever for harmony of expression.' Mr Ruskin condemns in the strongest terms 'the mourning and murky olive browns and verdigris greens, in which Claude, with the industry and intelligence of a Sevres china painter, drags the laborious bramble leaves over his childish foreground.' But Mr Ruskin himself acknowledges, with a reservation, Claude's charm in foliage, and pronounces more conditionally his power, when it was at its best, in skies—a region in which the greater, as well as the less, Poussin was declared to fail signally; 'a perfectly genuine and untouched sky of Claude,' Mr Ruskin writes, 'is indeed most perfect, and beyond praise, in all qualities of air; though even with him I often feel rather that there is a great deal of pleasant air between me and the firmament, than that the firmament itself is only air.'

When all has been said that can be said, let us look at a mellow or a sunny Claude on any wall where it may hang, and judge for ourselves of the satisfaction it is calculated to give.

Claude was fond of painting scenes on the Tiber and in the Roman Campagna, but while he tried to reproduce the hills and woodlands of Italy, he did not seek to paint the mountain landscapes of the Apennines.

Besides Claude's numerous works in England and scattered through other countries, some of his finest paintings are in the Doria and Sciarra palaces in Rome. He rarely put his name to his works; when he did so he signed it frequently 'Claudio,' sometimes 'Claudius.' I have spoken of his book of sketches, in which he had been wont to note on the back of the sketch the date of the completed picture, and to whom sold. This book he called the 'Libro di Verita,' or, Book of Truth, and its apparent use was to check the sale of spurious paintings in Claude's name, even during his lifetime. The ' Book of Truth' is in possession of the Duke of Devonshire, and has been employed in recent years with reference to the end for which it seemed designed, so woe to that country-house which has long prided itself on possessing a 'Claude,' if that 'Claude' does not happen to have a place in the 'Book of Truth,' though I do not know that it is at all certain that Claude took the precaution of inscribing *every* painting which he painted after a certain date in the 'Book of Truth.'

Claude Lorraine is well represented in the National Gallery. Engravings of his pictures are common.

Charles le Brun was born in Paris, in 1619. He was trained to be a painter, and went young to Rome, studying there for six years under the guidance of Nicolas Poussin. Le Brun returned to Paris, and, through the patronage of the Chancellor Segnier, was introduced to the court, and got the most favourable opportunities of practising his profession with worldly success. He speedily acquired a great name, and was appointed painter to the King, Louis XIV. Le Brun had enough influence with his royal master, and with the great minister Colbert, to succeed in establishing, while the painter was yet a young man, the Royal Academy of Art, of which he was the first member, and virtually the head, holding, in his own person, the directorship of the Gobelin tapestry works, which was to be the privilege of a member of the Academy. Le Brun continued in the utmost favour with the King, who, not content with employing the painter largely at Fontainebleau and in Versailles, invested him with the order of St Michael, bestowed on him letters of nobility, and visited him frequently at his work, occasions when there were not wanting adroit courtiers to liken the Grand Monarque to the Emperor Charles V., and Le Brun to Titian.

Le Brun seems to have been a man of energy, confidence, and industry, neither mentally before nor after his time, and by no means too retiring, meditative, or original, to fail to profit by his outward good fortune. He wrote, as well as painted, artistic treatises, which were received as oracular utterances, and entirely deferred to in the schools of his day. He died at Paris in 1690, when he was in his seventieth year.

Le Brun's real merits as a painter were limited to respectable abilities and acquirements, together with florid quickness and ease, and such an eye to what was splendid and scenic as suited admirably a decorator of palaces in an age which prized sumptuousness, and an exaggeration of dramatic effect, over every other quality. Nicolas Poussin's quiet refinement of style became in Le Brun what is called academic (conventionally learned), pompous, and grandiose, and men decidedly preferred the degeneration. But later critics, who have not the natural partiality of the French to the old master, return to their first loves, and condemn Le Brun's swelling violence, both in the tints and poses of his figures. Among his most famous works, which have been magnificently engraved, are his 'Battles of Alexander.'

Antoine Watteau was born at Valenciennes in 1684. A very different painter from Le Brun, he was yet as characteristic of French art in the reign of Louis XIV. I think my readers must be familiar with his name, and I dare say they associate it, as I do, not only with the fans which were painted largely after his designs, but with mock pastorals and Sèvres china. I don't know if his birth-place at Valenciennes, with its chief product of dainty lace, had anything to do with it, but the other items of poor Watteau's history are considerably removed from the very artificial grace which one connects with his name. He was the son of a carpenter, and struggled up, by the hard instrumentality of third-rate masters and of picture-dealers, to the rank which he attained among artists, taking his stand from the first, however, as the painter of well-bred, well-apparelled people — the frequenters of *bals masqués,* and *fêtes champêtres,* who were only playing at shepherds and shepherdesses.

Watteau was elected an Academician in 1717, when he was thirty-three years of age, and he afterwards came to England, but did not remain there. He died of consumption at Nogent-sur-Marne in 1721, when he was thirty-six years of age. [34] Watteau's gifts were his grace and brilliance on a small scale. He did not draw well; as to design, his composition may be said to be suited to such a work as the collection of 'fashionable figures,' which he engraved and left behind him. Yet, if we were to see at this moment some of his exquisite groups of ladies in sacques and Watteau hats, and cavaliers in flowing wigs and lace, cravats, I have no doubt that the most of us would admire them much, for they are exceedingly pretty, and exceeding prettiness is attractive, particularly to women. But I would have my readers to remember that this art is a finical and soulless art, after all. I would fain have them take this as their maxim, 'That the art is greatest which conveys to the mind of the spectator, by any means whatsoever, the greatest number of the greatest ideas.'

Jean Baptiste Greuze was born at Tournus in Burgundy in 1726. He studied painting from his youth in the studios of artists at Lyons, Paris, and Rome, and his studies resulted in his being a celebrated genre painter. He only painted one historical picture, but, with the touchy vanity which seemed natural to the man, he ranked his genre pictures as high art; and when he was placed in the ordinary list of genre painters on his election as a member of the French Academy of Painting, Greuze resented the imputation, and withdrew from the Academy. He died in 1805, aged seventy-nine years. Greuze was a showy, clever, but neither earnest nor truthful painter of domestic subjects and family pictures. His pictures of women and heads of girls, the expression in some of which has been severely condemned, are among his best known works, and by these he is represented in the National Gallery. [35]

CHAPTER XI.

HOLBEIN, 1494-1543 — VAN DYCK, 1599-1641 — LELY, 1618-1680 — CANALETTO, 1697-1768 — KNELLER, 1646-1723.

Hans Holbein, sometimes entitled Hans the Younger, was born at Augsburg about 1494 or 1495. He was the son of a painter, and belonged to a family of painters, one or more of whom had preceded Hans Holbein in leaving Augsburg, and taking up his residence at Basle. There Holbein was under the patronage of, and on terms of friendly intercourse with, the great scholar Erasmus. One bad result proceeded from this friendly familiarity, that of establishing or originating the charge that Holbein, as a young man, at least, was coarse and dissipated in his habits. The evidence is sufficiently curious. There is still in existence the copy of a Latin book, called the 'Praise of Folly,' written by Erasmus, which Holbein, not being a scholar, could not have read for himself, but which, according to tradition, Erasmus himself, or some other friend, read to him, while Holbein was so delighted with the satire that he covered the margin of the book with illustrative sketches. (The sketches remain, and are unmistakably Holbein's.) Opposite a passage, recording the want of common sense and energy in many learned men, Holbein had drawn the figure of a student, and written below, *'Erasmus.'* The book coming again into the hands of Erasmus, he was offended with the liberty taken by the painter., and sought to retaliate in kind by writing below the sketch of a rude boor drinking, *'Holbein.'* In spite of the rough jesting, the friendship between scholar and painter was not interrupted.

In these early days Holbein sometimes practised painting on glass, after the example of some of his kinsmen. At Basle, Holbein painted what is considered his finest work, the 'Meier Madonna,' now at Darmstadt, with a copy in the Dresden Gallery, and there he executed the designs for his series of woodcuts of the 'Dance of Death.'

At Basle Holbein married, while still a young man. The presumption that the painter's marriage, like that of his countryman, Albert Dürer, was unhappy, has rested on the foundation that he left his wife and her children behind when he repaired to England, and that although he re-visited Basle, and saw his wife and family, they did not return with him to England. A fancied confirmation to the unhappiness of the marriage is found in the expression of the wife in a portrait which Holbein painted of her and his children when he was at Basle. 'Cross-looking and red-eyed,' one critic calls the unlucky woman; another describes her as 'a plain, coarse-looking, middle-aged woman,' with an expression 'certainly mysterious and unpleasant.' Holbein's latest biographer [36] has proved that the forsaken wife, Elssbeth Schmid, was a widow with one son when Holbein married her, and has conjectured that she was probably not only older than Holbein, but in circumstances which rendered her independent of her husband. So far the critic has done something to clear Hans Holbein from the miserable accusation often brought against him, that he abandoned his wife and children to starve at Basle, while he sunned himself in such court favour as could be found in England. But, indeed, while Hans Holbein may have been honest and humane enough to have been above such base suspicions, there is no trace of him which survives that goes to disprove the probability that he was a self-willed, not over-scrupulous man, if he was also a vigorous and thorough worker.

Holbein came to England about 1526 or 1527, when he must have been thirty-one or thirty-two years of age, and repaired to Chelsea to the house of Sir Thomas More, to whom the painter brought a letter of introduction, and still better credentials in the present, from Erasmus to More, of the portrait of Erasmus, painted by Hans Holbein. There are so many portraits and copies of portraits of Erasmus, not only by Holbein, but by other painters—for Erasmus was painted by Albert Dürer and Quintin Matsys,—that this special portrait, like the true Holbein family portrait of the More family, remains very much a subject of speculation. Most of us must be well acquainted with the delightful account which Erasmus gave of Sir Thomas More's country-house at Chelsea, and the life of its occupants. It has been cited hundreds of times as an example of what an English family has been, and what it may be in dutiful discipline, simple industry, and high cultivation, when Sir Thomas's young daughters repeated psalms in Latin to beguile the time in the drudging process of churning the butter. During Holbein's residence in or visits to the Mores' house at Chelsea, he sketched or painted the original of the More family picture.

Holbein was introduced to Henry VIII, by Sir Thomas More, and was immediately taken into favour by the king. and received into his service, with a lodging in the palace, a general salary of thirty pounds a year, and separate payment for his paintings. According to Horace Walpole, Holbein's palace lodging was probably 'the little study called the new library' of square glazed bricks of different colours, designed by the painter at Whitehall. (This gateway, with the porch at Wilton, were the painter's chief architectural achievements.) By another statement, Holbein's house was on London Bridge, where it was destroyed in the great fire.

I have already alluded to the anecdote of the value which Henry VIII, put on Holbein. It was to this effect: that when an aggrieved courtier complained to the king that the painter had taken precedence of him—a nobleman, the king replied, 'I have many noblemen, but I have only one Hans Holbein.' In fact, Holbein received nothing save kindness from Henry VIII.; and for that matter, there seemed to be something in common between bluff King Hal and the equally bluff German Hans. But on one occasion Hans Holbein was said to have run the risk of forfeiting his imperious master's favour by the too favourable miniature which the painter was accused of painting of Anne of Cleves.

At Henry's court Holbein painted many a member of the royal family, noble and knight, and English gentleman and lady. His fortune had made him a portrait painter, but he was fully equal to other branches of art, as shown by his 'Meier Madonna,' and still more by the designs which have been preserved of his famous allegory of 'the Triumphs of Riches and Poverty,' painted for the hall of the Easterling Steelyard, the quarters of the merchants of Allemagne, then traders in London. In addition to painting portraits Holbein designed dagger hilts, clasps, cups, as some say after a study of the goldsmith's work of Cellini.

For a long time it was believed that Hans Holbein died after Mary Tudor succeeded to the English throne; indeed, some said that his death had been occasioned or hastened by that change in the affairs of men, which compelled him to quit his lodgings in the palace to make room for 'the new painter,' Sir Antony More, who came in the suite of Mary's well-beloved husband, Philip of Spain. There was even a theory, creditable to Hans Holbein, drawn from this conclusion, that he might have adopted the Protestant views of his late gracious master, and have stood by them stoutly, and so far forfeited all recognition from the bitter Catholic Mary. But, unfortunately for the tradition and theory, and for the later pictures attributed to Hans Holbein, his will has been discovered, and that quite recently, proving, from the date of its administration, his death of the plague (so far only the tradition had been right), when yet only in his forty-eighth year, as early as 1543, four years before the death of Henry VIII. In spite of court patronage Holbein did not die a rich man, and there is an impression that he was recklessly improvident in his habits.

Holbein had revisited Basle several times, and the council had settled on him a pension of fifty florins a year, provided he would return and reside in Basle within two years, while his wife was to receive a pension of forty florins a year during Holbein's two years' absence. Holbein did not comply with the terms of the settlement. About the time of his death his son Philip, then a lad of eighteen, was a goldsmith in Paris. Of Hans Holbein's portraits I have two to draw from; one, painted in his youth at Basle, shows the painter in an open doublet, and curious stomacher-like shirt, and having on his head a great flapping hat. His face is broad and smooth-skinned, with little hair seen, and the features, the eyes especially, rather small for such an expanse of cheek and chin. The other picture of Holbein to which I have referred belongs certainly to a considerably later period of his life, and represents him with short but bushy hair, and short bushy beard and moustache, a man having a broad stout person with a mixture of dauntlessness and *bonhommie* in his massive face.

Mr Ruskin says of Holbein, as a painter, that he was complete in intellect; what he saw he saw with his whole soul, and what he painted he painted with his whole might.

In deep and reverential feeling Holbein was far behind his countryman Albert Dürer, but Holbein was far more fully furnished than Dürer (unless indeed as Albrecht Dürer showed himself in that last picture of 'the Apostles') in the means of his art; he was a better draughtsman in the maturity of his powers, and a far better colourist. For Hans Holbein was not more famous for the living truthfulness of his likenesses ('a man very excellent in making physiognomies'), than for the 'inimitable bloom' that he imparted to his pictures, which 'he touched, till not a touch became discernible.' Yet beneath this bloom, along with his truthfulness, there was a dryness and hardness in Holbein's treatment of his subjects, and he is far below Titian, Rubens, and even Rembrandt as a portrait painter.

Holbein was in the habit of painting his larger portraits on a peculiar green, and his miniatures on a blue background. He drew his portrait sketches with black and red chalk on a paper tinted flesh-colour. It is said, that with the exception, of Philip Wouwermann, no painter has been so unfortunate in having the works of other painters attributed to him as Hans Holbein has been, and 'that three out of every four pictures ascribed to him are misnamed.' [37]

The 'Meier, or Meyer Madonna,' is otherwise called 'the Meier Family adoring the infant Christ in the arms of the Virgin.' The subject is understood to prove that it must have been painted in Holbein's youth, before Protestantism was triumphant at Basle. The figures are the Burgomaster Meier and his wife, whom Holbein painted twice; their son, with a little boy *nude* beside him; another woman, elderly, conjectured to be a grandmother of the family, and beside her the young daughter of the house. In the centre on a turkey carpet stands the Madonna, holding in her arms an infant stretching out its left hand to the group of worshippers. In course of time, and in its transfer from hand to hand, a doubt has arisen with regard to the subject of this picture. Some critics have regarded it as a votive picture dedicated in a private chapel to commemorate the recovery from sickness or the death of a child. This conjecture seems to rest mainly on the fact, that the child in the Dresden copy (it is said to be otherwise in the Darmstadt picture) is of an aspect so sickly, as to have given rise to the impression that it represented an ailing, or even a dead child, and no glorious child Christ. Critics have gone still farther, and imagined that the child is a figure of the soul of a dead child (souls were sometimes painted by the old painters as new-born children), or of the soul of the elder and somewhat muffled-up woman who might have been recently dead. Mr Ruskin regards the picture as an offering for the recovery of a sick child, and thus illustrates it:

'The received tradition respecting the Holbein Madonna is beautiful, and I believe the interpretation to be true. A father and a mother have prayed to her for the life of their sick child. She appears to them, her own child Christ in her arms; she puts down her child beside them, takes their child into her arms instead; it lies down upon her bosom, and stretches its hand to its father and mother, saying farewell.'

Yet another much more prosaic and less attractive interpretation of the picture has been suggested by Holbein's biographer, that the two children may represent the same child. The child standing by his brother may be the boy restored to health, the feeble child in the arms of the Virgin may indicate the same child in its sickness, while the extended arm may point to the seat of the disease in an arm broken or injured. After all, the child may simply be a child Christ, marred in execution. I have given this dispute at length, because I think it is interesting, and, so far as I know, unique in reference to such a picture. By an odd enough mistake this very picture was once said to be the famous More Family picture.

The idea of the 'Dance of Death' did not originate with Holbein, neither is he supposed to have done more than touch, if he did touch, the paintings called the 'Dance of Death,' on the wall of the Dominican burial-ground, Basle, painted long before Holbein's day, by the order of the council after the plague visited Basle, and considered to have for its meaning simply a warning of the universality of death. But Holbein certainly availed himself of the older painting, to draw from it the grim satire of his wood-cuts. Of these there are thirty-seven designs, the first, 'The Creation;' the second, 'Adam and Eve in Paradise;' the third, 'The Expulsion from Paradise;' the fourth, 'Adam Tilling the Earth;' the fifth, 'The Bones of all People;' till the dance really begins in the sixth. Death, a skeleton, as seen through the rest of the designs, sometimes playing on a guitar or lute, sometimes carrying a drum, bagpipes, a dulcimer, or a fiddle, now appearing with mitre on head and crozier in hand to summon the Abbot; then marching before the parson with bell, book, and candle; again crowned with ivy, when he seizes the Duke, claims his partners, beginning with the Pope, going down impartially through Emperor, King (the face is supposed to be that of Francis I.), nobleman, advocate, physician, ploughman, countess, old woman, little child, &c. &c., and leading each unwilling or willing victim in turn to the terrible dance. One woman meets her doom by Death in the character of a robber in a wood. Another, the Duchess, sits up in bed fully dressed, roused from her sleep by two skeletons, one of them playing a fiddle.

Granting the grotesqueness, freedom, variety, and wonderful precision of these woodcuts, I beg my readers to contrast their spirit with that of Albrecht Dürer's 'The Knight, Death, and the Devil,' or Orcagna's 'Triumph of Death.' In Holbein's designs there is no noble consoling faith; there is but a fierce defiance and wild mockery of inevitable fate, such as goes beyond the levity with which the Venetians in the time of the plague retired to their country-houses and danced, sung, and told tales, till the pestilence was upon them. It has a closer resemblance to the piteous madness with which the condemned prisoners during the French Reign of Terror rehearsed the falling of the guillotine, or the terrible pageant with which the same French, as represented by their Parisian brethren, professed to hail the arrival of the cholera.

Of the 'More Family' there are so many duplicates or versions, that, as in the case of Erasmus's picture, it is hard to say which is the original picture, or whether Holbein did more than sketch the original, or merely sketch the various heads to be afterwards put together by an inferior artist. A singular distribution of the light in the best authenticated picture has been supposed to favour this conjecture. But under any supposition, this, the second of the three noted English family pictures, is of the greatest interest. I shall record a minute and curious description given of this 'More Family,' which is still in the possession of a descendant of the Mores and Ropers.

'The room which is here represented seemed to be a large dining-room. At the upper end of it stands a chamber-organ on a cupboard, with a curtain drawn before it. On each end of the cupboard, which is covered with a carpet of tapestry, stands a flower-pot of flowers, and on the cupboard are laid a lute, a base-viol, a pint pot or ewer covered in part with a cloth folded several times, and *Boetius de Consolatione Philosophiæ*, with two other books upon it. By this

cupboard stands a daughter of Sir Thomas More's, putting on her right-hand glove, and having under her arm a book bound in red Turkey leather and gilt, with this inscription round the outside of the cover—*Epistolica Senecæ*. Over her head is written in Latin, *Elizabeth Dancy*, daughter of Sir Thomas More, aged 21.

'Behind her stands a woman holding a book open with both her hands, over whose head is written *Spouse of John Clements*. [38]

'Next to Mrs Dancy is Sir John More in his robes as one of the justices of the King's Bench, and by him Sir Thomas in his chancellor's robes (?), and collar of SS, with a rose pendant before. They are both sitting on a sort of tressel or armed bench, one of the arms and legs and one of the tassels of the cushion appear on the left side of Sir Thomas. At the feet of Sir John lies a cur-dog, and at Sir Thomas's a Bologna shock. Over Sir John's head is written, *John More, father, aged* 76. Over Sir Thomas's,

Thomas More, aged 50. Between them, behind, stands the wife of John More, Sir Thomas's son, over whose head is written *Anne Cresacre, wife of John More, aged* 15. Behind Sir Thomas, on his left hand stands his only son, John More, pictured with a very foolish aspect, and looking earnestly in a book which he holds open with both his hands. Over his head is written, *John, son of Thomas More, aged* 19.' (The only and witless son of the family, on whom Sir Thomas made the comment to his wife:—'You long wished for a boy, and you have got one—for all his life.')

'A little to the left of Sir Thomas are sitting on low stools his two daughters, Cecilia and Margaret. Next him is Cecilia, who has a boot in her lap, clasped. By her side sits her sister Margaret, who has likewise a book on her lap, but wide open, in which is written, *L. An. Senecæ—Oedipus—Fata si liceat mihi fingere arbitrio meo, tem-*

perem zephyro levi. On Cecilia's petticoat is written, *Cecilia Heron, Daughter of Thomas More, aged* 20, and on Margaret's, *Margaret Roper,*

daughter of Thomas More, aged 22.' (The best beloved, most amiable, and most learned of Sir Thomas's daughters, who visited him in the Tower and encouraged him to remain true to his convictions, while her step-mother urged him to abjure his faith. Margaret Roper intercepted her father on his return to the Tower after his trial, and penetrating the circle of the Guards, hung on his neck and bade him farewell. There is a tradition that she caused her father's head to be stolen from the spike of the bridge on which it was exposed, and, getting it preserved, kept it in a casket. She and her husband, William Roper, wrote together the biography of her father, Sir Thomas More.)

'Just by Mrs Roper sits Sir Thomas's lady in an elbow-chair (?), holding a book open in her hands. About her neck she has a gold chain, with a cross hanging to it before. On her left hand is a monkey chained, and holding part of it with one paw and part of it with the other. Over her head is written '*spouse of Thomas More, aged* 57.'

(Dame Alice More, the second wife of Sir Thomas More, a foolish and mean-spirited woman.)

'Behind her is a large arched window, in which is placed a flowerpot (a vase) of flowers, and a couple of oranges. Behind the two ladies stands Sir Thomas's fool, who, it seems, was bereft of his judgment by distraction. He has his cap on, and in it are stuck a red and white rose, and on the brim of it is a shield with a red cross on it, and a sort of seal pendant. About his neck he wears a black string with a cross hanging before him, and his left thumb is stuck in a broad leathern girdle clasp'd about him. Over his head is written *Henry Pattison, servant* of Thomas More. At the entrance of the room where Sir Thomas and his family are, stands a man in the portal who has in his left hand a roll of papers or parchments with two seals appendant, as if he was some way belonging to Sir Thomas as Lord Chancellor. Over his head is written *Joannes Heresius, Thomae Mori famulus.* In another room at some distance is seen through the door-case a man standing at a large bow-window, with short black hair, in an open sleeved gown of a sea-green colour, and under it a garment of a blossom-colour, holding a book open in his hands written or printed in the black letter, and reading very earnestly in it. About the middle of the room, over against Sir Thomas, hangs a clock with strings and leaden weights without any case.' [39]

It is notable that not one of Sir Thomas's sons-in-law is in this picture, neither is there a grandchild, though one or more is known to have been born at the date.

The miniature of Anne of Cleves, if it ever existed, is lost; it is probable that what was really referred to was the portrait of Anne by Holbein in the Louvre, where she appears 'as a kindly and comely woman in spite of her broad nose and swarthy complexion, but by no means such a painted Venus as might have deceived King Hal.' [40]

A well-known portrait by Holbein is that of a 'Cornish Gentleman,' with reddish hair and beard. I saw this portrait not long ago, as it was exhibited among the works of the Old Masters, and so much did it look as though the figure would step from the frame, that it was hard to believe that more than three hundred years had passed since the original walked the earth. [41]

Doubtless the last of Holbein's portrait pieces, which it is reported he left uncompleted when he died, is that of the 'Barber Surgeons,' painted on the occasion of the united company receiving their charter from the king, and including the king's portrait. This picture still hangs in the old company's hall.

I have only to say a few more words of those sketches which survive the destruction of the picture—Holbein's allegory of the 'Triumph of Riches,' and the 'Triumph of Poverty,' and of his portrait sketches. In the 'Triumph of Riches,' Plutus, an old man bent double, drives in a car, drawn by four white horses; before him, Fortune, blind, scatters money. The car is followed by Crœsus, Midas, and other noted misers and spendthrifts—for Cleopatra, the only woman present, is included in the group. In the 'Triumph of Poverty,' Poverty is an old woman in squalor and rags, who is seated in a shattered vehicle, drawn by asses and oxen, and guided by Hope and Diligence. The designs are large and bold. In the first, a resemblance to Henry VIII, is found in Crœsus. If the resemblance were intentional on Holbein's part, it showed the same want of tact and feeling which the painter early betrayed in his caricature of Erasmus.

But the best of Holbein's drawings are his portrait sketches with chalks, on flesh-tinted paper. These sketches have a history of their own, subsequent to their execution by Holbein. After being in the possession of the art-loving Earl of Arundel, and carried to France, they were lost sight of altogether for the space of a century, until they were discovered by Queen Caroline, wife of George II., in a bureau at Kensington. You will hear a little later that the finest collection of miniatures in England went through the same process of disappearance and recovery. [42] These original sketches, in addition to their great artistic merit, form a wonderful collection of speaking likenesses, belonging to the court of Henry VIII.,—likenesses which had been happily identified in time by Sir John Cheke (in the reign of Elizabeth), since the names of the originals have been inscribed on the back of each drawing, as it is believed, by Sir John Cheke's hand. The collection is now in the Queen's library, Windsor, with photographs at Kensington Museum. There are one or two of Holbein's reputed portraits at Hampton Court.

I must pass over some painters as not being sufficiently represented for my purpose. Among these is Sir Antony More, Philip II, of Spain's friend. It is recorded that Philip having rested his hand on the shoulder of More while at work, the bold painter turned round, and daubed the royal hand with vermilion. This gave rise to the courtier-saying that Philip 'made slaves of his friends, and friends of his painters.' Another is Zucchero, one of the painters who was requested by Queen Elizabeth to paint her picture without shade, the result being 'a woman with a Roman nose, a huge ruff and farthingale, and a bushel of pearls.' There are also Van Somer,—Janssens, who painted Lady Bowyer, named for her exquisite beauty, 'The star of the East,' and Susanna Lister, the most beautiful woman at court, when presented in marriage to Sir Geoffry Thornhurst by James I, in person, [43] —and Daniel Myttens, all foreigners, Flemish or Dutch, whom we must thus briefly dismiss. And now we come to Van Dyck.

Antony Van Dyck was born at Antwerp, in 1599. His father was a merchant; his mother was famous for painting flowers in small, and for needlework in silk. The fashion of painting 'in small' had prevailed for some time. Horace Walpole mentions that the mother of Lucas de Heere, a Flemish painter, born in 1534, could paint with such 'diminutive neatness' that she had executed 'a landscape with a windmill, miller, a cart and horse, and passengers,' which half a grain of corn could cover. At ten years of age, Van Dyck began to study as a painter, and he soon became a pupil, and afterwards a favourite pupil, of Rubens. In 1618, when Van Dyck was but a lad of seventeen years, he was admitted as a master into the painters' guild of St Luke. Two years later, he was still working with Rubens, who, seeing his lameness of invention, counselled him to abide by portrait painting, and to visit Italy. A year later, in 1621, when Van Dyck was twenty years of age, he came to London, already becoming a resort of Flemish painters, and lodging with a countryman of his own, worked for a short time in the service of James I.

On Van Dyck's return to Flanders, and on the death of his father, he was able to take Rubens' advice, and in 1623, when Van Dyck was still only twenty-two years of age, he set out for Venice, the Rome of the Flemish painters. Before quitting Antwerp, Van Dyck, in proof of the friendship which existed between the painters, presented Rubens with several of the former's pictures, among them his famous portrait of 'Rubens' wife.' As a pendant to this generosity, when Van Dyck came back to Antwerp, and complained to Rubens that he—Van Dyck—could not live on the profits of his painting, Rubens went next day and bought every picture of Van Dyck's which was for sale.

Van Dyck spent five years in Italy, visiting Venice, Florence, Rome, and Palermo, but residing principally at Genoa. In Italy, he began to indulge in his love of splendid extravagance, and in the fastidious fickleness which belonged to the evil side of his character. At Rome he was called 'the cavalier painter,' yet his first complaint on his return to Antwerp was, that he could not live on the profits of his painting! He avoided the society of his homelier countrymen.

At Palermo, Van Dyck knew, and according to some accounts, painted the portrait of Sophonisba Anguisciola, who claimed to be the most eminent portrait painter among women. She was then about ninety years of age, and blind, but she still delighted in having in her house a kind of academy of painting, to which all the painters visiting Palermo resorted. Van Dyck asserted that he owed more to her conversation than to the teaching of all the schools. A book of his sketches, which was recovered, showed many drawings 'after Sophonisba Anguisciola.' She is said to have been born at Cremona, was invited at the age of twenty-six by Philip II, to Spain, and was presented by him with a Spanish don for a husband, and a pension of a thousand crowns a-year from the customs of Palermo.

The plague drove Van Dyck from Italy back to Flanders, where he painted for a time, and presented his picture of the 'Crucifixion' to the Dominicans as a memorial gift in honour of his father, but in Flanders Rubens' fame overshadowed that of every other painter, and Van Dyck, recalling an invitation which he had received from the Countess of Arundel while still in Italy, came a second time to England, in 1630, when he was about thirty years of age, and lodged again with a fellow-countryman and painter named Gildorp. But his sensitive vanity was wounded by his not at once receiving an introduction to the king, or the countenance which the painter considered his due, and the restlessness, which was a prominent feature in his character, being re-awakened, he withdrew once more from England, and returned to the Low Countries in 1631. At last, a year later, in 1632, Van Dyck's pride was propitiated by receiving a formal invitation from Charles I., through Sir Kenelm Digby, to visit England, and this time the painter had no cause to complain of an unworthy reception. He was lodged by the king among his artists at Blackfriars, having no intercourse with the city, save by water. He had the king, with his wife and children, to sit to him, and was granted a pension of two hundred a-year, with the distinction of being named painter to his Majesty.

A year later Van Dyck was knighted. Royal and noble commissions flowed upon him, and the king, who had a hereditary love of art, visited the painter continually, and spent some of the happiest and most innocent hours of his brief and clouded life in Van Dyck's company. Thus began Van Dyck's success in England, and it rested with himself whether that success was to be real or only apparent, enduring or temporary.

To give you an example of how often, and in how many different manners, Van Dyck painted the king and royal family, I shall quote from a list of his pictures —

'King Charles in coronation robes.'

'King Charles in armour' (twice).

'King Charles in white satin, with his hat on, just descended from his horse; in the distance, view of the Isle of Wight.'

'King Charles in armour, on a white horse; Monsieur de St Antoine, his equerry, holding the king's helmet.'

'The King and Queen sitting; Prince Charles, very young, standing at the King's side; the Duke of York, an infant, on the Queen's knee.'

'The King and Queen holding a crown of laurel between them.'

'The Queen in white.'

'Prince Charles in armour' (two or three times).

'King, Queen, Prince Charles, and Princess Mary.'

'Queen with her five children.'

'Queen with dwarfs, [44] Sir Geoffrey Hudson having a monkey on his shoulder.'

Van Dyck had several great patrons, after the king. For the Earl of Arundel, in addition to portraits of the Earl and Countess, the painter designed a second Arundel family picture, which was painted by Fruitiers. For George, Duke of Buckingham, Van Dyck painted one of his finest double portraits of the Duke's two sons, when children. For the Northumberland family Van Dyck painted, besides portraits of Henry and Algernon, Earls of Northumberland, another famous picture, that of the two beautiful sisters, Lady Dorothy Percy, afterwards Countess of Leicester, and her sister, Lady Lucy Percy, afterwards Countess of Carlisle, whose charms figure frequently in the memoirs of her time. William and Philip, Earls of Pembroke, were also among his patrons, and for the second he painted his great family picture, 'The Wilton Family.' Sir Kenelm Digby, too, whose wife Venitia was more frequently painted than any woman of her day, and was not more distinguished for her beauty than for her lack of nobler qualities. Van Dyck alone painted her several times, the last after her sudden death, for her vain and eccentric, if gallant, husband, who in the end was no friend to Van Dyck.

But these high names by no means exhaust the list of patrons of a painter who, among various contradictory qualities, was indefatigably industrious. His work is widely distributed among the Scotch as well as the English descendants of the nobility whom he painted, so that the possession of at least one ancestral 'Van Dyck' accompanies very many patents of nobility, and is equivalent to a warrant of gentle birth.

The Earl of Clarendon, in the next reign, had a great partiality for Van Dyck's pictures, and was said to be courted by gifts of them until his apartments at Cornbury were furnished with full-length 'Van Dycks.' A third of his collection went to Kitty Hyde, Duchess of Queensberry, one of the Earl's three co-heiresses. Through the Rich family many of these 'Van Dycks' passed to Taymouth Castle, where by a coincidence they were lodged in the company of numerous works of George Jamieson of Aberdeen, who is said to have been for a short time a fellow-pupil of Van Dyck's under Rubens, who has been called 'the Scotch Van Dyck,' and who is certainly the first native painter who deserves honourable mention. Since the death of the last Marquis of Breadalbane these travelled 'Van Dycks' have gone back to the English representative of the Rich family.

Van Dyck had forty pounds for a half, and sixty pounds for a whole-length picture;—for a large piece of the King, Queen, and their children, he had a hundred pounds. For the Wilton family picture he had five hundred and twenty-five pounds. But Van Dyck soon impaired his fortune. He was not content with having a country-house at Eltham in Kent, where he spent a portion of each summer; he would emulate in his expenditure the most spendthrift noble of that reign. 'He always went magnificently dressed, and had a numerous and gallant equipage, and kept so good a table in his apartment that few princes were more visited and better served.' His marriage was not calculated to teach him moderation. In his thirty-ninth year the King gave him the hand of Marie Ruthven, who was nearly related to the unhappy Earl of Gowrie. She was his niece, her father having been the scarcely less unhappy younger brother Patrick, a physician, who, apprehended when a young man on the charge of being concerned in the treason of his elder brothers, spent his manhood in the Tower. He was kept a prisoner there from 1584 to 1619, nearly forty years, and was only released in his age and infirmity when his mind was giving way. Patrick Ruthven's infant daughter had been adopted, either through charity or perversity, by Anne of Denmark, and brought up first at the court of Anne, and afterwards at that of Henrietta Maria. The assertion that Marie Ruthven was a very beautiful woman has been contradicted. It was said that 'she was bestowed in marriage on Sir Antony Van Dyck as much to humble further the already humbled and still detested family of Ruthven, as to honour the painter; but this does not seem consistent with King Charles's known favour for Van Dyck. Yet such a view might have been entertained by Marie Ruthven herself, who, according to tradition, held herself degraded by the marriage, and never forgave the degradation. She was not a loving wife to a man who could hardly have been a very loving or loyal husband. And certainly the marriage did not unite the painter closer to the king.

With his professional industry, Van Dyck combined an equally unquenchable love of pleasure, which, with his luxurious and sedentary habits, induced paroxysms of gout, from which Rubens also suffered severely. This must have ultimately disqualified him for good work, and when his debts accumulated in greater proportion even than his receipts, in place of having recourse, like Rubens, to his painting-room, Van Dyck tried a shorter road to get rich, by following the idle example of Sir Kenelm Digby in his pursuit of alchemy and the philosopher's stone.

In the year of his marriage, Van Dyck re-visited Flanders, in company with his wife, and then repaired to France, it is understood with the intention of settling there. He was instigated to the step by his wife, and his own ambition of rivalling Rubens' triumphs at the Luxembourg; but the preference which the French gave to the works of their countryman, Nicolas Poussin, roused his latent jealousy, and so mortified him as to induce him to renounce his intention. He determined to return to England, and was, to his credit, confirmed in his resolution by the threatening civil war which was to shake his royal master's throne to the foundation, rather than deterred from it.

Again in England, Van Dyck employed Sir Kenelm Digby to make an offer on the painter's part that for eight hundred pounds he would paint the history, and a procession of the Knights of the Garter on the walls of the Knights' banqueting-room at Whitehall—that palace which was to have surpassed the Louvre, the Tuileries, and the Escurial, and from one of the windows of which Charles stepped out on his scaffold. But the proposal was rejected, and immediately afterwards the civil war broke out, and was speedily followed by the death of Van Dyck, about a year after his marriage, when he was a little over forty years old, at Blackfriars, in 1641. He was buried in old St Paul's, near the tomb of John of Gaunt. His daughter, Justiniana, was born a short time—some say only eight days—before her father died, and was baptized on the day of his death. Van Dyck left effects and sums due to him to the amount of twenty thousand pounds; but the greater part of the debts were found beyond recovery at the close of the civil war. His daughter grew up, and married a Mr Stepney, 'who rode in King Charles's life guards.' His widow re-married; her second husband was a Welsh knight.

Van Dyck's character was one of those that are made of very contradictory elements. He was actuated by opposite motives which are hard to analyze, and which in their instability have within themselves, whatever their outward advantages, the doom of failure in the highest excellence. He was a proud man, dissatisfied both with himself and his calling, resenting, with less reason than Hans Holbein showed, that he should be condemned to portrait painting, yet by no means undervaluing or slurring over his work. He 'would detain the persons who sat to him to dinner for an opportunity of studying their countenances and re-touching their pictures,' 'would have a sitter, sitting to him seven entire days, mornings and evenings, and would not once let the man see the picture till it pleased the painter.' Van Dyck appears to have been a man with the possibilities in him of greater things than he attained, possibilities which were baffled by his weakness and self-indulgence, leaving him with such a sense of this as spoiled his greatest successes.

I have the varying indications of two pictures of Van Dyck from which to get an impression of his personal appearance. The first picture is that of a youthful face, soft, smiling, with dark eyes, finely-formed nose, a slightly open mouth, having a full-cleft under lip, the hair profuse and slightly curled, but short, and no beard or moustache. The dress is an open doublet, without a collar, a lace cravat, and one arm half bare. The second is the picture of Van Dyck in the Louvre, which is judged the best likeness of the painter. In this his person is slender, his complexion fair, his eyes grey, his hair chestnut brown, his beard and whiskers red. He wears a vest of green velvet, with a plain collar.

In his art, Van Dyck, with something of the glow of Rubens, and with a delicacy peculiarly his own, was decidedly inferior to his great master, both in power and in fertility of genius. In the superficial refinement which was so essential a part of Van Dyck, he had the capacity of conferring on his sitters a reflection of his own outward stateliness and grace. When he painted at his best his portraits were solid, true, and masterly, but he has been reproached with sacrificing truth to the refining process which he practised. Even in the case of Charles I., whose portraits are our most familiar examples of Van Dyck, and who thus lives in the imagination of most people as the very personification of a noble and handsome cavalier, there have not been wanting critics who have maintained that Charles, — the son of a plain uncouth father, and of a mother rather floridly buxom than delicately handsome, and who was in his childhood a sickly rickety child, — was by no means so well endowed in the matter of manly beauty as we have supposed. These students of old gossip and close investigation, have alleged that Charles was long and lanky, after he had ceased to be Baby Charles; that his nose was too large, and, alas! apt to redden; that his eyes were vacillating; and his mouth, the loosely hung mouth of a man who begins by being irresolute, and ends by being obstinate. [45] Again, in the hands of a sitter, which Van Dyck was supposed to paint with special care and elegance, it has been argued that he copied always the same hand, probably his own, in ignorance, or in defiance of the fact that hands have nearly as much and as varying character as a painter can discover in faces. Though Van Dyck painted many beautiful women, he did not excel in rendering them beautiful on canvas, so that succeeding generations, in gazing on Van Dyck's versions of Venitia, Lady Digby, and Dorothy Sydney — Waller's Sacharissa, — have wondered how Sir Kenelm, Waller, and their contemporaries, could find these ladies so beautiful.

Van Dyck certainly owed something of the charm of his pictures to the dress of the period, with regard to which he received this credit that 'Van Dyck was the first painter who e'er put ladies' dress into a careless romance.' But in reality never was costume better suited for a painter like Van Dyck. The hair in the men was allowed to flow to the shoulders or gathered in a love knot, while the whiskers and beard formed a point. In the women the hair was crisped in curls round the face. The ruff in men and women had yielded to the broad, rich, falling collar, with deep scallops of point lace. Vest and cloak were of the richest velvet or satin, or else, on the breaking out of the civil war, men appeared in armour. The man's hat was broad and flapping, usually turned up at one side, and having an ostrich feather in the band; his long wide boots were of Spanish leather, and he wore gauntlet gloves, and rich ruffles at his wrists. The women wore hoods and mantles, short bodices, ample trains, and wide sleeves terminating in loose ruffles at the elbow, which left half of the arm bare. Pearl necklaces and bracelets, round feather fans, and 'knots of flowers,' were the almost universal ornaments of women. Another ornament of both men and women, which belonged to the day, and was very common in the quarters I have been referring to, was a miniature enclosed in a small case of ivory or ebony, carved like a rose, and worn on the left side in token of betrothal. [46] Van Dyck, along with the appreciation of black draperies which he held in common with Rubens, was specially fond of painting white or blue satin. He is said to have used a brown preparation of pounded peach-stones for glazing the hair in his pictures.

In the end, with all the aids that critics may have given him, and all the faults they may find in him, Van Dyck was a great, and in the main an earnest portrait painter. Perhaps 'Charles in white satin, just descended from his horse,' is the best of the single portraits which were held to be Van Dyck's forte.

I must try to give my readers some idea of Van Dyck's 'Wilton Family.' It has been so praised, that some have said 'it might have been covered with gold as a price to obtain it;' on the other hand, it has not escaped censure. One critic asserts that there is no common action uniting the figures, and that the faces are so different in complexion—one yellow-faced boy appearing either jaundiced or burnt by a tropical sun, that the family might have lived in different climates.

This is the story of the picture. 'Earl Philip of Pembroke having caused his family to meet, informs them with great emotion of the necessity of his eldest son Charles, Lord Herbert, going into the army of the Grand Duke of Tuscany, there to acquire military honour and experience, notwithstanding his having just married Mary, daughter of George, Duke of Buckingham. Lord Herbert is receiving the news with ardour, the young bride is turning aside her fair face to hide her tears. (Charles Lord Herbert was married Christmas, 1634, went to Florence, and died there of small pox, January, 1636.)

'In the Pembroke picture (or "Wilton Family") there are ten figures. The Earl and Countess are seated on a dais, under a coat of arms. He wears a great lace collar, an order on his breast, a key at his girdle, and has great shoes with roses. She has flowing curls, hanging sleeves, arms crossed, necklace on the bare neck. (The Countess of Pembroke was the Earl's second wife, Anne Clifford, daughter of George, Earl of Cumberland, the brave lady who defied Cromwell, and was fond of signing her name with the long string of titles derived from her two husbands, "Anne Dorset, Pembroke, Montgomery.") Robert Dormer, Earl of Carnarvon, is introduced with his wife, Lady Anne Sophia Herbert, daughter of Earl Philip; they are on the Countess's left hand. The daughter-in-law, about to be parted from her husband, stands on the lowest step of the dais; she is elegantly dressed, with hanging sleeves knotted with bows from shoulder to elbow. Two young men, the bridegroom and his brother, are at their father's right hand; they wear great falling collars and cloaks. There are three half-grown boys in tunics without collars, and great roses in their shoes, with a dog. The three little angels in the clouds are three daughters of the family who died in infancy.'

Van Dyck's finest sacred pictures were his early 'Crucifixion,' and a Pieta, at Antwerp. In these he gave a promise of nobler and deeper pathos than he afterwards fulfilled. His pictures are to be found freely, as I have written, in old English mansions, such as Arundel and Alnwick Castles, Knowsley, Knole, Petworth, &c. A head said to be by Van Dyck is in the National Gallery.

Van Dyck had few pupils: one, an Englishman named Dobson, earned an honourable reputation as a painter.

From Sir Antony More's time down to that of Leily and Kneller, the rage for portraits was continually increasing, and took largely the form of miniatures, which were painted chiefly by foreigners; notably by Hilliard and two Olivers or Oliviers, a father and son of French extraction, and by a Swiss named Petitot. A collection of miniatures by the Oliviers, including no less than six of Venitia, Lady Digby, had a similar fate to that of Holbein's drawings. The miniatures had been packed in a wainscot box and conveyed to the country-house in Wales of Mr Watkin Williams, who was a descendant of the Digby family. In course of time the box with its contents, doubtless forgotten, had been transferred to a garret, where it had lain undiscovered for, it has been supposed, fully a hundred years. It was two hundred years after the date of the painting of the miniatures, that on some turning over of the lumber in the garret, the exquisite miniatures, fresh as on the day when they were painted, were accidentally brought to light. [47]

Sir Peter Lely was born in Westphalia in 1618. His real name was Vander Facs, and his father was a 'Captain of Foot,' who, having chanced to be born in rooms over a perfumer's shop which bore the sign of a lily, took fantastically enough the name of Du Lys, or Lely, which he transmitted to his son. Sir Peter Lely, after studying in a studio at Haarlem, came to England when he was twenty-three years of age, in 1641, and set himself to copy the pictures of Van Dyck, who died in the year of Lely's arrival in England, and whom he succeeded as court painter. Lely was knighted by Charles II., married an English woman, and had a son and a daughter, who died young. He made a large fortune, dying at last of apoplexy, with which he was seized as he was painting the Duchess of Somerset, when he was sixty-two years of age, in 1680.

With regard to Lely's character, we may safely judge from his works that he was such a man as Samuel Pepys, 'of easy virtue,' a man holding a low enough standard by which to measure himself and others. Mr Palgrave quotes from Mr Leslie the following characteristic anecdote of Lely, which seems to prove that he was aware of, and coolly accepted, the decline of art in his generation and person. A nobleman said to Lely, 'How is it that you have so great a reputation, when you know, as well as I do, that you are no painter?' 'True, but I am the best you have,' was the answer. Lely's punishment followed him into his art, for beginning by copying Van Dyck, it is said of Lely that he degenerated in his work till it bore the very 'stamp of the depravity of the age.'

Lely's sitters were mostly women. Among them was one who deserved a fitter painter, Mistress Anne Killigrew, Dryden's—

'Youngest virgin daughter of the skies.'

In Lely's portrait of her, she is a neat, slightly prim, delicate beauty, with very fine features, and such sleepy eyes, as were probably the gift of Lely, since he has bestowed them generally on the women whom he painted. Mistress Anne Killigrew's hair is in curls, piled up in front, but hanging down loosely behind. Her bodice is gathered together by a brooch, and she has another brooch on one shoulder. She wears a light pearl necklace, and 'drops' shaped like shamrocks in her ears.

Lely painted both Charles I, and Cromwell, who desired his painters to omit 'no pimple or wart,' but to paint his face as they saw it.

Among less notable personages Lely painted Monk, Duke of Albemarle, and his rough Duchess, once a camp follower, according to popular rumour, and named familiarly by the contemptuous wits of the day 'Nan Clarges.' It is with not more honourable originals than poor 'Nan Clarges' that Lely's name as a painter is chiefly associated. We know what an evil time the years after the Restoration proved in England, and it was to immortalize, as far as he could, the vain, light women of the generation that Lely lent what skill he possessed. There their pictures hang in what has been called 'the Beauty Room' at Hampton Court, and no good man or woman can look at them without holding such beauty detestable.

At Hampton Court also there are several of the eleven portraits of Admirals whom Lely painted for James II, when Duke of York.

Antonio Canal, called **Canaletto,** incorrectly Canaletti, was born at Venice in 1697. He was the son of a scene painter at the theatre. In his youth he worked under his father; a little later he went to Rome, and studied for some time there. Then he came to England, where he remained only for two years. I have hesitated about placing his name among those of the foreign painters resident in England, but so many of his works are in this country that he seems to belong to it in an additional sense. He is said to have 'made many pictures and much money.' He died at Venice when he was seventy years of age, in 1768. As a painter he was famous for his correctness of perspective and precision of outline (in which it is alleged he aided himself by the use of the camera), qualities specially valuable in the architectural subjects of which he was fond, drawing them principally from his native Venice. But his very excellence was mechanical, and he showed so little originality or, for that matter, fidelity of genius, that he painted his landscapes in invariable sunshine.

The great wood-carver **Grinling Gibbons** deserves mention among the artists of this date. He was a native of Rotterdam, where he was born in 1648. He came to London with other carvers the year after the great fire of London, and was introduced by Evelyn to Charles II., who took him into his employment. 'Gibbons was appointed master carver in wood to George I., with a salary of eighteen-pence a day.' He died at his house in Bow Street in the sixty-third year of his age, in 1721. It is said that no man before Gibbons 'gave to wood the lightness of flowers.' For the great houses of Burghley, Petworth, and Chatsworth, Gibbons carved exquisite work, in festoons for screens, and chimney-pieces, and panels for pictures, of fruit, flowers, shells, and birds.

Sir Godfrey Kneller was born at Lübeck in 1646, and was the son of an architect. He is said to have studied under Rembrandt; but if this be true, it must have been in Kneller's early youth. It is more certain that he travelled in Italy and returned to settle in Hamburg, but changing his plans, he came to England, when he was about thirty years of age, in 1675. London became his home. There he painted portraits with great success; his prices being fifteen guineas for a head, twenty if with one hand, thirty for a half, and sixty for a whole-length portrait. Charles II, sat at the same time to Kneller and to Lely. Not Titian himself painted more crowned heads than it fell to the lot of Kneller to paint—not less than six reigning kings and queens of England, and, in addition, Louis XIV. of France, Charles VI, of Spain, and the Czar Peter of Russia.

William III, created Kneller a knight, and George I, raised the painter's rank to that of a baronet. Sir Godfrey was notorious for his conceit, irritability, and eccentricity, and for the wit which sparkled more in his conversation than in any originality of observation displayed in his painting. Walpole attributes to Kneller the opposite qualities of great negligence and great love of money. The negligence or slovenliness, whether in the man or the artist, did not interfere with an immense capacity for work, such as it was, but if Horace Walpole be right, that Kneller employed many Flemish painters under him to undertake the wigs, draperies, &c. &c., the amount of work in portrait painting which Sir Godfrey Kneller accomplished is so far explained. He attained the end of being a very rich man, and married an English woman, but left no family to succeed to his wealth and his country-seat of Whitton, when he died at his house in London in his seventy-eighth year, in 1723.

As a painter Sir Godfrey Kneller showed considerable talent in drawing, and a certain cumbrous dignity of design, but he had much more industry of a certain kind than artistic feeling or taste. When he and Lely painted Charles II, together, Kneller's application and rapidity of execution were so far before those of Lely, who was technically the better painter of the two, that Kneller's picture was finished when Lely's was dead-coloured only. Kneller was highly praised by Dryden, Addison, Prior, and Steele. Apropos of these writers, among the most famous works of Kneller are the forty-three portraits, painted originally for Tonson, the bookseller, of the members of the Kit Cat club, the social and literary club of the day, which got its name from the chance of its holding its meetings in a house the owner of which bore the unique name of Christopher Cat. Another series of portraits by Kneller are what ought to be, in their designation, the Hampton Court Beauties. These are still, like the other 'Beauties,' at Hampton. The second series was proposed by William's Queen Mary, and included herself, Sarah Jennings, Duchess of Marlborough, and Mary Bentinck. To Sarah Jennings men did award the palm of beauty, but poor Queen Mary, who had a modest, simple, comely, English face as a princess, had lost her fresh youthful charm by the time she became Queen of England, and was still further disfigured by the swelling of the face to which she was liable. Her proposal to substitute the worthier women of her court for the unworthy beauties of her uncle King Charles' court was not relished, and helped to render Mary unpopular—among the women, at least, of her nobility. Neither was Sir Godfrey Kneller qualified to enhance the attractions of Mary's maids of honour and ladies in waiting, who, to complete their disadvantages, lived at a period when it had become the fashion for women to crown their persons by an erection on their natural heads of artificial 'edifices of three heads.'

To Kneller, as I have already written, we owe the preservation of Raphael's cartoons.

CHAPTER XII. [48]

ITALIAN MASTERS FROM THE FOURTEENTH TO THE SEVENTEENTH CENTURIES—TADDEO GADDI, 1300, SUPPOSED TO HAVE DIED 1366—FRA FILIPPO, 1412-1469—BENOZZO GOZZOLI, 1424-1496—LUCA SIGNORELLI, 1441, SUPPOSED TO HAVE DIED ABOUT 1524—BOTTICELLI, 1447-1515—PERUGINO, 1446-1522—CARPACCIO, DATE AND PLACE OF BIRTH AND DEATH UNKNOWN—CRIVELLI—FILIPPINO LIPI, EARLIER THAN 1460—ANTONELLA DA MESSINA, BELIEVED TO HAVE

DIED AT VENICE, 1496—GAROFALO, 1481-1559—LUINI, DATE OF BIRTH UNKNOWN, SUPPOSED TO HAVE DIED ABOUT 1530—PALMA, ABOUT 1480-1528—PARDENONE, 1483-1538—LO SPAGNA, DATE OF BIRTH UNKNOWN, 1533—GIULIO ROMANO, 1492-1546—PARIS BORDONE, 1500-1570—IL PARMIGIANINO, 1503-1540—BAROCCIO, 1528-1612—CARAVAGGIO, 1569-1609—LO SPAGNOLETTO, 1593-1656—GUERCINO, 1592-1666—ALBANO, 1578-1660—SASSOFERRATO, 1605-1685—VASARI, 1513-1574—SOFONISBA ANGUISCIOLA, 1535, ABOUT 1620—LAVINIA FONTANA, 1552-1614.

Taddeo Gaddi, the most important of Giotto's scholars, was born in 1300, and was held at the baptismal font by Giotto himself. Gaddi rather went back on earlier traditions and faults. His excellence lay in his purity and simplicity of feeling. His finest pictures are from the life of the Virgin, in S. Croce, Florence. He was, like his master, a great architect as well as painter. He furnished the plans for the Ponte Vecchio and the Ponte della Trinità, and conducted the works of the campanile, Florence, after Giotto's death. He was possessed of great activity and industry. He is supposed to have died in 1366, and rests in the scene of his labours, since he was buried in the cloisters of S. Croce.

Fra Filippo, 1412-1469, a Carmelite friar. The romantic, scandalous life, including his slavery in Barbary, attributed to him by Vasari, the great biographer of the early Italian painters, has received no corroboration from modern researches. It is rather refuted. He always signed his pictures 'Frater Filippus,' and his death is entered in the register of the Carmine convent as that of 'Frater Filippus.' In all probability he was from first to last a monk, and not a disreputable one. He describes himself as the poorest friar in Florence, with six marriageable nieces dependent on him, and he is said to have been involved in debt.

His colouring was 'golden and broad,' in anticipation of that of Titian; his draperies were fine. He was wanting in the ideal, but full of human feeling, which was apt to get rude and boisterous; his angels were 'like great high-spirited boys.' Withal, his style of composition was stately. Among the best examples of his work are scenes from the life of St John the Baptist in frescoes in the choir of the Duomo at

Prato. His panel pictures are rather numerous. There are two lunette
⁴⁹ pictures by Fra Filippo in the National Gallery.

Benozzo Gozzoli, 1424—1496, a scholar of Fra Angelico, but resembling him only in light and cheerful colouring. He is said to
have been the first Italian painter smitten with the beauty of the
natural world. He was the first to create rich landscape backgrounds, and he enlivened his landscapes with animals. He displayed a fine fancy for architectural effects, introducing into his
pictures open porticoes, arcades, balconies, and galleries. He liked
to have subsidiary groups and circles of spectators about his principal figures. In these groups he introduced portraits of his contemporaries, true to nature and full of expression and delicate feeling.
His best work is in the Campo Santo, Pisa, scenes from the history
of the Old Testament, ranging from Noah to the Queen of Sheba.
The Pisans were so pleased with his work as to present him, in 1478,
with a sarcophagus intended to contain his remains when they
should be deposited in the Campo Santo. He survived the gift
eighteen years, dying in 1496. His easel pictures are rare, and do not
offer good representations of the master. There is one in the National Gallery—a Virgin and Child, with saints and angels.

Luca d'Egidio di Ventura, called also **Luca 'da Cortona,'** from his
birthplace, and **Luca Signorelli,** 1441, supposed to have died about
1524. His is a great name in the Tuscan School. He played an important part in the painting of the Sistine Chapel, though he is only
represented by one wall picture, the History of Moses. At his best he
anticipated Michael Angelo in power and grandeur, but he was
given to exaggeration. His fame rests principally on his frescoes at
Orvieto, where, by a strange chance, he was appointed, after an
interval of time, to continue and complete the work begun by Fra
Angelico, the master most opposed to Signorelli in style. Luca added the great dramatic scenes which include the history of Antichrist,
executed with a grandeur which 'only Lionardo among the painters
sharing a realistic tendency could have surpassed.' These scenes,
which contain The Resurrection, Hell, and Paradise, bear a strong
resemblance to the work of Michael Angelo. In his fine drawing of
the human figure Signorelli may be known by 'the squareness of his
forms in joints and extremities.' A conspicuous detail in his pictures

is frequently a bright-coloured Roman scarf. His work is rarely seen north of the Alps.

Sandro Filipepi, called **Botticelli,** 1447—1515. He was an apprentice to a goldsmith, and then became a scholar of Filippo Lipi's. Botticelli was vehement and impetuous, full of passion and poetry, seeking to express movement. He was the most dramatic painter of his school. Occasionally he rises to a grandeur that allies him to Signorelli and Michael Angelo. His circular pictures of the Madonna and Child, with angels, are numerous. Like Fra Filippo, Botticelli's angels are noble youths, some of them belonging to the great families of the time. They are prone to be ecstatic with joy or frantic with grief. There is a grand Coronation of the Virgin, by Botticelli at Hamilton Palace, and a beautiful Nativity by the old master belongs to Mr Fuller Maitland. His Madonna and Child are grand and tragic figures always. Botticelli's noble frescoes in the Sistine Chapel are apt to be overlooked because of Michael Angelo's 'sublime work' on the ceiling. There has been a revival of Botticelli's renown within late years, partly due to the new interest in the earlier Italian painters which Mr Browning has done something to stimulate.

I quote some thoughtful remarks on Botticelli by W.C. Lefroy in *Macmillan's Magazine*: 'Mr Ruskin, we know, divides Italian art into the art of faith, beginning with Giotto, and lasting rather more than 200 years, and the art of unbelief, or at least of cold and inoperative faith, beginning in the middle of Raphael's life. But whatever division we adopt, we must remember that the revival of Paganism, as a matter of fact, affected men in different ways. Right across the schools this new spirit draws its line, but the line is not a hard and sharp one. Some men lie wholly on one side of it, with Giotto, Angelico, and Orcagna; some wholly upon the other, with Titian and Correggio, but there are some on whom it seems to fall as a rainbow falls upon a hill-side. Such, for instance, is Botticelli. Now he tries to paint as men painted in the old days of unpolluted faith, and then again he breaks away and paints like a very heathen.

'The interest which this artist has excited in the present generation has been exaggerated into something like a fashion, and recent criticism has delighted to find or imagine in him the idiosyncrasies of recent thought. To us it may be he does in truth say more than he or his contemporaries dreamed of, but while true criticism will sternly refuse to help us to see in his pictures that which is purely subjective, it will, I think, recognise the fact that a day like ours is capable of reading in the subtle suggestions of ancient art thoughts which have only now come to be frankly defined or exquisitely analysed. To us, moreover, Botticelli presents not only the poem of the apparition of the young and beautiful manhood of humanism before the brooding and entranced, yet half expectant, maidenhood of mediævalism, but also the poem of the painter's own peculiar relation to that crisis. For us there is the poetry of the thing itself, and also the poetry of Botticelli's attempt to express it. The work of Botticelli does not supply a universal utterance for mankind like Shakespeare's plays, but when we stand before the screen on which his "Nativity" is hung, or contemplate in the adjoining room his two perplexed conceptions of "Aphrodite," we are face to face with a genuine outcome of that memorable meeting, mediævalism, humanism, and Savonarola, which no generation can afford to ignore, and our own especially delights to contemplate. There has been much dispute about the date of Botticelli's "Nativity," and some defenders of Savonarola have hoped to read 1511 in the strange character of its inscription, so that this beautiful picture, standing forth as the work of one for many years under the influence of "the Frate," may refute the common calumny that that influence was unfriendly to art. Our catalogue, indeed, unhesitatingly asserts of Botticelli, that "he became a follower of Savonarola and no doubt suffered from it;" but though there seems to be really little doubt that the "Nativity" was painted in 1500, the inscription, with its mystic allusion to the Apocalypse, and the whole character of the picture, afford unmistakable evidence of the influence of Savonarola.'

Pietro Perugino, 1446, died of the plague at Frontignano in 1522. Perugino is another painter who has been indebted to the last Renaissance. His fame, in this country rested chiefly on the circumstance that he was Raphael's master, whom the generous prince of painters delighted to honour, till the tide of fashion in art rose suddenly and floated old Pietro once more to the front. At his best he had luminous colour, grace, softness, and enthusiastic earnestness, especially in his young heads. His defects were monotony, and formality, together with comparative ignorance of the principles of his art. His conception of his calling in its true dignity was not high. His attempts at expressing ardour degenerated into mannerism, and he acquired habits and tricks of arrangement and style, among which figured his favourite upturned heads, that in the end were ill drawn, and, like every other affectation, became wearisome. In the process of falling off as an artist, when mere manual dexterity took the place of earnest devotion and honest pains, Perugino had a large studio where many pupils executed his commissions, and where, working for gain instead of excellence in art, he had the satisfaction, doubtless, of amassing a large fortune. Among his finest works is the picture of an enthroned Madonna and Child in the gallery of the Uffizi. Another fine Madonna with Saints is at Cremona. His frescoes in the Sala del Campio at Perugia are among his best works. The subjects of these frescoes are partly scriptural; partly mythological. In the execution there is excellence alike in drawing, colouring, and the disposal of drapery. A *chef d'œuvre* by the master is the Madonna of the Certosa at Pavia, now in, the National Gallery. Yet it is said to have been painted at the very period when Michael Angelo ridiculed Perugino's work as 'absurd and antiquated.' **Vittore Carpaccio,** date and place of birth unknown, though he is said to have been a native of Istria. He was a historical painter of the early Venetian School and a follower of the Bellini. His romantic *genre* pictures show the daily life of the Venice of his time, and are furnished with landscape and architectural backgrounds. His masterly and rich work is mostly in Venice. He introduces animals freely and well in his designs.

Carlo Crivelli was another master of the fifteenth century who deserves notice. He had strong individuality, yet was influenced by the Paduan and Venetian Schools. He displayed an old-fashioned preference for painting in tempera. Sometimes his drawing approaches that of Mantegna, while he has a gorgeousness of colouring all his own. His pictures occasionally show dignity of composition in combination with grace and daintiness; but he could be guilty of exaggerated vehemence of expression. He frequently introduced fruit, flowers, and birds in his work. He is fully represented in the National Gallery, his works there ranging from 'small tender pictures of the dead Christ with angels, to a sumptuous altar-piece in numerous compartments.'

Filippino Lipi was an adopted son and probably a relation of Fra Filippo's, though a scholar's use of his master's name was not uncommon. The date of his birth is earlier than 1460. Filippino was also a pupil of Botticelli's, while there was a higher sense of beauty and grace in the pupil than in the teacher. Among his last works is the Vision of St Bernard, an easel picture in the Badia at Florence. The apparition of the Madonna in this picture is said to be 'full of charm.' In his larger works he is one of the greatest historical painters of his country. Roman antiquities had the same keen interest for him which they held for the greatest of his contemporaries, and he made free use of them in the architecture of his pictures. He has fine work in the Carmelite Church, Florence, and in S. Maria Sopra Minerva, Rome. Much of some of his pictures is painted over. The National Gallery has a picture of Filippino's 'of grand execution,' though almost colourless — the Madonna and Child, with St Jerome and St Francis.

Antonella da Messina was the Neapolitan painter who brought the practice of painting in oils from the Netherlands into Italy, though it is now believed, from stubborn discrepancies in dates, that the story of his great friendship with Jan Van Eyck, as given by Vasari, is apochryphal. Very likely Hans Memling, called also 'John of Bruges,' was the real friend and leader of Antonella. His best work consisted of portraits. He is believed to have died at Venice in 1496.

Benvenuto Tisio, surnamed from the place of his birth **Garofalo,** was born in 1481, and died in 1559. He passed from the early school of Ferrara to that of Raphael. His conception was apt to be fantastic, while his colouring was vivid to abruptness, and he was deficient in charm of expression. He fell into the fault of monotonous ideality. At the same time his heads are beautiful, and his drapery is classic. His finest work is an 'Entombment' in the Borghese Palace, Rome. There is an altar-piece by Garofalo, a Madonna and Child with angels, in the National Gallery.

Bernardo Luini, who stands foremost among the scholars of Lionardo da Vinci, was born by the Lago Maggiore, the date unknown, came to Milan in 1500, was elderly in 1525, and is supposed to have died not long after 1530. His work is chiefly found in Milan. His great merit has been only lately acknowledged. He is not 'very powerful or original,' but for 'purity, grace, and spiritual expression,' he ranks very high. He unites the earnestness of the older masters with the prevailing feeling for beauty of the great masters of Italian Art. His pictures were long mistaken for those of his master, Lionardo, though it is said that when the difference between them is once pointed out, it is easily recognised; indeed, the resemblance is confined to a smiling beatific expression in the countenances, which abounds more in Luini's pictures. His heads of women, children, and angels present every degree of serenity, sweet cheerfulness and happiness, up to ecstatic rapture. 'Christ Disputing with the Doctors,' in the National Gallery, formerly called a Lionardo, is now known to be a Luini. He painted much, whether in tempera, fresco, or oil. His favourite subjects in oil were the Madonna and Child, with St John and the Lamb, and the Marriage of St Catherine. Probable he appears to greatest advantage in frescoes. He is said to have reached his highest perfection in the figure of St John in a Crucifixion in the Monasterio Maggiore, Milan.

Jacopo Palma, called **Il Palma Vecchio,** was born about 1480 near Bergamo, and died in 1528. He is believed to have studied under Giovanni Bellini, while he is also the chief follower of Giorgione. His characteristics are ample forms and gorgeous breadth of drapery. His female saints, with their large rounded figures, have a soft yet commanding expression. He had an enchanting feeling for landscape, which seems to have been the birthright of the Venetian painters. To Palma is owing what are called 'Santa Conversazione,' where there are numerous groups round the Virgin and Child, as if they are holding a court in a retired and beautiful country nook. Palma rivalled Giorgione and Titian as a painter of women's portraits. Among these is that of his daughter Violante, believed to have been loved by Titian. 'Palma's three Daughters,' in the Dresden Gallery, is a masterpiece of 'fair, full-blown beauty.' The hair of the women is of the curiously bleached yellow tint affected then by the Venetian ladies. Palma painted many pictures, leaving at his death forty-our unfinished.

Giovanni Antonio da Pardenone, born 1483, died 1538. He had
many names, 'Pardenone' from his birthplace, 'Corticellis' from that
of his father, and he is believed to have assumed the name 'Regillo'
after he received knighthood from the King of Hungary. He was
Venetian in his artistic qualities. Many of his works are in his native
Pardenone and in obscure towns near. All have suffered and some
are now hidden by whitewash. His chief strength lay in fresco. His
scenes from the Passion in the cathedral, Cremona, are greatly dam-
aged and wretchedly restored, but they still reveal the painter as a
great master. They have 'fine drawing, action, excellent colouring,
grand management of light and shade, with freedom of hand and
dignity of conception.' In the prophets and sybils around the cupola
of the Madonna di Campagna, Piacenza, Pardenone's power is fully
proven. His immense works in fresco account for the rarity of his oil
pictures and their comparative inferiority. There is only one picture,
and that a portrait, indisputably assigned to Pardenone in England,
in the Baring Collection.

Giovanni di Pietro, known as **Lo Spagna (the Spaniard),** was a
contemporary of Raphael's, a fellow-pupil of his under Perugino.
There is no record of the time and place of Lo Spagna's birth. He
died in 1533. He was a careful, conscientious follower of Perugino
and Raphael, doing finished and delicate work; an 'Assumption' in
a church at Trevi is a fine example of his qualities. His best picture
was painted in 1516, and is at Assisi. It represents the Madonna
enthroned with three saints on each side. In his later works he betrayed feebleness. Pictures by Lo Spagna are often attributed to
Raphael.

Giulio Pippi, surnamed **Romano,** born in 1492, died in 1546, was
a very different painter, while he was the most celebrated of Raphael's scholars. He had a vigorous, daring spirit, with a free hand and
a bold fancy. So long as he painted under Raphael, Giulio followed
his master closely, especially in his study of the antique, but he
lacked the purity and grace of his teacher, on whose death, the pupil leaving Rome, pursued his own coarser, more vehement impulses. The frescoes in the Villa Modama, Rome, are good examples of
his style, so is the altar-piece of the Martyrdom of St Stephen in S.
Stefano, Genoa. Giulio Romano was the architect who designed the
rebuilding of half Mantua. His best easel picture in England is the

'Education of Jupiter by Nymphs and Corybantes,' in the National Gallery. In Raphael's lifetime his principal scholar was accustomed to work on the master's pictures, and on his death Giulio, together with another pupil, Gianfrancesco Penni, were left executors of Raphael's will and heirs of his designs.

Paris Bordone was born at Treviso in 1500 and died in 1570. He was educated in the Venetian School, and remained remarkable for delicate rosy colour in his flesh tints and for purple, crimson, and shot hues in his draperies, which were usually small and in crumpled folds. His *chef d'œuvre* is in the Venetian Academy. It is a fisherman presenting a ring to the Doge, and is a large and fine picture with many figures. He dealt frequently in mythological or poetic subjects. There is an example of the first in the National Gallery. He was great in single female subjects and women's portraits. There is a portrait by Bordone of a lovely woman of nineteen belonging to the Brignole family, in the National Gallery. He had often fine landscape and grand architecture in his pictures.

Il Parmigianino, born 1503, died 1540, was a follower of Correggio's. In Parmigianino's case the danger of the master's peculiarities became apparent by the lapse into affectation and frivolity. 'His Madonnas are empty and condescending, his female saints like ladies in waiting.' Still there were certain indestructible beauties of the master which yet clung to the scholar. He had clear warm colouring, decision, and good conception of human life. He was highly successful in portraits. There is a splendid portrait by Parmigianino, said to be Columbus, in Naples. Among his celebrated pictures is 'The Madonna with the Long Neck,' in the Pitti Palace. An altarpiece in the National Gallery, which represents a Madonna in the clouds with St John the Baptist appearing to St Jerome, is a good example of Parmigianino. It is said that he was engrossed with this picture during the siege of Rome in 1527. The soldiers entered the studio intent on pillage, but surprising the master at his work, respected his enthusiasm and protected him.

Federigo Baroccio, of Urbino, born in 1528, died in 1612, was also a follower of Correggio's, and made a stand against the decline of art in his day. He was tender and idyllic, though apt in his turn to be affected and sentimental. When painting in the Vatican, Rome, his rivals sought to take his life by poison. The attempt caused Baroccio to return to Urbino, where he established himself and executed his commissions.

Amirighi da Caravaggio was born at Caravaggio in 1569, and died at Porto Ercole in 1609. He was chief of the naturalistic school, the members of which painted common nature and violent passions in bitter opposition to the eclectics, especially the Caracci. The feud was sometimes carried on appositely enough on the side of the naturalistic painters by poison and dagger. Caravaggio was distinguished by his wild temper and stormy life, in keeping with his pictures. He resided principally in Rome, but dwelt also in Naples. He is vulgar but striking, even pathetic in some of his pictures. The 'Beheading of John the Baptist,' in the Cathedral, Malta, is one of his masterpieces. His Holy Families now and then resemble gipsy *ménages*.

Guiseppe Ribiera, a Spaniard, and so called **Lo Spagnoletto,** was born 1593 and died 1656. He followed Caravaggio, while he retained reminiscences of the Spanish School and of the Venetian masters. Some of his best pictures, such as 'the Pieta with the Marys and the Disciples,' and his 'Last Supper,' are in Naples. He had a wild fancy with a preference for horrible subjects—executions, tortures—in this respect resembling Domenichino. Lo Spagnoletto is said to be particularly unpleasant in his mythological scenes. Many of his pictures have blackened with time. His 'Mary of Egypt standing by her open Grave' is a remarkable picture in the Dresden Gallery.

Giovanni Francesco Barbiera, surnamed Guercino da Cinto, approached the school of the Caracci. In his art he resembled Guido Reni, with the same sweetness, greater liveliness, and fine chiaroscuro. 'Dido's Last Moments' and 'St Peter raising Tabitha' in Rome and in the Pitti Palace are fine examples of Guercino's work. His later pictures, like Guido's, are fascinating in softness, delicate colouring and tender sentiment, degenerating, however, into mannerism and insipidity, while his colouring becomes at last pale and washy.

Albano, born 1578, died 1660. He had elegance and cheerfulness which hardly rose to grace. He painted mostly scenes from ancient mythology, such as 'Venus and her Companions.' Religious subjects were comparatively rare with him; one, however, often repeated was the 'Infant Christ sleeping on the Cross.'

Giovanni Battista Salvi, surnamed from his birthplace **Sassoferrato,** was born in 1605 and died in 1685. He followed the scholars of the Caracci, but with some independence, returning to older and greater masters. His art was distinguished by a peculiar but slightly affected gentleness of conception, pleasing and sweet—with the sweetness verging on weakness. He finished with minute care. He gave constant representations of the Madonna and Child and Holy Families in a domestic character. In one of his pictures in Naples the Madonna is engaged in sewing. His most celebrated, 'Madonna del Rosario,' is in S. Sabina, Rome. The Madonna bending in ecstatic worship over an infant Christ lying on a cushion is in the Dresden Gallery.

Giorgio Vasari was born at Arezzo in 1512 and died at Florence in 1574. He was an architect, or jeweller, and a historical painter of heavy crowded pictures. His lives of the early Italian painters and sculptors up to his own time, the sixteenth century, though full of traditional gossip, are invaluable as graphic chronicles of much interesting information which would otherwise have been lost.

Sofonisba Anguisciola, born 1535, died about 1620, was a pupil of Bernardino Campi about the close of the sixteenth century at Cremona. She is justly praised by Vasari. Though her works are rare there are a few in England and Scotland. Three of her pictures which are mentioned with high commendation by Dr. Waagen are, 'a nun in the white robes of her order, nobly conceived and delicately coloured,' in Lord Yarborough's collection; in Mr Harcourt's collection, 'her own portrait, still very youthful, delicate, charming, and clear;' and in the collection of the late Sir W. Stirling Maxwell, 'another portrait of herself at an easel painting the Virgin and Child on wood, delicately conceived, clear in colour, and very careful.'

Lavinia Fontana, born in 1552, died 1614, was a daughter of Prospero Fontana, who belonged to the fast degenerating Bolognese artists at the close of the sixteenth and beginning of the seventeenth century. She was a better artist than her fellow painters, worked cleverly and boldly, and showed truth to nature. She has left excellent portraits. In the late Sir W. Stirling Maxwell's collection there is a picture by her, 'Two girls in a boat with a youth rowing,' on wood, 'of very graceful motive and careful treatment,'

CHAPTER XIII. [50]

GERMAN, FLEMISH, AND DUTCH ARTISTS FROM THE FIFTEENTH TO THE EIGHTEENTH CENTURY—VAN DER WEYDEN, A CONTEMPORARY OF THE VAN EYCKS, 1366-1442—VAN LEYDEN, 1494-1533—VAN SOMER, 1570-1624—SNYDERS, 1579-1657—G. HONTHORST, 1592-1662—JAN STEEN, 1626-1679—GERARD DOW, 1613-1680—DE HOOCH, DATES OF BIRTH AND DEATH UNKNOWN—VAN OSTADE, 1610-1685—MAAS, 1632-1693—METZU, 1615, STILL ALIVE IN 1667—TERBURG, 1608-1681—NETCHER, 1639-1684—BOL, 1611-1680—VAN DER HELST, 1613-1670—RUYSDAEL, 1625 (?)-1682—HOBBEMA, 1638-1709—BERCHEM, 1620-1683—BOTH, 1610 (?)-1650 (?)—DU JARDIN, 1625-1678—ADRIAN VAN DE VELDE, 1639-1672—VAN DER HEYDEN, 1637-1712—DE WITTE, 1607-1692—VAN DER NEER, 1619(?)-1683—WILLIAM VAN DE VELDE THE YOUNGER, 1633-1707—BACKHUYSEN, 1631-1708—VAN DE CAPELLA, ABOUT 1653—HONDECOETER, 1636-1695—JAN WEENIX, 1644-1719—PATER SEGERS, 1590-1661—VAN HUYSUM, 1682-1749—VAN DER WERFF, 1659-1722—MENGS, 1728-1774.

Roger van der Weyden was a contemporary of the Van Eycks, born at Tournai. His early pictures in Brussels are lost. He visited Italy in 1439, and was treated with distinction at Ferrara. His Flemish realistic cast of mind and artistic power remained utterly unaffected by the grand Italian pictures with which he came in contact; so did his profound earnestness, which must have been great indeed, since its effects are felt through all impediments down to the present day. His expressive realism chose subjects in which the sentiments of grief and pity could be most fitly shown. He sternly rejected any suggestion to idealise the human form, and paint heads, hands, or feet different from those in ordinary life. 'It is the simplicity with which he gives expression by large and melancholy eyes, thought by projections of the forehead, grief by contracted muscles, and suffering by attenuation of the flesh which touches us.' The deadly earnestness of the man impresses the spectator at this distant date. 'There is no smile in any of his faces, but there is many a face wrung with agony, and there is many a tear.' He objected to shadow in every form, and filled his pictures with an invariable atmosphere and light—those which belong to dawn before sunrise. Among his finer works are a triptych [51] belonging to the Duke of Westminster, a 'Last Judgment' in the Hospital at Bearne, and a large 'Descent from the Cross' in Madrid. In the triptych in the centre is Christ with black hair, which is unusual, in his left hand the globe. On his right is the Virgin Mary, on his left St John the Evangelist; on the right wing is St John the Baptist, on his left the Magdalene.

Lucas Van Leyden was born in 1494 and died in 1533. He painted both scriptural subjects and everyday scenes, being a man of varied powers. He worked admirably for his time, and added to his art that of an engraver. He followed the Van Eycks, but lowered their treatment of sacred subjects. In incidents taken from common life he showed himself full of observation, and possessed of some humour. His pictures are rare. A 'Last Judgment,' in the Town House, Leyden, is a striking but unpleasant example of Lucas Van Leyden's work.

Paul Van Somer was born at Antwerp in 1570, and died in 1624. He worked for many years in England, where his best works—portraits—remain. He was truthful, a good colourist, and finished carefully. His portraits of Lord Bacon at Panshanger and of the Earl and Countess of Arundel at Arundel Castle are well known.

Frans Snyders was born in 1579, and died, at Antwerp in 1657. After Rubens, Snyders was the greatest Flemish animal painter. He painted along with Rubens often, Snyders supplying the animals and Rubens the figures. Frans Snyders paid a visit to Italy and Rome, from which he seems to have profited, judging by his skill in arrangement. This skill he displayed also in his kitchen-pieces (magnificent shows of fruit, vegetables, game, fish, &c.), which, like his animal pictures, are numerous. In one of these kitchen-pieces in the Dresden Gallery, Rubens and his second wife are said to figure as the cooks. Princes and nobles bade for Snyders' pictures. There is a famous 'Boar Hunt' in the Louvre, in Munich 'Lionesses Pursuing a Roebuck,' in Vienna 'Boar attacked by Nine Dogs.' Snyders' animal pictures are full of energetic action and fierce passion. To these qualities is frequently added hideous realism in detail. There are many Snyders in English galleries.

Gerard Honthorst was born at Utrecht in 1592, and died in 1662. He was a follower of Caravaggio. He visited Italy and found favour in Rome, where he got from his night-pieces Correggio's name, 'Della Notte.' Honthorst was summoned to England by Charles I., for whom he painted several pictures. He entered the service of Prince Frederick Henry of Orange, and painted also for the King of Denmark. He left an extraordinary number of works, sacred, mythological, historical, and latterly many portraits. He drew well and painted powerfully, but was coarsely realistic in his treatment. At Hampton Court there are two of his best portraits, those of the unfortunate Queen of Bohemia and the Duke of Buckingham and his family. Gerard Honthorst's younger brother, William, was a portrait painter not unlike the elder brother in style.

Jan Steen was born at Leyden in 1626, and died in 1679. He was great as a *genre* painter. He is said to have been, after Rembrandt, the most humorous of Dutch painters, full of animal spirits and fun. At his best, composition, colouring, and execution were all in excellent keeping. At his worst, he was vulgar and repulsive in his heads, and careless and faulty in his work. He was very rarely either kindly or reverent in his subjects, though, in spite of what is known to have been his riotous life, he is comparatively free from the grossness which is often the shame of Flemish and Dutch art. Jan Steen succeeded his father as a brewer and tavern-keeper at Delft. He renounced the brewery, in which he did not succeed, and joined the Painters' Guild, Haarlem; but his position as a tavern-keeper is reflected in his pictures, of which eating and drinking, card-playing, &c., are frequently the *motifs*. His family relations were not conducive to higher principles and tastes. He is said to have been so lost to common feeling as to have painted his first wife when she was in a state of intoxication. [52] His second wife may have been a worthier woman, but she was drawn from the lowest class, and had been accustomed to sell sheeps' heads and trotters in the butchers' market. Without doubt Jan Steen had extraordinary genius coexisting with his coarse, careless nature and jovial habits, and he must have worked with great facility, since, in spite of his idleness and comparatively early death, he left as many as two hundred pictures, of which two-thirds are in this country, where his broad humour has rendered him extremely popular. Besides his favourite subjects, such as 'The Family Jollification,' 'The Feast of the Bean King,' 'Game of Skittles,' he has pictures in a slightly higher atmosphere, such as 'A Pastor Visiting a Young Girl,' 'The Parrot,' 'Schoolmaster with Unmanageable Boys,' 'The Pursuit of Alchemy.' Among the latter a good example is 'The Music Master' in the National Gallery.

Gerard Dow was born in 1613 and died in 1680. He was a *genre* painter of great merit. He belonged to Leyden, and was a pupil of Rembrandt. He began with portraiture, often painting his own face, and went on to scenes from low and middle-class life, but rarely attempted to represent high society. Compared to Jan Steen, however, he is refined. He had a curious fondness for painting hermits. The lighting of his pictures is frequently by lantern or candle. They are mostly small, and without animated action, but are full of picturesqueness. He was a good colourist, 'with a rare truth to nature and a marvellous distinctness of eye and precision of hand.' Minute as his execution was, his touch was 'free and soft.' His best pictures are 'like nature's self seen through the camera obscura.' An instance often given of his exquisite finish is that of a broom in the corner of one of his pictures. Some contemporary had remarked how careful and elaborate was the labour bestowed on it, when the painter answered that he was still to give it several hours' work. He must have been exceedingly industrious as well as painstaking, since he left two hundred pictures as his contribution to Dutch art. Among his finer pictures are 'An Old Woman reading the Bible to her Husband,' in the Louvre; 'The Poulterer's Shop,' in the National Gallery. His *chef d'œuvre*, 'The Woman Sick of the Dropsy,' is in the Louvre. His candlelight is the finest rendered by any master. There is a good example of it in 'The Evening School,' in the Amsterdam Gallery.

Peter de Hooch—spelt often, **De Hooge** —was the *genre* painter of full, clear sunlight. The dates of his birth and death can only be guessed by those of his pictures, which extend from 1656 to 1670. His groups are generally playing cards, smoking, drinking, or engaged in domestic occupations—almost always in the open air. No other *genre* painter can compare with him in reproducing the effects of sunlight. His prevailing colour is red, varied and repeated with great delicacy. English lovers of art brought De Hooch into favour, and many of his pictures are in England. There are fine examples—'The Court of a Dutch House' and 'A Courtyard'—in the National Gallery.

Adrian van Ostade was born at Haarlem in 1610 and died in his native town in 1685. He has been called 'the Rembrandt of *genre* painters,' and, like Rembrandt, he was without the sense of human beauty and grace, for even his children are ugly; yet it is the purer, happier side of national life which he constantly represents, and he had great feeling for nature, with picturesqueness and harmony of design and colouring, as well as mastery of the technique of his art. He suffered many hardships in his youth, and grew up a quiet, industrious, family man. He left a very large number of pictures, nearly four hundred, many of them good, and not a few in England. 'The Alchemist' [53] is in the National Gallery.

Maas, born in 1632, died in 1693, is a much-prized *genre* painter, whose pictures are rare. He was a pupil of Rembrandt. He is said to have treated 'very simple subjects with naïve homeliness and kindly humour.' His pictures are 'well lit, with deep warm harmony, and a vigorous touch.' 'The Idle Servant-maid,' in the National Gallery, is a masterpiece.

Metzu, like Terburg, is *par excellence* one of the two painters of Dutch high life. Metzu was born in 1615, and is known to have been alive in 1667. He painted both on a large and a small scale, and occasionally departed from his peculiar province to represent market-scenes, &c. He is the most refined and picturesque of *genre* painters on a small scale. Among his *chefs d'œuvre* are a 'Lady holding a Glass of Wine and receiving an Officer,' in the Louvre; and a 'Girl writing, a Gentleman leaning on her chair and another girl opposite playing the Lute,' in the Hague Gallery. The fine 'Duet,' and the 'Music Lesson' are both in the National Gallery.

Gerard Terburg was born at Zwol, in 1608, and died in 1681. He visited Germany and Italy in his youth. His small groups and single figures, taken from the wealthier classes, with their luxurious surroundings, are 'given with exquisite delicacy and refinement.' Included in his masterpieces are a 'Girl in white satin (a texture which he rendered marvellously) washing her hands in a basin held before her by a maid-servant,' in the Dresden Gallery; an 'Officer in confidential talk with a Young Girl, and a Trumpeter who has brought him a Letter,' in the Hague Gallery; a 'Young Lady in white satin sitting playing the Lute,' in the Chateau of Wilhelmshöe, at Cassell. There are twenty-three Terburgs in England and Scotland.

Caspar Netcher, born in 1639, died in 1684. He formed himself upon Metzu and Terburg. He is the great Dutch painter of childhood. His finest works are in the Dresden Gallery. In the National Gallery is his 'Children blowing Bubbles.'

Ferdinand Bol was born at Dordrecht in 1611, and died at Amsterdam in 1680. He was a student of Rembrandt's, and distinguished himself in sacred and historical pictures, and especially in portraits. He followed his master in his youth, fell off in his art in middle life, but became again excellent in his later years. Among his fine pictures are 'David's Charge to Solomon,' in the Dublin National Gallery; and 'Joseph presenting his father Jacob to Pharaoh,' in the Dresden Gallery. His last portraits are considered very fine. They are taken in the fullest light, and have a surprising amount of animation. Such a portrait, called 'The Astronomer,' is in the National Gallery. [54]

Jacob Ruysdael was born in 1625(?) at Haarlem. In 1668 he was in Amsterdam, and acted as witness to the marriage of Hobbema, whose lack of worldly prosperity Ruysdael shared. He himself was unmarried, and maintained his father in his old age. In the prime of life Jacob Ruysdael in turn fell into extreme poverty, and died an inmate of the Haarlem Almshouse in 1682 — a sad record of Holland's greatest landscape painter, for 'beyond dispute' Ruysdael is the first of the famous Dutch landscape painters.

'In no other is there the feeling for the poetry of Northern nature united with perfect execution, admirable drawing, great knowledge of chiaroscuro, powerful colouring, and a mastery of the brush which ranged from the minutest touch to broad, free execution.' His prevailing tone of colour is a full, decided green, though age has given many of his pictures a brown tone. A considerable number of his pictures are in a greyish, clear, cool tone (good examples of the last are to be seen in the Dresden Gallery). He generally painted the flat Dutch country in tranquil repose. He dealt usually in heavy clouded skies which told of showers past and coming, and dark sheets of water overshadowed by trees, lending a melancholy sentiment to the picture. He was fond of wide expanses of land and water, fond also of introducing the spires of his native Haarlem, touching the horizon line. He has left a few sea-pieces, always with cloudy heavens and heaving or raging seas; [55] where he has given sketches of sea, and shore, the ærial perspective is rendered in tender gradations 'full of pathos.' He has other pictures representing hilly, even mountainous, landscapes. In these foaming waterfalls form a prominent feature. Ruysdael was weak in his drawing of men and animals, in which he was occasionally assisted by fellow-artists, such as Berchem and Van de Velde. Among his finest pictures are 'A View of the Country round Haarlem,' in the Museum of the Hague; 'A flat country, with a road leading to a village and fields with wheat sheaves,' in the Dresden Gallery; 'A hilly bare country through which a river runs; the horseman and beggar on a bridge, by Wouvermans,' in the Louvre. His most remarkable waterfall is in the Hague Museum. In the Dresden Gallery there is 'A Jewish Cemetery,' 'full of melancholy.' Three of Ruysdael's fine waterfalls are in the National Gallery. Of two very grand storms which he painted one is in the Louvre, the other in the collection of the Marquis of Lansdowne at Bowood. There are many of Ruysdael's pictures in England. In the great landscape painter, as in the other renowned Dutch artists of the seventeenth century, the influence of Rembrandt is marked.

Meindert Hobbema was born in 1638, married in 1638, and died in poverty at Amsterdam in 1709. His works, which were neglected in his lifetime, now fetch much more than their weight in gold. Sums as large as four thousand pounds have been paid more than once for a Hobbema, yet his name was not found in any dictionary of art or artists for more than a century after his death. The English were the first to acknowledge Hobbema's merit, and nine-tenths of his works are in England, where he is the most popular Dutch landscape painter. But he is said by judges to have less invention and less poetic sensibility than his contemporary and friend Ruysdael. Hobbema's subjects are usually villages surrounded by trees like those in Guelderland, water-mills, a slightly broken country, with groups of trees, wheatfields, meadows, and small pools, more rarely portions of towns, and still more seldom old castles and stately mansions. [56] He has all the lifelike truthfulness of the Dutch artists. In tone he is as warm and golden as Ruysdael is cool in his greens. In the National Gallery there are excellent specimens of Hobbema, such as 'The Avenue Middelharnis' and 'A Landscape in Showery Weather.'

Nicolas Berchem, often spelt **Berghem,** was born at Haarlem in 1620, and died at Amsterdam in 1683. He was an excellent Dutch landscape painter. He had evidently visited Italy, and displayed great fondness for Italian subjects. His pictures show 'varied composition, good drawing, fine ærial effects, freedom, playfulness, and spirit.' As a colourist he was unequal, being often warm and harmonious, but at other times heavy and cold. It is clear that he was no student of life, from the monotony of his shepherds and shepherdesses and the sameness of his animals. He was naturally industrious, and was spurred on, as a still greater artist is said to have been, by the greed of his wife. He painted upwards of four hundred pictures, besides doing figures and animals for other painters. The great northern European galleries are rich in his works. One of his best pictures, 'A Shepherdess driving her cattle through a ford in a rocky landscape,' where the cool tone of the landscape is contrasted with the golden tone of the cattle, is in the Louvre. Another fine picture, 'Crossing the Ford,' is in the National Gallery.

Jan Both, born in 1610 (?), died in 1650 (?), was another Dutch landscape painter still more spellbound by Italy, [57] which he visited, and where he fell under the influence of Claude Lorraine. Both devoted himself thenceforth to Italian landscape to a greater degree than was practised by any other Dutch painter. He was excellent in drawing and skilful in rendering the golden glories of Italian sunsets. He painted freely and with solidity. The figures of men and animals in his pictures were often introduced by his brother Andreas. Jan Both excelled both in large and small pictures, but he was most uninterestingly uniform in design. He had generally a foreground of lofty trees, and for a background a range of mountains rising step by step, with a wide plain at their feet. Sometimes he introduced a waterfall or a lake. He rarely painted particular points in a landscape. His life was not a long one, so that his pictures do not number more than a hundred and fifty. Occasionally his warm

tone of colouring degenerates to a foxy red. One of Both's best pictures—a landscape in which the fresh light of morning is apparent—is in the National Gallery.

Karil du Jardin, born in 1625, died in 1678, is a third great Dutch
landscape painter, whose fancy Italy laid hold of, so that he settled
in the country, dying at Venice. He was, it is said, a pupil of Berchem's, from whom he may have first drawn his Italian proclivities.
He has more truth and feeling for animated nature than Berchem.
Indeed, in this respect Du Jardin followed Paul Potter. According to
contemporary accounts, Du Jardin, who had his share of the national humour, wasted his time in the pursuit of pleasure, and did not
leave more pictures behind him than Both left. Du Jardin's best
works are in the Louvre, but there are also many of his pictures in
England. Among his masterpieces, 'Cattle of all kinds in a meadow
surrounded by rocks, and watered by a cascade; a horseman giving
alms to a peasant boy;' and his celebrated 'Charlatan,' full of observation and humour, are in the Louvre. A fine picture, 'Figures of
Animals under the shade of a Tree,' is in the National Gallery.

Adrian Van de Velde, born in 1639, died in 1672, the younger
brother of a great marine painter, ranks almost as high as Paul Potter in cattle painting. If 'inferior in modelling and solidity' to his
rival, Adrian Van de Velde is superior in variety, taste, and feeling.
Like the great English animal painter, Landseer, Van de Velde was a
distinguished artist when a mere boy of fourteen. Like his compat-
riot, Paul Potter, Van de Velde died young, at the age of thirty-two.
He generally disposed of his cattle among broken ground with trees
and pools of water. Sometimes he has a herdsman or a shepherdess,
sometimes there is a hunting party passing. His scenery is reckoned
masterly. It is mostly taken from the coast of Scheveningen. He
often painted in men, horses, and dogs for other painters. He must
have been very industrious, with great facility in his work, since, in
spite of his premature death, he had painted nearly two hundred
pictures. 'A brown cow grazing and a grey cow resting,' which is in
the Berlin Museum, was done at the age of sixteen, yet it is full of
observation, delicacy, and execution. 'Cattle grazing before a peasant's cottage,' which is in the Dresden Gallery, is considered very
fine. A fine 'Winter Landscape,' and a 'Farm Cottage,' are in the

National Gallery. Some of Adrian Van de Velde's best work, as well as his brother's, is in England.

Jan Van der Heyden, 'the Gerard Dow of architectural painters,' was born in 1637 and died in 1712. He combined an unspeakable minuteness of detail with the closest observation of nature. His subjects, which he selected with great taste, were chiefly well-known buildings, palaces, churches, and canal banks in Holland and Belgium. He painted in a warm transparent tone, with close application of the laws of perspective. The figures in his pictures, in excellent keeping, were often introduced by Adrian Van de Velde. Van der Heyden's productiveness as a painter was lessened by the circumstance that his mechanical talent led him to make an invention by which the construction of the fire-engines of his day was greatly improved. In consequence he was placed by the magistrates of Amsterdam at the head of their fire-engine establishment, which had thus many claims on his time. A beautiful 'Street in Cologne' is in the National Gallery.

Emanuel De Witte, born in 1607, died in 1692, was great in architectural interiors, especially in churches of Italian architecture. He stood to this branch of Dutch art in the same relation that Ruysdael did to landscape and William Van de Velde to seascape.

Aart Van der Neer was born in 1619(?), died in 1683. He is famous for his canal banks by moonlight, and fine disposal of broad masses of shadow. After his moonlights come his sunsets, conflagrations, and winter scenes. He rarely painted full daylight. He sometimes painted on the same canvas with Cuyp. There is a fine small moonlight picture by Van der Neer in the National Gallery. Many of his works are in England.

William Van de Velde the younger, the elder brother of Adrian Van de Velde, the cattle painter, was born at Amsterdam in 1633, and died at Greenwich in 1707. His early life was spent in Holland. He followed his father, William Van de Velde, a painter also, to England, where, under the patronage of Charles II, and James II., William the younger painted the naval victories of the English over the Dutch, just as in Holland he had already painted the naval victories of the Dutch over the English. He was a greater and more consistent artist than he was a patriot. Without question he is the first marine painter of the Dutch School. He was untiring in his study of nature, so that his perfect knowledge of perspective and the incomparable mastery of technical qualities which he inherited from his school, enabled him to render sea and sky under every aspect. His vessels 'were drawn with a knowledge which extended to every rope.' He has been an exceedingly popular painter both with the Dutch and the English. Of upwards of three hundred pictures left by him many are in Holland and still more in England, where in his lifetime he was largely employed by the English nobility and gentry. William Van de Velde has a great picture in the Amsterdam Museum, where the English flag-ship, the *Princess Royal*, is represented as striking her colours to the Dutch fleet in 1666. In the companion picture, also by Van de Velde, 'Four English men-of-war brought in as prizes,' the painter introduces himself in the small boat from which he witnessed the fight. William Van de Velde's triumphs in calm seas are seen especially in his pictures at the Hague and in Munich. Some of Van de Velde's best works are in the National Gallery.

Backhuysen born in 1631, died at Amsterdam in 1708, was another admirable marine painter. He did not study painting till he had followed a trade up to the age of eighteen years; he then gave himself with ardour to art, making many studies of skies, coasts, and vessels. He was inferior to William Van de Velde in his colouring, which was heavy, with a cold effect. But he had in full a Dutch painter's truthfulness, while his 'stormy waves and rent clouds' are given with poetic feeling. He was an industrious and successful man, painting nearly two hundred pictures, and receiving many commissions from the King of Prussia, Grand Duke of Tuscany, &c. One of his finest works, 'A View of the River from the Landing-place called the Mosselsteiger,' is in Amsterdam Museum. In the Louvre is 'A view of the Mouth of the Texel, with ten Men-of-war Sailing before a Fresh Wind.' 'Dutch Shipping' is in the National Gallery.

Van de Capella is another capital marine painter, though little is known of him. He was a native of Amsterdam about 1653. His favourite subject is a quiet sea in sunny weather. His work bears some resemblance to that of Cuyp. His best pictures are in England. 'A Calm at Low Water' is in the National Gallery.

Melchior de Hondecoeter, born in 1636, died in 1695, chose the feathered tribe for his subjects. He has been called 'the Raphael of bird painters.' He painted especially poultry, peacocks, turkeys, and pigeons, which he usually represented alive, and treated with great truthfulness and picturesque feeling. Among his best pictures are 'The Floating Feather,' a feather given with singular lightness drifting in a pool, with different birds on the water and the shore—a pelican prominent—in Amsterdam Museum, and 'A Hen defending her Chickens against the attacks of a Pea-hen, with a Peacock, a Pigeon, a Cassowary, and a Crane,' also in Amsterdam.

Jan Weenix, born in 1644, died in 1719. He was a painter of 'still life,' and was especially famous for his dead hares, 'which in form and colour, down to the rendering of every hair, are marvels of execution.' He painted sometimes, though rarely, a living dog in his pieces. A fine example of his work, 'Dead Game with a Dog,' is in the National Gallery. Weenix sometimes painted flower pieces. [58]

Pater Segers, so called because he was a Father in a Jesuit convent, which he entered at twenty-four years of age. He was born in 1590, and died in the Jesuit convent, Antwerp, 1661. He was a famous flower painter, but did not paint flowers by themselves; he painted them in conjunction with the historical and sacred subjects of other painters. He added many a wreath to the Virgin and Child. He worked in this fashion with Rubens, but painted more frequently along with painters of a lower rank in art. Pater Segers' flowers are finely drawn and tastefully arranged. The red of his roses has remained unchanged by years, while the roses of other painters have become violet or faded altogether. He had endless royal commissions. There are six of his pictures of much merit in the Dresden Gallery.

Besides the elder and younger De Heem and Maria Von Oesterwyck mentioned at page 258, **Jan Van Huysum,** 1682—1749, was great in flower painting, choosing flowers rather than fruit for his brush. If De Heem has been called the Titian, Van Huysum has been defined as the Correggio, of flowers and fruit. He reversed the ordinary course of artists by beginning in a broad style, and progressing into an execution of the finest details. In masterly drawing and truthfulness he was not inferior to De Heem, though hardly reckoned his equal in other respects. Even in Van Huysum's lifetime there was an eager demand for his pictures, of which he left more than a hundred. There is an excellent fruit and flower piece by him in Dulwich Gallery, and a masterpiece, 'A Vase with Flowers,' is in the National Gallery.

Andrian Van der Werff was born in 1659, and died in 1722. He is honourably distinguished for his pursuit of the ideal, in which he stood alone among the Dutch artists of his day. He showed much sense of beauty and elegance of form with great finish, but he had more than counterbalancing faults. His grouping was artificial, his heads monotonous, his colouring 'cold and heavy,' with a frosty feeling' in his pictures. His flesh tints resembled ivory, yet his elegance was so highly prized that he had many royal and noble patrons, for whom he executed sculptural and mythological pieces. Many of his pictures are in the Munich Gallery.

Anton Raphael Mengs was born in Bohemia 1728, and died in Rome 1774. His father was a distinguished miniature painter, and gave his son a careful education, training him to copy the masterpieces of Michael Angelo and Raphael from his twelfth year. Unfortunately he remained a copyist and an eclectic. He drew well, learnt chiaroscuro from studying Correggio, and colouring from analysing Titian. He was acquainted with the best technical processes in oil and fresco. All that teaching could do for a man was done, and to a great extent in vain. For though he worked with great conscientiousness, fancy and feeling were either originally lacking, or they were overlaid and stifled by his excess of culture and severe education. The most successful of his works are portraits, in which masterly treatment makes up to some extent for the absence of originality and subtle sympathy. But in his day, and with some reason, Raphael Mengs was greatly prized, since he figured among a host of ignorant, careless, and conceited painters. At the age of seventeen he was appointed court painter to King Augustus of Saxony. He was summoned to Spain by Charles III., who gave him a high salary. Among his good works is an 'Assumption' on the high altar of the Catholic Church, Dresden. An allegorical subject in fresco on the ceiling of the Camera de Papini in the Vatican has 'beauty of form, delicate observation, and masterly modelling.' Mengs wrote well on art, though in his writing also his eclecticism comes out.

NOTE TO PAGE 96.

'I have been told that I have not done justice to Lionardo in this short sketch. I give in an abridged form the accurate and appreciative analysis of the man and his work in Sir C, and Lady Eastlake.'—Kugler. It is stated that the versatility of Lionardo was against him. He attempted too much for one man and one life. An additional impediment was produced by his temperament, 'dreamy, perfidious, procrastinating,' withal desirous of shining in society. His ideal of the Lord's head is the highest that art has realised. The apostles' heads are among the truest and noblest. The countenances of his Madonnas are full of ineffable sweetness and pathos. 'At the same time he analysed the monstrous and misshapen, and has left us caricatures in which he seems to have gloated over hideousness half human, half brute. He altered and retouched without ceasing, always deferring the conclusion of the task which he executed with untiring labour and ceaseless dissatisfaction.' The wonder is not that he should have left so little, but that he left enough to prove the transcendent nature of his art. 'There is nothing stranger in history than the fact that his great fame rests on one single picture—long reduced to a shadow—on half-a-dozen pictures for which his hand is alternately claimed and denied, and on unfinished fragments which he himself condemned.' Lionardo was too universal to be of any school.

INDEX.

Rosa

Signorelli	Snyders	Somer, Van	Spagna
Spagnoletto	Steen	Teniers, Father and Son	Terburg
Tintoretto	Titian	Van Dyck	Vasari
Velasquez	Velde, Van de	Velde, Van de, The Younger	Veronese
Watteau	Weenix	Werff	Witte
Wouvermans			

FOOTNOTES:

Note 1: (return) It is in their unconsciousness and earnestness that a parallel is drawn between the first Italian painters and the Elizabethean poets. In other respects the comparison may be reversed, for the early Italian painters, from their restriction to religious painting, with even that treated according to tradition, were as destitute of the breadth of scope and fancy attained by their successors, as the Elizabethean poets were distinguished by the exuberant freedom which failed in the more formal scholars of Anne's reign.

Note 2: (return) Kugler's Handbook of Art.

Note 3: (return) While writing of goldsmiths that became painters, I may say a word of a goldsmith who, without quitting his trade, was an unrivalled artist in his line. I mean Benvenuto Cellini, 1500 – 1571, a man of violent passions and little principle, who led a wild troubled life, of which he has left an account as shameless as his character, in an autobiography. Cellini was the most distinguished worker in gold and silver of his day, and his richly chased dishes, goblets, and salt cellars, are still in great repute.

Note 4: (return) Kugler's *Hand-book of Painting.*

Note 5: (return) Kugler's *Hand-book of Painting.*

Note 6: (return) See note, page 422.

Note 7: (return) Mrs Roscoe's *Life of Vittoria Colonna*

Note 8: (return) Michael Angelo's will was very simple. 'I bequeath my soul to God, my body to the earth, and my possessions to my nearest relations.'

Note 9: (return) Lady Eastlake, *History of Our Lord.*

Note 10: (return) Hare, *Walks in Rome.*

Note 11: (return) Lanzi, in Hare's *Walks in Rome.*

Note 12: (return) Rio. *Poetry of Christian Art*, in Hare's *Walks in Rome.*

Note 13: (return) Mrs Jameson.

Note 14: (return) Dean Alford.

Note 15: (return) *Imperial Biographical Dictionary.*

Note 16: (return) Titian's age is variously given; some authorities make it ninety-nine years, placing the date of his death in 1570 or 7.

Note 17: (return) Kugler.

Note 18: (return) The term originated in the French expression, '*du genre bas.*'

Note 19: (return) He had a peculiar fondness for blue and bronze hues.

Note 20: (return) It is due to Tintoret to say, that there are modern critics, who look below the surface, and are at this date deeply enamoured of his pictures. Tintoret's name now stands very high in art.

Note 21: (return) Mrs Jameson.

Note 22: (return) Guido said of Rubens: 'Does this painter mix blood with his colours?'

Note 23: (return) *Life of Rubens.*

Note 24: (return) If I mistake not, this is the same Countess of Arundel who, in her widowhood, resided in Italy in order to be near her young sons then at Padua. Having provoked the suspicion of the Doge and Council of Venice, she was arrested by them on a charge of treason, and brought before the tribunal, where she successfully pled her own cause, and obtained her release, the only woman who ever braved triumphantly the terrible 'ten.'

Note 25: (return) Here is the description of a very different Rembrandt which appears in this year's Exhibition of the Works by Old Masters: 'There is no portrait here which equals Rembrandt's picture, from Windsor, "A Lady Opening a Casement;" a not particularly appropriate name, because the picture represents no such action. The lady is simply looking from an open window, her left hand raised and resting at the side of the opening. We believe there is nothing left to tell who this lady was, with the grave, sad eyes, and lips that seem to quiver with a trouble hardly yet assuaged by time. She wears a lace coif, and broad rich lace collar, almost a tippet, for it falls below her shoulders, together with lace cuffs. A triple band of large pearls goes about her neck, and she has similar ornaments round each wrist. She wears a mourning robe and black jewellery.... This picture, which resembles in most of its qualities a pair, of somewhat larger size, which were here last year, and also came from the Royal collection, is signed and dated "Rembrandt, F. 1671." It is, therefore, a late work of his. What wonderful harmony is here, of light, of colour, of tone. How nearly perfect is the keeping of the whole picture; as a whole, and also in respect of part to part. Could anything be truer than the breadth of the chiaroscuro? Notice how beautifully, and with what subtle gradations, the light reflected from her white collar strikes on her slightly faded cheek; how tenderly it seems to play among the soft tangles of the hair that time has thinned.'—*Athenæum.*

Note 26: (return) He had been called the Titian of flower and fruit painters. He preferred fruit for his subject. His works are not common in England. His masterpiece, 'The Chalice of the Sacrament,' crowned with a stately wreath, and sheaves of corn and bunches of grapes among the flowers, is at Vienna.

Note 27: (return) Sir W. Stirling Maxwell.

Note 28: (return) Sir W. Stirling Maxwell.

Note 29: (return) Hare, *Wanderings in Spain.*

Note 30: (return) Hare's *Wanderings in Spain.*

Note 31: (return) The spelling is an English corruption of the French Claud.

Note 32: (return) Poussin had a villa near Ponte Molle, and the road by which he used to go to it is still called in Rome 'Poussin's walk.'

Note 33: (return) Claude's summer villa is still pointed out near Rome.

Note 34: (return) *Imperial Biographical Dictionary.*

Note 35: (return) Madame Le Brun, whose maiden name was Vigée, born 1755, died 1842, was an excellent portrait painter.

Note 36: (return) Wornum.

Note 37: (return) Wornum.

Note 38: (return) Supposed to be a niece of Sir Thomas More's.

Note 39: (return) Rev. J. Lewis, 1731.

Note 40: (return) Wornum.

Note 41: (return) A still more famous picture by Holbein is that called 'The Two Ambassadors,' and believed to represent Sir Thomas Wyatt and his secretary.

Note 42: (return) Walpole.

Note 43: (return) Walpole.

Note 44: (return) Dwarfs figured at Charles's court, as at the court of Philip IV. of Spain.

Note 45: (return) The notion that Van Dyck sacrificed truth to grace is absolutely contradicted by certain critics, who bring forward as a proof of their contradiction what they consider the 'over-true' picture of the Queen Henrietta Maria, shown at the last exhibition of the works of Old Masters. The picture seems hardly to warrant the strong opinion of the critics.

Note 46: (return) Walpole.

Note 47: (return) Walpole.

Note 48: (return) Lady Eastlake and Dr. Waagen's works on Italian, Flemish, and Dutch Art, modelled on Kugler.

Note 49: (return) A lunette is a small picture, generally semicircular, surmounting the main picture in an altar-piece.

Note 50: (return) The Dutch still more than the Italian artists belonged largely to families of artists bearing the same surnames.

Note 51: (return) A picture with one door of two panels is called a diptych, with two doors of three panels a triptych, with many doors and panels a polyptych.

Note 52: (return) Fairholt's 'Homes and Haunts of Foreign Artists.'

Note 53: (return) Alchemists, like hermits, still existed in the seventeenth century.

Note 54: (return) **Bartholomew Van der Helst,** 1613-1670, was another great Dutch portrait painter. His portrait pieces with many figures are famous. An 'Archery Festival,' commemorating the Peace of Westphalia, includes twenty-four figures full of individuality and finely drawn and coloured. One of his best works is 'In the Workhouse,' at Amsterdam. Two women and two men are conversing together in the foreground. There is a man with a book, and a preacher delivering a sermon in the background.

Note 55: (return) It may be that Ruysdael's straggling life was reflected in his lowering skies and stormy seas.

Note 56: (return) Other eminent painters, such as Van de Velde, Wouvermans, and Berchem often supplied cattle and figures to Hobbema's landscapes.

Note 57: (return) Was the apparently greater success of these partly denaturalised Dutch landscape painters, as contrasted with the adversity of Ruysdael and Ttobbema, due to the classic mania?

Note 58: (return) Peter Gysels was another painter of 'still life.' His butterflies are said to have been rendered with 'exquisite finish.'

ISBISTERS' PRIZE AND GIFT BOOKS FOR YOUNG READERS.

"Charming prize books. If anything can make the children of the present day take kindly to useful information, it will be such books as these, full of excellent illustrations, and in easy as well as interesting language." — Guardian.

ONE SHILLING VOLUMES.

ANIMAL STORIES FOR THE YOUNG.

In Three handsome little Volumes full of Illustrations.'

1. HEADS WITHOUT HANDS;
Or, Stories of Animal Wisdom.

2. HEARTS WITHOUT HANDS;
Or, Fine Feeling among Brutes,

3. SENSE WITHOUT SPEECH;
Or, Animal Notions of Right and Wrong.

MOU-SETSÉ.

A Negro Hero. By L.T. MEADE.
With Illustrations. Small 8vo.

HALF-CROWN VOLUMES.

Profusely Illustrated. Crown 8vo, cloth extra.

AMONG THE BUTTERFLIES.

A Book for Young Collectors.
By B.G. JOHNS, M.A.
With Twelve Full-page Plates, &c. Crown 8vo.

"This is such a book as should be abundantly given as a prize in schools."
Glasgow Herald.

MOTHER HERRING'S CHICKEN.

An East-end Story. By L.T. MEADE.
Illustrated by BARNES. Crown 8vo.
"One of the most pleasing little tales which was ever written for young people; ay,
and even for old people."—*Newcastle Chronicle.*

A DWELLER IN TENTS.

By L.T. MEADE. With Illustrations. Crown 8vo.
"It surprises us with a study of human character of no ordinary merit and intensity."
Pall Mall Gazette.

ANDREW HARVEY'S WIFE.

By L.T. MEADE. With Illustrations. Crown 8vo.
"The characters are well drawn, and the story well developed."—*Literary World.*
"Decidedly strong and well wrought out."—*Scotsman.*

IN PRISON AND OUT.

By HESBA STRETTON.
10th Thousand. Illustrated by R. BARNES. Crown 8vo.
"Told with all the pathos and captivating interest of the authoress of 'Jessica's
First Prayer.'"—*Guardian.*

COMPLETE CATALOGUE FREE BY POST.

TWO SHILLING VOLUMES.

Profusely Illustrated. Crown 8vo, cloth extra, gilt edges.

THREE LITTLE HEROES.

WILLIE HARDY.—LITTLE RAINBOW.—JEAN BAPTISTE.
By Mrs. CHARLES GARNETT. With Thirty Illustrations.
"Touching and graceful sketches."—*Literary World.*
"Drawn from life we should say.... So vivid and natural in colour-ing."

Church Bells.

NOBODY'S NEIGHBOURS.

A Story of Golden Lane. By L.T. MEADE.
With Thirty Illustrations.
"In every respect entitled to a place among the best reward books of the season." —
Schoolmaster.

KING FROST.

The Wonders of Snow and Ice. By Mrs. THORPE.
With Seventy Illustrations.
"Exceedingly able, and without an unattractive page." — *School Board Chronicle.*
"Full of charming little pictures and instructive descriptions of the phenomena
which attend the presence of the Ice King." — *Christian World.*

UP THE NILE.

A Boy's Voyage to Khartoum. By H. MAJOR, B. Sc.
With Forty Illustrations.
"Must be placed amongst the best of the books for boys and girls which have been
issued this season. A very excellent book." — *Nottingham Guardian.*

THE STRENGTH OF HER YOUTH.

A Story for Girls. By S. DOUDNEY. With Twenty Illustrations.
"The story is simple enough, but Miss Doudney handles it well." —
Spectator.
"Sound and healthy in tone, yet not without movement and variety. Carefully
illustrated and tastefully bound." — *Daily News.*

WE THREE;

A Bit of Our Lives.
By the Author of "Worth a Threepenny Bit," &c.
With Thirty Illustrations.

TWO SHILLING VOLUMES.

Profusely Illustrated. Crown 8vo, cloth extra, gilt edges.

A BAND OF THREE.

By L.T. MEADE, Author of "Scamp and I," &c.
Illustrated by Barnes.
"An exquisite little tale. Since the days of 'Little Meg's Children' there has been
no sketch approaching the pathos of child-life in 'A Band of Three.'"
Christian Leader.
"Full of pathos and interest."—*Guardian.*

MY BACK-YARD ZOO.

A Course of Natural History. By Rev. J.G. WOOD, M.A., Author of "Homes without Hands," &c.
With Seventy Illustrations.
"A book that will delight young people. It is well illustrated and thoroughly
reliable."—*Morning Post.*

"Really a complete course of natural history."—*Times.*

FROM THE EQUATOR TO THE POLE.

IN THE HEART OF AFRICA. By JOSEPH THOMSON.
CLIMBING THE HIMALAYAS. By W.W. GRAHAM.
ON THE ROAD TO THE POLE. By Captain A.H. MARKHAM.
With Forty-five Illustrations.
"A more delightful prize or present for boys than this it would be hard to find."
Record.

FAITHFUL FRIENDS.